EASY STREET

(THE HARD WAY)

EASY STREET

(THE HARD WAY)

a memoir

Ron Perlman

with Michael Largo

Da Capo Press
A Member of the Perseus Books Group

Copyright © 2014 by Ron Perlman

Published by Da Capo Press
A Member of the Perseus Books Group
www.dacapopress.com

Da Capo Press books are available at special discounts for bulk purchases in the U.S.
by corporations, institutions, and other organizations. For more information,
please contact the Special Markets Department at the Perseus Books Group,
2300 Chestnut Street, Suite 200, Philadelphia, PA 19103, or call (800) 810-4145, ext. 5000,
or e-mail special.markets@perseusbooks.com.

Library of Congress Cataloging-in-Publication Data is available for this book.
ISBN 978-0-306-82344-2 (hardcover)
ISBN 978-0-306-82345-9 (e-book)

Editorial production by Marrathon Production Services. www.marrathon.net

DESIGN BY JANE RAESE
Set in 12-point Dante

2 4 6 8 10 9 7 5 3 1

This book is dedicated to the believers,
quintessential of whom are my beautiful wife and best friend, Opal Stone,
my kids, Blake and Brandon Perlman, who always direct me to true north,
and my dear, dear Mom, Dorothy Rosen Perlman Kestenbaum.
And equally important, to the unbelievers,
who have shaped me as surely as the waters shape the mountains.

contents

Foreword by Guillermo del Toro ix

1   A Coupla Cannibals Are Eating a Clown . . . 1

2   A Coupla Drunks Walk Out of a Bar . . . 14

3   Out of the Drink 33

4   Grinding Machine 52

5   Forever-ness 63

6   Godfather 79

7   Just Good Enough to Not Get Paid 91

8   My Cave or Yours? 100

9   Wanna Set the Night on Fire . . . 109

10 Get a Real Job 122

11 Stage or Scream 134

12 Name of the Rose 142

13 Birth of the Beast 153

14 Beauty in the Beast 163

15 How You Doin'? 173

16 Not So Good . . . Until 187

17 They Call Them Shrinks for a Reason 197

18 Enfants Perdus 208

CONTENTS

19 Como Day Peliculas . . . 215

20 The Doctor Will See You Now 228

21 Piled Higher and Deeper 241

22 Meanwhile . . . 255

23 Mudville 267

24 Legacy 275

25 The Power and the Glory 286

Acknowledgments 297

foreword

Memory is, by definition, imperfect.

In reading Ron's memoirs, I am delighted to discover nuances and details I had long forgotten. This proves to me that it is not enough to have lived one's life if you have no one to share it with. The Perl and I have been friends now for well over two decades. He is my brother, my blood, and my confidant. I love him because he is, as you are about to discover, one of the most imperfect, most charming human beings on the planet. Agent Myers in the first *Hellboy* film expresses one of the few maxims I have been able to verbalize and one that I live by day to day: "We like people for their qualities, but we love them for their defects." In writing this line I meant to say that we must not simply "accept" imperfection when it is revealed to us—we must celebrate it. This, I assure you, is the true sign of friendship.

Ron and I hide nothing from each other, and we are, therefore, able to be at ease when we hang out. Ron wears his imperfection with great pride, but he went through a long and painful process to be able to achieve such a state of grace. This process is detailed in several chapters of the book you are about to read. The Perl has embellished every anecdote in which I am involved, that much I know.

I am glad he recalls—or has fabricated—so many details. It makes no difference whether I agree with them because I would much rather hear Ron tell the story than pursue accuracy. You see, Ron happens to be the best raconteur I have ever met. All the stories he tells have a setup and a punch line and are always entertaining.

You can and will spend hours with the Perl and learn more about yourself, what it means to be human, by hearing him tell you tales in which he fumes, cringes, or grovels at the feet of life. His triumphs and struggles are instructive and entertaining in equal measure. He is not gossipy, but he stays compelling. He gives you a map of his flaws but is kind enough to be mum about the many flaws of others. He is Virgil to his own Dante and takes us all on a travelogue of self-discovery and acceptance.

Ron's journey as an actor is woven tightly with my own growth as a director. I was a fan of his early enough that we caught each other in the infancy of our careers. He neglects to tell the story, but he stood by me on *Cronos* when his team advised him to leave the production. We were entirely broke and unable to pay him his due weekly salary, but he trusted me. I gave him my word that he would get paid every cent if he stayed and finished the production. I never forgot this, and I, in turn, stood by him as my choice for Hellboy. Back then it didn't make the financing of the movie any easier.

I didn't really care. I stuck to my belief that Ron was Hellboy. It was a simple fact because, naturally, I had written the part for him. All those lines in both movies, the ones that seem improvised and spontaneous, seem so because I know the man as well as I do and have such kinship with him. Ron is Hellboy, yes, but I will always look upon Ron wishing I could be him when I grow up. That has proven to be out of the question as I turn fifty and my only growth is now lateral. But one can hope . . .

Ron and I are not afraid of a good fight or a verbal dustup when we get too big for our britches. We knock each other around from time to time, but we always end up standing on a burnt-out battlefield when everyone else has toppled. We have gone through day shoots, night shoots, all nighters, seventy-two-hour days, lack of funds, mutiny or bliss, explosions, slime, blood, freezing rain, six-hour makeup jobs, and each other's tempers, and we've got each other's back every time.

Our friendship is stronger than ever. I love Ron. I love his defects and love the fact that he has chosen to ignore mine. We are fallible as humans and very exacting as artists, and that is a combination you can only reveal to your closest companions and accomplices. I have seen Ron grow into the most unlikely of leading men, and he has remained my constant partner in crime. Some of our adventures together are chronicled in this book, but most of them are not. Each movie we've made would give enough chill and thrill to fill a book this size, but Ron is chronicling his most important endeavor: his truce with himself and the long journey to being able to live at peace in one's skin.

I read speedily and hungrily through every page and discovered details and episodes in Ron's life that I knew nothing about. This book is bound to surprise you too, even if you are already a fan, and it will turn you into one if you are not. May we all love Ron for those precious defects he has made all his own, and may we all live long enough to witness and share his earnest, pratfall-laden journey into full realization.

Love the Perl. You will too.

Guillermo del Toro
Pan's Labyrinth, Hellboy, Pacific Rim

EASY STREET

(THE HARD WAY)

CHAPTER 1

A Coupla Cannibals Are Eating a Clown . . .

The year 1969 was a culturally packed dividing line, or a closing of many circles that changed scores of things, not only for me but also for history. Nixon was sworn in as president, and the death toll in Vietnam reached 320,000. A man had actually walked on the moon. The Jets, quarterbacked by "Broadway Joe" Namath, had won the Super Bowl, and the underdog Mets would win their first World Series. There were student protests and the Chicago Eight, and madman Charles Manson would go on his Helter Skelter senseless killing spree. The Academy Award for Best Picture would go to *Midnight Cowboy*, John Wayne would win a long-awaited Best Actor Oscar for his performance in *True Grit*, and the young and dashing Newman-and-Redford duo would bust the box offices and hearts of American women in *Butch Cassidy and the Sundance Kid*. And on the radio that year the counterculture had gone commercial: the big hits blaring from every transistor and car tuner were the songs "The Age of Aquarius / Let the Sun Shine In," "Come Together," "Crimson and Clover," and "In the Year 2525."

Theater was also at an apex—culturally well regarded and important and probably never to return to the status in which it was held then. The thing we now call Off-Off Broadway was invented in the basements and factory lofts of the Lower East Side. And during that very week when my girlfriend and cousin tracked me down, there were over one hundred thousand people converging on Max Yeager's farm in Woodstock.

This is how the script was written for me that day: a guy walks out of a restaurant in late summer of 1969. He's about to get the big kind of news that happens only a few times in life, a notice of the caliber that packs a *For Whom the Bell Tolls*–type of emotional gut punch, which he surely didn't want to hear just then, not when for the first time in his life he was actually feeling sort of good about himself.

He's in the quaint little New England town of Stockbridge, Massachusetts, nestled in the Berkshire Mountains. It's a beautiful sunny day, the kind with blue-eyed skies and air as fresh as a fucking dinner mint. He's laughing, joking around with his buddies, as he steps out onto the sidewalk, though he has absolutely no warning and no clue of what's going to happen in the next few minutes. He'd just finished lunch in a cheap eatery, a hole-in-the-wall joint named Alice's Restaurant, the same one made famous by folksinger Arlo Guthrie, the one where "you can get anything you want." Although when he spotted these two people who were very special to him—up here in the green mountains, a three-hour drive from the city—showing up unannounced and walking toward him, he knew he was about to get something he surely didn't want or need.

This guy—whose future would have him being a Neanderthal; a lion-faced man; a red-tailed, red-bodied, wiseass devil; a Romulan; a hunchback; a cross-dresser; a cop; a lawyer; a biker; and a hundred other personas—was just a nineteen-year-old kid then. He was six foot two with piercing blue eyes and curly blondish hair. He was thick boned, as they used to call it, though not noticeably overweight as he had been the majority of his childhood. He did, however, have a unique face, a distinctive kisser, as he'd been told a thousand times, with a pronounced jaw and high forehead. It was the kind of face that was not ugly but surely one of its kind, and he'd gotten accustomed to people sometimes taking a double look. He had learned to counter this seemingly endless barrage of negativity with a tough-guy, good-humored bravado, which he had learned as a necessity to survive when growing up on the streets of Washington Heights, NYC.

But that day in Stockbridge he was working as an intern for a theater troupe and was thrilled, pumped up to be finally hanging around with real, working actors. He had just finished his first year in college studying drama and had had the luck of getting an internship as an assistant stage manager, or a PA, which was really a glorified coffee getter in the hierarchy of theater, but it was still an opportunity this kid was just ecstatic to have. He'd spent the previous weeks with the troupe as it rehearsed toward bringing a play, a Leonard Melfi experimental piece titled *The Jones Man*, to the stage. He had been aboard since early June as the play was rehearsed in East Village Off-Off Broadway playhouses and then went to the Provincetown Theater Festival on Cape Cod. And now he was on the second leg of this magical summer, having moved to the Berkshire Theater Festival to assist in still another out-of-town tryout of a brand-new American play, this one starring Ed Setrakian and Richard Lynch, two up-and-coming and highly regarded downtown New York actors.

It all changed and came to a halt when these two people came toward him. It took a second of focusing to recognize his girlfriend, Linda, and cousin, Kenny. He immediately got a warm smile at such a surprise, but within less than a second a sense of dread filled him with the speed of those internal light switches we have that change our emotional reactions from lights-on to lights-out like the snap of a finger. It was the simple fact these two people, who were so dear to him, just being together that didn't compute. They had never been in each other's company in their lives. It was this incongruity that made him know that something cataclysmic had happened. He could see this incredible sadness and dread on his girlfriend's face. Her usual beautiful, big brown eyes were red and puffy as if she had just forced herself to stop crying.

They seemed so afraid of the news they had to give and what it might engender that he already almost knew what it was he was about to learn. Linda looked so sad, and even though his first reaction was, "Holy shit, here's my girl," and a surprise that brought a big smile to his face, his stomach knotted up a moment later as her usual warmth was oddly not reciprocated—that was the giveaway. Then he looked at his cousin's face, one that had mastered the street look of neutrality, and he too seemed uncharacteristically forlorn.

To an observer it might've appeared like some heartbreaking romantic turn was about to tear apart the young man. Maybe his girlfriend and cousin were here to personally reveal their affair. But in reality, on that day that type of idea never crossed his mind, nor could he imagine either to be disloyal. Instinctively he knew it was something else, a betrayal of a much grander kind.

He turned to Kenny, because his girl was in too much pain to mouth the words, to intone this news he was about to get . . .

"It's bad, isn't it?"

Kenny took a deep breath, and the young man waited for a response that seemed like a million years in coming until his cousin finally spoke: "Yeah. It's your dad . . . he died."

It was impossible, he first thought. His pop was only forty-nine years old and had seemed healthier than an ox the last time the kid saw him, only a few weeks earlier. He was the rock, the inspiration, the steadfast example of fortitude. What would happen to his family now, himself, his older brother with his special needs, and his mother, who by temperament was not built to handle even the smallest changes and challenges—and now this?

That kid was me, of course, or how I remember myself, now at age sixty-three, looking back on that day. I didn't have my shit together at that age, not by any means, although I took the news stoically—or at least I appeared to. I knew I needed to get home, take charge. I told my girlfriend and cousin to stand by and give me a half hour to gather my things and tell the bosses in the company that I needed to leave and that I was unlikely to return to finish the summer internship. Death is a thief, the grandest perpetrator of larceny of all. It robs the potential of all the things left undone and reimburses the living with bits of memories that, with each day, pass through the fingers like a handful of sand.

It would take more than two hours to drive back home to find out exactly how my father died, which would be the most moving and poetic way a man's life could end. He had taught me to have big dreams and convinced me that I would one day grab the world by the balls—or at least try to with all I had by dedicating my life to acting. He had told me that I could silence the naysayers by showing them what I had. When I got this news I went into action because that's what always worked to subdue the overwhelming bouts of self-doubt and self-loathing that plagued me.

I was sorry I had to leave, because that summer, finally, I was feeling good, like a million bucks, even if I only actually had twenty-five in my pocket and was sleeping on a mattress on the floor in a shack of a cottage the theater company provided for our class of peons, or PAs. I had been doing it—actually being in theater, mingling among people who were real performers who had dedicated their lives to the art, as I planned to do too. During that summer it had become absolutely clear that I not only *wanted* to pursue acting but also *needed* to. Before, my exposure to performing arts had been fundamental, sophomoric, but the last six weeks had been eye-opening and an epiphany.

In life it seems like events go from point A to point B, but that's not the way it really is. These are all only segments that end up making circles, some that never get closed and some that intersect with only another circle, until one's whole time on earth is a chain of these seminal rings. That's how life is, or at least how it seems to me now after enough water has passed under the bridge to have given the illusion of some grand plan.

After giving notice I raced back to my cousin's car and asked him to let me drive. They had been through enough—with the effort it must've taken to find out where I was and truck all the way up here—and besides, I needed to be doing something. I needed an activity to keep me from disintegrating. He handed over the keys to his big, wide Buick and sat in the backseat. My girl squeezed next to me, in the days before seatbelts were required, and pressed her shoulder against mine and put her hand on my leg. Me, I was gripping ten-and-two on the wheel, the windows were down, the radio was off, and I beelined down toward the city. Gunning along the two-lane, tree-lined parkways with the speed of the gushing wind and the whoosh of passing cars created a welcomed sound to fill the car's deadly silence.

Everyone in the theater company—the director, producers, the other PAs, and even the actors—had been exceptionally sympathetic and understanding, which was a surprise considering how low I was on the totem pole. Most of what I'd been assigned to do had been basically busywork and hardly of value. I especially remembered the heartfelt reaction of the principal actor, Richard Lynch. He was then and continued to be throughout my life a genuinely stand-up guy, despite the demons he battled. In the last few weeks my job had been to get Richard onstage sober each night and keep him away from the vodka. Sometimes I was successful, and other times, not so much. I went from being a protector to an enabler in about five seconds flat on occasion because Richard could charm the keys right off of the warden.

That was the first time I was drawn into the wilds of the performing arts and exposed to the internal torments so many actors dealt with in trying to get through the day's performance. It comes to that thin line between creativity and self-destruction. I stopped at the liquor store whenever he pleaded, as he promised to have only a quick guzzle and no more. The director would scold me when I brought Richard to the stage in a cloud of booze breath: "I told you he was going to charm you into a fucking bottle."

Richard was an incredibly handsome guy, so much so that it was hard to stop yourself from staring at him even though it might be construed as a bit gay. Richard was one of the next generation of young actors around whom there was buzz that he was about to break into the big time. On top of his amazing good looks, he had the acting chops of Brando. Yet already he also had this very toxic combination of forces working on him. He was very ambivalent about success, and he was very pro-substance abuse.

His claim to fame was that two years before I met him he had dropped acid and lit himself on fire in Central Park. So the Richard Lynch I knew, even though you could actually still see how naturally good looking he was, had suffered third-degree burns that nearly destroyed his face. He had to be completely surgically reconstructed. I remained active friends with him after our time in Stockbridge, and over the years there was this wonderful, real simpatico between us every time we met.

When he found out my dad had died, he stepped up and made sure I knew he was sending his love and support. He was a really talented and kind-hearted man who, unfortunately, would go on to battle a lifelong drinking problem. But watching him that summer, as he transformed into the actor's persona, was absolutely thrilling to me, and he inspired and taught me so much. Richard died at age seventy-two in 2012 after playing a wide array of heinous villains in film and television. He made his feature acting debut in 1973's *Scarecrow* alongside Gene Hackman and Al Pacino. Like myself to a degree, Richard became very popular on the sci-fi and horror circuit later in his career.

Somewhere on the Taconic Parkway I looked in the rearview and caught my cousin's eyes looking at me.

"My brother," I asked, "is he around?" I was hoping, for my mother's sake, he wasn't having one of his episodes, as we called them long before the mental health disorder from which my brother suffered even had a name.

"Yeah," Kenny said. "He's at your place. He's cool." And then he named my uncles and aunts who were staying with Mom in the apartment. The last time I had called home, from a pay phone, my mom told me they were heading out on their annual vacation. Even though we didn't have much money, my folks always took a two-week trip to the Catskills or the Poconos, to the resorts that Jews went to in the fifties and sixties. That year they had been gone only a week to the

Tamiment Resort in the Poconos, so I knew something must've happened to my dad while they were there.

There is always a selfish side to death. There's often an emotional response of feeling betrayed, as crazy as this may seem, that we sometimes get when the person we love goes and fucking dies on us when we need them most. As I drove I wondered to whom I could tell my stories now, as my dad, having been in the music business during the Swing Era, was the only one who understood. I would've told him how that summer I spent time with a local New York kid from the Bronx who would go on to have one of the most heralded movie careers of our time. I spent days with him after our troupe caravanned up to Provincetown.

I had met this Italian guy, then in his mid-twenties, six weeks earlier when I was assigned to drop off a script to his walk-up cold-water flat on Fourteenth Street, between Second and Third Avenues. He had just gotten out of the shower and answered my knock on his door wearing only a towel. He was very friendly to me: "Hey man, I appreciate that a lot. Who are you? Great. Cool, man, thanks." That guy was Al Pacino.

Provincetown, at the tip of Cape Cod, was a saltwater taffy, boardwalked seaside resort that in those days had turned into a tie-dyed, acid-dropping hippie hangout. It was where a lot of the New York out-of-work actors went to escape the city and chill with friends who were acting in the Festival. Pacino was up there basically on the lam, hiding out from his agent and managers, who were getting movie offers coming out the wazoo. There was a huge buzz about him, and the world was suddenly after him. He was going to be anointed as the next big thing in movies, though at the time he wanted no part of it and was undecided about making the leap from being a serious theater actor to getting swallowed up into the Hollywood machine.

In Provincetown I spent a lot of time with Al, playing pick-up baseball games. Baseball was my thing, so he and I got along great, spending four or five hours a day shagging flies or hitting grounders with a Fungo bat and smoking doobies. I look back at those days and wonder about the whole stardom thing. Then, Pacino's dues card was paid up and he'd been chosen, a process that is both baffling and magical. When I knew him he was just a regular kid who grew up in the Bronx on Arthur Avenue. Yet even then he was an extraordinary person with incredible charisma. I'll always remember my time hanging with Pacino that summer when he was on the verge of launching his amazing career.

I never worked with Al, but I'd see him around town. We seemed to have the same tastes in real Italian food. Out of respect for his privacy, I never went over to his table. But recently I thought, *Why the fuck not?* and crossed the restaurant to shake his hand. "Yeah, man, I know you. What's up? Pull up a chair." We then kibitzed about our summer. He got more and more into it when he recalled the details I described. "Yeah, man, we did that. I remember. Kids, man, we were fucking kids. How cool, I had forgotten that. Age fucking sucks." Al Pacino went on from that summer in 1969 to amass a two-page list of major awards that he was either nominated for or won, including an Oscar for *Scent of a Woman* in 1993. He is an inerasably talented man and a deserved living cinema icon.

The long and silent car ride back to the city came to an end, and I was apprehensive as we finally found a parking spot. Holding my girlfriend's hand, I made my way to the family's apartment building, which by then was still in the Heights but a bit further uptown. Our apartment was on the first floor, a remnant of the doctor's instruction to remove the three-flight walk-up my dad should avoid, having suffered what I thought was a mild heart attack a couple of years earlier. Little did I know . . . I guess my folks thought it best to protect me from the true gravity of that first episode, how devastatingly damaging it had been.

The apartment smelled different when I entered, maybe from me coming from the fresh mountain air or maybe from the smell that tears make, as if sorrow has its own aroma. When I got my mom to calm down, which she did after a few moments of knowing I was there, she told me how it had happened. My dad was the most easy-going, likable person you could ever wanna meet. He played drums in the forties, during the era of the big bands like Bennie Goodman, Glenn Miller, Artie Shaw, and the likes, but he had put his sticks away twenty-five years earlier when we kids came along. Making the kind of living it takes to support a family was an honor that distinguished the very few when it came to music. But wherever he found a band, he always managed to charm his way onto the stage to sit in for a few numbers.

My mom told me it was no different at the Tamiment, with Dad getting up on stage each night and doing these crowd-awing drum solos. On that final night he had the house on its feet as he moved the drumsticks like magic wands in his hands until the ultimate note. Near the finale his stick hit the cymbal in the sweetest of tones, and then . . . suddenly he was on the ground. According to my mom and the coroner's report, he was dead before he hit the floor, victim of a massive coronary.

When I opened up this chapter about my childhood, referring to the tolling bell, a phrase used by poet John Donne and the title of Hemingway's masterpiece novel, I was thinking of the sound that Dad's final slam on the cymbal must've made. I can still hear it. Although I wasn't there, I imagine this echo of his very last reverberation rippling out like a widening circle, the kind made by a stone thrown in a pond, until the very essence of his last harmonic act is still rippling endlessly across the galaxy.

It was the saddest story I ever heard my mother tell, yet, even at age nineteen, I was struck by how his death was the most poetically perfect thing that could ever have happened to him. Poetic because if you could name the thing that you wanted to do when you died and your death occurred when you were doing the thing you loved most, then my father went out big! There was no pain, no lingering, but instead he died in that last moment of glory with the sound of the drumbeats and cymbals ringing in his ears.

Jews bury their dead quickly, and within an hour of arriving home I went to the viewing where my dad was laid out. It was an open coffin and the first time I had actually seen anybody dead. My father looked so at peace and still so young, as if I could shout, "Cut!" and the scene would be over and he'd step out of the box as if nothing had happened. But it wasn't a movie; it was real. And my dad was gone. For good.

Neither Dad nor I, then or now, had ever been too enamored with many of the Jewish traditions or dogma, but what we did find useful were gestures that were truly humane and helped move people through tough times in ways that were helpful, instructive, cathartic. Such was the traditional weeklong Shiva that Jews "sit" after a death. For one week the family stays home, the doors remain open for all to come pay respects, the food and booze are flowing, and a life is celebrated. All the people my dad knew—relatives, neighbors, coworkers—came to the apartment. You go through scrapbooks, you reminisce about what had been happening behind the scenes of old photos and snapshots, you tell stories and anecdotes, you hear things you never might have heard before. Because death provides a kind of perspective that life can never offer: it's a way to make sense of a person's life.

For me, I was seeing clearly the cloth from which I'd been cut. Performers must use even the cruelest and saddest emotional experiences as their source of inspiration. That's what brings authenticity and raises the level of a performance from being "staged," or fake, into one that transcends and becomes real. Sitting next to my aunt, I looked at a photo of me in my dad's arms when I was born. Then in another black-and-white snapshot, there I was riding my first bike, Dad steadying the back fender.

I wish I could've told that kid as he sat there in this deep grief and loss, even if he appeared pleasant, polite, and strong for his mom in front of the visitors, that understanding and coming to peace with his youth would be so important. He would have to come to own it all. By owning I mean that each of the memories from our childhood must be appreciated, or at least come to terms with, because this foundation is what made us who we are, is what gave us our values and ways to cope.

For some, the weirdness and dysfunction and pain of their early years may have been great, but all of it, good and bad, has to be owned. No matter what line of work you do, success cannot truly be achieved until you own who you are. The most offensive liability then becomes an asset. It makes you perform your best, regardless of the challenges you might face.

When you're acting and must get into character on command, these emotional experiences you have lived through and learned, every one of them, are each essential tools. Once tapped into, they make for the best performances and create the most believable presentations. When I go into character I use all the feelings—from loss, my perception of my physical and mental awkwardness, and my joys—to transform into character and make it real. I must, no matter the role, find the internal connection that makes me understand how the character I'm playing ticks and attempt to understand and emotionally connect to each role's particular mindset, as written in the script. No matter the walk of life pursued, even if not in performing arts, owning and knowing the cloth from which you were cut makes you better, makes you succeed at anything you dare to dream, and helps you achieve it.

At that age I felt so much self-loathing at times. With my father gone, who would center me, encourage me, and boost me? No one from the outside world could give criticism with that kind of no-strings-attached, fatherly advice meant from the heart to help the way he did. Later, much later, all of these memories would become paramount in my effort to get better and persevere in the profession I love. But then, when my dad had just died, I looked at those handsome photos of my father and laughed—how did I miss that arrangement of good-looking bones? Sigmund Freud, quoting Napoleon Bonaparte, said, "Anatomy is destiny."

Look what that little general did to quell the naysayers. Damn, he nearly conquered the world. Through his persistence to show how *big* he was, Napoleon is still remembered to this day, and he is not merely lost atoms, ashes of a person's life scattered into obscurity. That day in August 1969, there in that apartment of grief, I would tell my past self to listen to me, this guy you would become. Your face is perfect, exactly as it was meant to be. That's how you accomplished every dream you ever wanted and achieved goals bigger than even imagined—because of that anatomy you once cursed. I wanted to tell him that someday he would look in the mirror and say, "Yes, fuck them all. I may not be as financially well off as I'd like—whoever is?—but I have what's better than gold. I have self-satisfaction and, simply, I like myself . . ."

A coupla cannibals are eating a clown. One says to the other, "Does HE taste funny to you?"
                                        —Bert Perlman, 1919–1969

(CHAPTER 2)

A Coupla Drunks Walk Out of a Bar . . .

My first address was 633 West 171st Street. My apartment was on the third floor in a building with no elevator, or what we haltingly called a *walk-up*. The neighborhood was called Washington Heights, so named because it was the highest point in Manhattan. It was the place that allowed General George Washington to have the vantage point he needed to attack and defeat the British as they made their march for New York. It made for a decisive turning point in the war for America's freedom—no small accomplishment. That was the second-most important fact regarding Washington Heights, with the first, of course, being that it was the eventual birthplace of yours truly.

My building was located between Broadway to the north and Fort Washington Avenue to the south. The neighborhood mirrored New York in general insomuch as it was a melting pot: some Chinese, some Italians, some Irish, and a burgeoning population of Puerto Rican, a trend that led to the imagining of the greatest musical of all time, *West Side Story*. But what Washington Heights had in most abundance were European Jewish émigrés, some arriving before the insanity of the onslaught of the Third Reich and some actual survivors of the Holocaust. My family was the former, my mom being first-generation American, and my dad, third or fourth generation. (Every time I go to ancestry.com to get the answer to that, all I get is chopped liver!)

My apartment was the old-fashioned railroad flat, quite popular in a city where living space was at a premium. Let me describe the set, so to say, of this apartment, which had been the "stage" where my childhood years were played out.

Our place had one long hallway. You opened the door, and just to your left was the first bedroom, the one my brother and I shared. It had twin beds on opposite sides of the room, with his, as the older brother, of course, in the better spot next to the window. Our room was completely unadorned. Maybe there was a picture that he cut out of *Downbeat* magazine, of Charlie Mingus, Miles Davis, or some jazz player he was into at the time, tacked to his side of the room. I had a chest at the bottom of my bed for my baseball bats and gloves and maybe some roller skates. That's it. There were no pictures or posters on my side. Neither of us had bikes; we couldn't afford them. Then you go down the hallway another four feet and you were in a cramped bathroom with one of those bathtubs on four legs taking up most of the space. Then you go down that same hallway another four feet and you were in the kitchen that had a Formica table and four chrome frame chairs with vinyl checkerboard-patterned seat covers. And the cheapest fuckin' stove no money could buy. As for the dishwasher— her name was Dotty Perlman.

Go down the hallway again and you were in the living room, which had a sofa and two chairs. There was a big cabinet of a furniture box that housed the TV with its small screen, which we used throughout the fifties and early sixties. There was an upright piano against one wall, and catty corner to that was a Victrola in a cabinet with all of our records. There was no small amount of LPs and 45s inside the cabinet, with more stacked on either side, because my dad had tons of music; there was always something playing on the turntable, mostly Sinatra. Then the last room of the hallway, which was a straight line from beginning to end, was my parents' bedroom. Hence, railroad flat. It's a floor plan meant to imitate coaches on a train—what poor guy and his family wouldn't want to live their entire fuckin' lives on a train?!

My earliest memory was my dad teaching me how to turn on a baseball. I was around two and a half. Of course he taught me that skill, one for which I became quite prodigious, from the right side of the plate, never stopping to realize that I was wiping my ass with my left hand, thus setting off a lifetime of dyslexia and all the joys that engenders. To this day I can only read one word at a time, which translates into my reading time for Tolstoy's *War and Peace* taking four and a half years. On this count, however, I must give the old man a pass, 'cuz at two and a half years old I don't think I was wiping my own ass yet anyway!

At home it was a sanctuary, because mostly everywhere else I was always feeling like the odd man out, at least during the elementary and middle school years. It was like I was always wearing two left shoes. I went to PS 173, followed by junior high school at PS 115. I wasn't a problematic kid, neither excelling in studies nor getting in trouble. I remember, without exaggeration, that all the way from my first day in kindergarten and throughout middle school I never failed to be the biggest kid in every class. There was simply nowhere for me to hide, and no matter where I went, it was impossible for me to be anonymous. The only life I had before school was completely surrounded by family. I thought everything was cool. Then when I got to school I was one of thirty students in a classroom every year, and for the first eight years, known as the fat kid. There are always two or three of us fat kids, and I was one of 'em. That was my identity: "Oh that's Ron. He's the fat kid." Put my head down so they wouldn't call on me; put my head down so I don't get in any fights with anybody; put my head down so nobody has to know how shitty I feel about myself. Just keep my head down except to pick it up to make a quick joke about myself. Before somebody else could.

I remember, even as a kid, thinking there's something wrong with this reality. It was okay with my mom and most of my family for me to be this big kid, but in truth, it was costing me a lot to be this guy out in the world. Thankfully I found baseball in my younger years, and that provided moments of salvation. I hung with a very small group of neighborhood kids who accepted me for who I was. Of course, these guys, who I still love, were all losers and outcasts in other ways. I didn't have to be anything more or less with them, and at least I was the king of our little oddball group because of my skills at playing ball. For as long as I was on the field or playing at the school lot or park, I had a new identity, with a reputation as a kid who could hit the ball farther than anybody else. When choosing up teams I was always the first picked and batted fourth. That's why I played ball every chance I could as a kid. It was a way to take my mind off the fact that I was basically a misfit everywhere else.

My second-oldest memory, a tradition that started almost as early as I was able, was walking from our apartment on 171st Street down to 155th Street, crossing the bridge over the East River to the Bronx, then walking up to 161st Street and River Avenue, buying general admission tickets (around six bucks and change), and taking our seats in the upper deck of the right field stands at . . . you guessed it, the house that Ruth built, the old Yankee Stadium. The seats may have been cheap and the view to the field was close to "rumor-like" insofar as you could barely see the field (we were so far from the field we had to keep asking our neighbors whether the game started yet!), but for some reason when the old man and I watched a game I felt like Rockefeller.

Once you were able to focus on the field, what you saw was pure magic: left field, Enos "Country" Slaughter; right field, Héctor López and, eventually, Roger Maris; center field, Mickey Mantle, my—and every other New Yorker's—very first larger-than-life, straight-out-of-central-casting, mythological, dyed-in-the-wool hero; third base, Cletis Boyer and, eventually, Greg Nettles; shortstop, Tony Kubek; second base, Billy Martin, then Gil McDougle, and, eventually, Bobby Richardson, the fifties version of Derek Jeter; first base, Moose Skowron; on the mound, either Whitey Ford, Don Larsen (only World Series perfect game!), "Bullitt" Bob Turley, and the renowned, heat-throwing Rhyne Duren. In fact, here's a little-known side note about old

Rhyne: he was a relief pitcher—never came in before late in the eighth or the ninth inning. I think he was the first one I knew of to throw a hundred-mile-an-hour fastball. And he wore coke-bottle glasses—blind as a fucking bat! And wild to boot. Now back in the early fifties there was no net behind home plate, nuthin' to protect the fan from the screaming foul tip. So you sat there at your own risk; there were even signs posted to that effect. Well, old Rhyne Duren would come in in the ninth inning, and his first warm-up pitch usually soared into the sixteenth row. He managed to get his second and third into about the third row. Now not only would this terrify the guy in the on-deck circle he was about to face, but he was also giving poor, unsuspecting fans who were in the middle of a cracker-jack transaction concussions routinely. I mean who'da thought ya had to pay attention during warm-up tosses! So if ya wanna know why there's a net behind every home plate in the majors . . . it's because of old blind-as-a-bat Rhyne Duren, the most explosively exciting relief pitcher to ever wear the pinstripes.

Wait, I ain't done! Catching, Yogi (yes, that Yogi) Berra. Or Elston Howard. That team was the one I watched throughout my childhood all through the fifties. That team was second only to the '27 Yankees. That team went to the World Series almost every year. And I'm not sure if you heard me, but that team had "The Mick" in center. And oh, by the way, all those guys I mentioned stayed Yankees their entire careers. 'Cuz there *were* no sports agents, there *were* no lawyers, there *was* no such thing as "free agency"—there was only loyalty. And grit. And if you were a Yankee fan, magic! I mean jeez, how can a Rockefeller feel any better'n that? All that and *hot dogs* too. All that seeping into me courtesy of the biggest Yankee fan of all, my dad. His love for the game, its purity, its meritocracy, its nuances of strategy, its fairness—all seeping their way into me. If that ain't as American as Horatio Alger and apple pie, I don't know what is!

If you walked out of my building and went to the right, you'd be on Fort Washington Avenue. There was kind of nothing down there except other apartment buildings—very residential. But if you walked out and went left, you were on Broadway, the longest street in America. But on my little patch of Broadway there was just one business after another business, after another business, after a restaurant, after a deli, after a meat shop, after a candy store, after a movie theater, and so on and so forth and so on. Broadway had everything. If you went south on Broadway from 171st Street to 170th, you'd find an optometrist, a luncheonette, hair dressers, barbers, and you'd eventually hit Columbia Presbyterian Hospital and then Audubon Ballroom, made famous as the site of Malcolm X's assassination, and the Museum of the American Indian—hadn't reached the status of "Native" yet; after all, it was only the fifties!—and a whole bunch of shit.

But the main reason I went south on Broadway was to hit the deli on the corner of 170th; I mean a real, bona fide deli, which even now makes my stomach growl just thinking about it. In the fifties and early sixties there were delis on every street in New York—*good* delis. There were also Chinese restaurants on every street. And they were all good, all authentic. Delis and Chinese, everywhere ya looked—a Jewish kid's dream!! There was also a pizza shop on every block. So on the next block down from my apartment, between 170th and 169th Streets, there was this place called Como's. It was where I had the first slice of pizza in my life, where I learned how to fold it so the oil could run down your elbow. Pizza. To this day my number-one favorite and the one reason I will never, ever be svelte! And heroes: chicken parm, meatball, eggplant! If I was hooked on Italian food—and trust me when I tell ya I am—it's 'cuz of Como's Pizzeria on 169th and Broadway.

Then if you went left on Broadway, heading further uptown, halfway up the block you'd come to Epstein's drugstore. This drugstore is where you went for everything from filling prescriptions or, if you got something in your eye, the druggist would take it out with a Q-tip or clean out a scraped knee and put a bandage on it. The druggists knew everybody on a first-name basis, and they were very protective of the neighborhood kids. You went to Epstein's if you couldn't find your parents or if you got locked out of your apartment. I felt safe with those guys. They knew me; they knew my family. Next door to Epstein's was a candy store. And I'm talking about penny candies, every kind of penny candy you could possibly want. It had a fountain with seltzer and had been there probably exactly as it was since the 1930s. The place had a small counter with a few stools where they made, before your eyes, homemade egg creams, floats, chocolate sodas, sundaes—you name it. Everything you could do with a soda fountain was in there. Plus, every newspaper, magazine, or comic book that you would ever want to buy as well as pink rubber balls called Spaldings, stickball bats, balsawood airplanes, crossword puzzle books, and dime novels.

When I went two blocks up to 173rd Street I was at my elementary school, PS 173. The school yard was great for baseball. They had one major diamond and a couple of minor diamonds, but they also had handball courts where we played stickball. We rarely went east, toward the East River, because the neighborhoods got more dangerous, what with the dramatic influx from Puerto Rico, thus making the 'hood way more territorial than it had been.

There was a park on 174th Street and Fort Washington Avenue, called Jay Hood Wright Park. That was famous because it had a low wall around it, which was a popular hangout. The wall had been a meeting spot when my parents were growing up, both of whom were born in Washington Heights. They met on that wall. And then I met my first girlfriend on that wall. I don't think anybody's hanging out on that wall anymore, but boy, back in the day the Heights was some 'hood.

My father even scrimped and saved to pay for me to take piano lessons for five years on that upright that sat in the living room. I sat through every hour dutifully, but it was plainly clear to my piano teacher and eventually my parents that the only time I hit that piano was during the hour a week the teacher showed up; I never practiced. Thus, the pattern that informed my entire life was set out then and there: in order for me to find things I could excel in, it would have to be things that came to me as naturally as hitting a baseball.

All the things I ended up loving to do were things my dad loved to do. It was me and him through most of my early years. Going to

Yankee Stadium nearly once a week during season, going bowling—it was me and him. When I first started learning how to shoot pool—me and him. We used to go shoot pool at least once a week. It was me and him when we went to the movies, it was me and him watching TV shows, and I developed this insatiable love for all those things . . . well, except for bowling; I never could stand bowling. I'm sure the fact that I sucked at it had nothing to do with it. But all the rest of that stuff . . . still favorite things to do.

When you think about it, especially as I see it now from my vantage point, the memories of our childhood years get cut up into editorial pieces. Like in making movies, a scene is filmed from a variety of angles, in a number of different sizes. The director later figures out how he wants it interpreted, deciding what's needed and more potent when telling his vision of the story. What you see on TV or in cinema is often not actually as it happened but rather the result of editorial decisions made during the slicing-and-dicing process after all the scenes are in the can. It's more or less the same sort of method applied to our childhood memories in terms of the "scenes" we wish to recall. The majority of what we experienced gets left on the cutting-room floor. In other words, what we wish to hold onto as memories can be very revealing.

There's a longstanding squabble in psycho-therapeutic circles concerning "nature versus nurture" (we'll tackle that way more when we get up to *Hellboy*), as to which is more formative and important in determining the ideals we come to hold as true, what we believe in, and who we become. Or, more simply, is how and by whom we were raised more vital than the fixed set of genetic traits we were dealt when we landed on this planet? Obviously, you can't pick the family you were born to or the era in which you came of age, but there's a palpable argument that we wouldn't be who we are—and what we ultimately make of our lives—without looking at the forces that formed our core values during our earliest years. If I ask the question, "Who are you?" you might say I'm a student at a university, studying whatever, or a mom, a banker, a taxi driver, an actor, a writer, a sister, a father. And yes, that's what you're doing, but who are you? What do you believe in, and what is the purpose of you being here?

I could not even begin to answer that question in complete honesty until I was well into my forties. Even after big studio film credits, a Golden Globe win and Emmy nominations, and having a cover of *US* magazine as the year's sexiest man (although it was in my Vincent mask from *Beauty and the Beast*), I still felt like I was this undeserving fraud. Yes, I was a fuckin' beast on screen, but I was also still one in my perceptions of myself. No praise seemed to change my self-inflicted slow death by this false perception of myself. When the pain got to be too much I was forced to get my ass to a place where I got to look at all these perceptions for what they were: bullshit! I had it all wrong, backward.

Who I was depended on others' accolades, how much money I made, the gigs I had, what I owned, what my TVQ was, whether my phone was ringing (meaning my manager was calling with work). It took a long, dark decade and a good dosage of therapy to finally turn inward before this change happened. But the amazing thing is that despite of, or perhaps because of, my career's twists and struggles, which were anything but facile, I did, in fact, find relief. And *then* some!

Anyway, another abiding and burnished memory from back in the day were our summer vacations, which during the early, early years were all spent at this little Catskill dive called the Heiden Hotel. It didn't of course compare to the crème de la crème places in the Catskills, like Grosingers or the Concord or one of those places you see in movies like *Dirty Dancing*. This was a resort for poor people, people who didn't have a whole lotta discretionary income, but the place had all the bells and whistles to make you feel like you had escaped the ordinary, if only for a brief bit. It had a day camp for the kids and a swimming pool. It had a little restaurant where you went every night and ate dinner and where you had your breakfast in the morning, and that was our summer vacation. We did this for the first fourteen years of my life. Then when my brother, who was four years older than me, segued into being a professional musician, he started doing gigs up in the Catskills at the ritzier places. My mom, dad, and I would then go to wherever he was playing. My dad eventually found a way to play at these places too. While my bro played in bands that might be doing anything from jazz to the Beatles, there was usually another house band that played for the Perry Como and Sinatra generation. Dad always fandangled his way onto the stage.

I remember feeling so good to see my brother's fucking genius and marveled at his instinctual talent on the drums. It was also great to see my dad become a totally different man when he had the sticks in his hands. I mean, the focus was incredible. He had this crazy and furious zeal when he played. He had this heat coming off his back and a sizzle about him because he was so fuckin' happy. Really, his connection to whatever true passion he had in life was playing those drums. When he wasn't on the drums he was just this ordinary, schlepping lower-middle-class dude trying to make a living and be the best dad he could be. But when he was behind the drums . . . well, it was something else. Something mythical touched him.

Back in the neighborhood the other thing my dad and I did was go to the movies. There was a Lowe's on 175th, which eventually turned into Reverend Ike's tabernacle, with gilded ceilings and gorgeous murals, built when movie houses were Victorian classic beauties, decorated in full detail like stages that had once only been meant for kings and crowned heads. Dad and I would go at least once a week for the admission of a handful of coins; we could feel like royalty for two hours in the dark theater, just for two bits and a ten-cent bar of candy. If I was on Easter break or summer vacation or Christmas vacation, we went to the movies two or three times in a week. We also went to the RKO Coliseum on 181st and Broadway. So between those theaters, which had had different distribution deals with 20th Century Fox, Paramount, or Warner Bros., for example, Dad and I watched pretty much every movie that came out all through my childhood.

As I write this it makes me remember how important my father's total absorption and near-fanaticism for watching movies was to me. It's a big part of the "who" I became. It was also one of those magical moments I still see vividly. It was so enthusiastically contagious to watch my dad's reaction to a film. It was like I was the dad and he was the kid. That's how much movies floated his boat. Whenever there was a cheaper ticket for a film revival going on at one of the movie houses we might go every day to see one classic masterpiece after another. I went with him to see the 1939 version of *Robin Hood* at least ten times. That one was made for the big screen and in color. It was one of the very first experimentations in Technicolor in Hollywood history. For my dad, it was his number-one movie of all time, and Errol Flynn was his number-one guy.

Flynn was an overnight sensation from the moment he hit Hollywood in 1935 with the release of *Captain Blood*. He was instantly typecast as a swashbuckling romantic. In the early days of film *typecast* was a big part of the contracted actor agreements the studio made with talent. You were a cop type, villain thug, happy brainless guy, sexy, or whatever box you could fill. It still happens to this day, and getting typecast can be a blessing or a curse. But Flynn rode that golden crest of fame with the full pedal to the metal. He also made some of the biggest box office–grossing movies for the next ten years. In life he was as suave and debonair during his heyday as he was on film, although he was a heavy drinker from the start. Unfortunately Flynn possessed a dark side. A dashing heroic golden boy in the eyes of the world, his genius ultimately was no match for his penchant for self-destruction. He would eventually squander all the majesty his magical side had accumulated. He became destitute in the fifties and spiraled down to an early death. Indeed, the curse of creativity versus self-destruction that so many in the arts struggle with had beaten Flynn in the end. He died at age fifty of heart disease, degeneration, and cirrhosis of the liver.

I was ten years old when Kennedy got elected. With Kennedy, it was toes all the way up: this guy appealed to you and broke through all this American hard-held tradition. You think the Presbyterians wanted to give up power to some Catholic upstart? No way, man. All they had going for them was power. Well, that's not all they had going for them, but the ruling class had always been WASPishly dominant in positions of higher power. I remember all of these discussions in our house between my father and his friends: "Oh, a Catholic guy will never get to be president." That's when I began to realize that there are forces at work in America that are bigger than anything I ever could discriminate.

One time I asked my dad and his buddies a question: "You mean a Catholic or a Jew has never been president?"

"All been Presbyterian," one guy answered, which, of course, is not totally accurate. But I began to wonder what the fuck is a Presbyterian anyway? If you were a kid growing up like me in the neighborhood and someone says Presbyterian, he could've been saying Hindu. I knew a lot of Catholics and I knew a lot of Jews, but I didn't know any Presbyterians—those were people who lived in a different neighborhood from mine. In fact, it didn't seem like they were even on the same planet as I was.

Yeah, we all grew up with the air-raid shelters and the Red menace. On the radio the House of Un-American Activities was playing out in the news and was the background noise I heard while doing my homework. But when I was a kid the first time I could recall a connection to anything other than sports figures and movie stars was JFK. From 1959, when he started running for office, you could sense this was going to be a game-changer. It was so palpable that you couldn't avoid it, even if you were a kid like me who didn't give a shit about any of that. It happened because Kennedy was this guy who looked like he stepped off a wedding cake and had this twinkle in his eye. He seduced men and women alike as good as any movie star on the planet.

Before Kennedy there was the fifties, with Eisenhower, who was just plain vanilla. I mean, there was nothing distinctive about him. He was more like a banker—completely unsexy, completely unspectacular, and completely unremarkable. In the 1960 election it was either Kennedy or Nixon. Nixon was politics as usual, and you knew what you'd get. He was another boring empty suit, with no personality, but he was supposed to be the next president of the United States because he'd been the vice president. Then this upstart kid comes along, this young guy with this stunning wife and brothers galore, and this father who pushed around kings, and there was just all this legend surrounding him. He starts giving press conferences, and every fourth question he has the floor laughing because his wit is so unbelievably sophisticated. He was always on point and was a truly witty guy who dared to take the ordinary events of the day and make them into something extraordinary.

It was a thrilling time, even as a kid, during those three years when he was president. We got a place in the world; we were the envy of the world because we had JFK and Jackie Kennedy in the White House. It was not like Camelot; it *was* Camelot. I actually was deeply invested in being alive during the Kennedy years and very deeply invested when the assassination took place, because that was a kind of end of innocence. I cried, just as I had done at my own father's funeral.

But in the early sixties Kennedy, in only three years, gave us a symbol that was worth living and dying for. He was as much of a prince as anything you've seen in this country in the last 150 years. He was charismatic, gorgeous, brilliant, and strong. He stared down the Russians and created the Peace Corps. Imagine giving seventeen-year-olds, who had all of this energy and idealism but didn't know what to do with it, an opportunity to put their energy and ideals to incredibly good use helping those less resourceful, all while seeing the world. He created the space program, thus opening the door to a new age of technology. He was a man who did not like to lose and took on any competition. He was going to make America the first to put a man on the moon. This sudden frenzied attention to science and technology was the initial catalyst that transformed our world into the techno age in which we currently exist, in full digitization, right now. He also ushered in an agenda to fix the broken promise of the American Constitution that said all men are created equal—it said nothing about color. He had the balls to finally say enough is enough, bringing the civil rights conversation to national attention.

Then all of the promise and all of the innocence and all of the purity, whatever it is that inspires somebody deep down into the bowels of their emotion, was removed in a couple of bullets. His death gave way to the entire cultural shift in the sixties. Once you took our innocence away, you created an environment for rebellion. How did they rebel? Rock 'n' roll, baby. Bob Dylan, man. The Beatles, the Stones. Bell-bottoms, long hair. Fuck you. Fuck me? Fuck you. That's when I was coming of age, right when JFK jumpstarted the modern era and lit the fuse that became the sixties.

I was thirteen and in middle school when the civil rights movement came to its head. I don't remember a lot of discussion about race in my family or among my friends. New York was already a melting pot, and I knew and liked all kinds of kids. It did play out on the TV news, though, with images of students being barred from entering college because they were black. Then you started seeing the news flooded with Cronkite reporting on the images of people having fire hoses turned on them because they were marching for something and Rosa Parks making a stink by not giving up her seat on the bus, such that you began to see this pattern of discontent, so you couldn't help but feel the sand shifting under your feet. There was no avoiding it, whether you had discussed it with your parents or not. If the news was on at your house always between six and seven at night, which it was, as it was in every house that owned a TV in America, this was what you were seeing.

When I think about how core values are formed, this one was forced upon me because of the era in which I lived. I guess I felt I needed to make kind of a call, thinking, *Holy shit, there's a big world out there*. It's so big that you need to know about it because you need to figure out where you stand in all of it. I agreed with everything the civil rights movement tried to achieve—it was common sense. I empathized with the spirit that was at the heart of this ostracized segment of the population: "We've eaten the crumbs for long enough, and we've gotten kicked in the face for long enough, and we've been hung from trees for long enough, and we've been led to believe that we're second-class citizens for long enough."

It was those feelings I got as a kid watching police-held German Shepherds biting people who were protesting when I began to see the blacks' real struggle. I had an automatic default of sympathy for this cause that was not superficial, was not passing—it was deep. I remember talking with one of my black friends from school: "Of course you guys should be fucking mad, of course you guys should be fighting for your rights. This is insane, and it's insane that anybody could be judged by the color of their skin."

My friend said he just hoped it'd play out without warfare.

If not for Kennedy and then LBJ taking up the mantle, there might've been just that, or at least a lot more bloodshed. So yeah, I was not just witnessing; I was also forming my own opinions about what it all meant to me and my own values. It altered me in such a way that runs deep and is deeply personal to me: the family I have created is with a woman of color from Jamaica, and my two kids have the blood of many cultures streaming through them. We have a family who was at one time against the law—can you imagine that? We don't think about color but rather about love and devotion and loyalty and admiration. I learned this watching the civil rights movement. If you think that what your kids are seeing and hearing from the age of five to thirteen is unimportant, you are seriously mistaken. A kid who plays hours of violent video games every day for all those years, for example, is going to have issues to deal with as an adult, of that you can be certain, and I bet it won't be pretty. What core values are being formed?

Two months before Kennedy was assassinated and Martin Luther King gave his epic "I Have a Dream" speech, I was going to temple to get trained for bar mitzvah. My gang of neighborhood buddies who I had been hanging with since kindergarten went too. I got through it, and we had the ceremony. My entire family came from all over, even an aunt who flew in from California. It's a big deal when a kid gets bar mitzvahed in the Jewish religion. Everybody shows up, everybody wears their spruced-up best at the temple. There's a ritual in which the kid gets up and sings a portion of the Torah. That's what your bar mitzvah is, and then you're part of the whole congregation. You participate in it, and when you get through the ordeal you are, so to speak, a man, and there's coffee and cake by the temple. Then you throw a party afterward at some reception hall. Depending on how much money you have, some people go on fuckin' safaris. My family had hotdogs. But we had a party, and people came with presents: fountain pens, US war bonds, and all the other shit people gave back then. I still have bonds from my bar mitzvah that I haven't cashed.

What I remember as the most formative aspect from this experience was a chance to see the guys in the group who were really committed, the guys in the group whose families had real skin in the game, and which guys in the group were going through the motions because their parents wanted them to. I concluded I was one of the guys doing it because my grandmother wanted it, but it wasn't anything I knew my dad could give a flying fuck about. He listened when I told him about what I learned at temple, about ritual and the tradition of it all, what it means to go through this rite of passage. He didn't relate to it on any level, but he said nothing to negate it. He dropped me off at Hebrew school. That was the extent of it. And he picked me up. He helped me buy the suits we both wore on the day of the ceremony. That was it.

When it was over, one day we were driving somewhere and had passed the temple. I asked him, "What is your view?"

He started to talk about a book he was reading by a guy named Robert Ingersoll, who had taken agnosticism to a philosophical level. Ingersoll was the Sigmund Freud of agnosticism. And he wrote a lot of books about his position and was a famous orator in the late 1800s during the "Golden Age of Free Thought."

> I will not attack your doctrines nor your creeds if they accord liberty to me. If they hold thought to be dangerous—if they aver that doubt is a crime—then I attack them one and all, because they enslave the minds of men.
>
> —*Robert Green Ingersoll*

My dad found sense in these books and gave me some quotes as we drove. "I just like the guy," my father said. "The guy says shit like this: 'Let us put theology out of religion. Theology has always sent the worst to heaven, the best to hell.' Or how about this: 'Happiness is the only good. The place to be happy is here. The time to be happy is now. The way to be happy is to make others so.'"

I don't remember any of his opinions being forced down my throat, and I said nothing after he told me what he believed in. In hindsight, my takeaway from all that is that it made me start to look around. I did see a lot of people who went to temple and synagogue and church who were the most racist muthafuckas I've ever seen, who were always throwing really bad words around. They had this attitude about anyone who wasn't like them. Whether you were black, Puerto Rican, Asian, or whatever—there was this blatant hypocrisy. On one hand, they were church-going, religion-keeping people, but on the other hand, they were as far from what religion was intended to embody as you could possibly imagine. Whereas my dad was the only completely nonreligious committed person I ever met, and he had the type of ethics I wanted. He was never racist, he was really kind, and he would go out of his way to help anybody who was down and out. By his actions he embodied the Golden Rule, and I realized you don't need to belong to any fuckin' edifice or ascribe to any dogma to have a relationship with God, to be a good person. You just have to be a good person.

What's the point in having a hero in name only? What good is it to admire someone and not be willing to emulate them and to try to live up to the qualities that made them inspirational to you in the first place? They stood for things that were noble, spoke about the human condition. What good is it to complain about cowardice or the lack of backbone or resolve that you see in others if you're going to do the same things? Whenever I catch myself being hypocritical I chastise myself, have trouble sleeping at night. Over the years I developed a reputation in the industry as a guy who doesn't keep his mouth shut when I see some injustice or disrespect happening around me. Even when I didn't have the self-respect I have now or was loathing who I was, I still didn't sit back and take it. In making movies there's egotistical, greed-driven fuckers at every turn. If I saw crews or actors being mistreated or taken advantage of, I got into people's faces.

Many looked at me sideways: "This Perlman doesn't mind his own business. We hired him for a job, and he's like some fuckin' unionizer."

I like being this guy who says we're all in this together. I've gone right up to the top and said, "You might be the producer, the guy with all the money, but treat people with respect goddammit, because if you don't, you're going to hear from me. We're all equal here, from the lowliest guy to the filmmaker. We are all trying to bring our A-game here, so don't fuck with people."

Sometimes this instinct that I learned when I was a kid was to the detriment of my own career and reputation. But this was core stuff, which I eventually learned how to grow into, to find the proper balance and regulate it to be most effective and do more good than harm. All of it came from what I learned as a young man, from people I admired.

But of all the gifts I borrowed out of my old man's passions and then went on to make my own, the most enduring sprung from the aesthetic. To this day the artists he taught me to love are the artists I revere the most—in fact, way more intensely these days than when I was first discovering them. Because—and to my enduring regret—those artists who exploded off the screen, out of the Victrola, through the TV box remain unsurpassable: Gable, Tracy, Bogie, Cagney, the Coop, Eddie G, Erroll, Fred and Gene, the Marx Boys, Bette Davis, Myrna Loy, Stanwyck, Jean Arthur, Olivia de Havilland and Joan Crawford, Jimmie, Cary and Kate, Garbo and Harlowe, Capra and Curtiz, Irene Dunne, Fonda, the Duke, Kirk and Burt, Monty and Brando, Malden and Freddie March, Steiger and George C, the "kings of cool," Lee Marvin and Bob Mitchum and "Wild Bill" Wildman, F and Dan Dailey and Michael Kidd, Ford, Wilder, Hawkes, Chaplin, Keaton, George Stevens, William Wyler—I could go on and on. And Gleason,

Sid Ceasar, Red Skelton, Uncle Milty, Hope and Crosby, Dino and Sam, Lucy and Abbot and Costello, Laurel and Hardy, the Stooges, and Martin and Lewis. Need I say more? And Frankie and Ella and Mel Torme and Donald O'Connor and, and, and . . . these were his heroes.

And why not?! No disrespect for the current crop but . . . well, you know what I mean. All these artists were walking the earth when I was figuring out what was good, some at the peak of their powers. These beauties who my dad passed down to me, they were the stuff that dreams truly were made on. Shit, they were the ones who started me dreaming. Dreaming bigger than the biggest $200 million tent pole can buy. Those are the shoulders we have stepped down from to assume the mantle of progress in modern-day cinema. That step has yielded . . . well, let's put it this way: we've replaced humanity with technology. We went from an obsession with figuring out the glory of being human to the desensitization of the very same. And so I don't write this book, this letter to my kids and my kid's friends, and every fuckin' kid who dreams big and aspires to a life in the arts with anything less than the fiercest sense of urgency. 'Cuz although the progress we've made has taken us to lots of unimaginable places, the price we paid is vast. And the chasm is widening with every passing day. So for me, this shit is personal!

A couple of drunks walk out of a bar. One sez to the other, "I betcha a hundred bucks if I shine this flashlight up to the sky, you can't climb up the beam of light." The other one sez, "Ah, I know you. When I'm halfway up you'll shut the fuckin thing off!"
—Bert Perlman, 1953

CHAPTER 3

Out of the Drink

George Washington High School was built in 1925 and took up an entire city block. It had architecture like you'd see in Philly, with a doom cornice on top and looking very historical from the onset. Inside, the drab hallways had been livened up to help motivate our class of neighborhood kids who went there. Some halls had been painted by famous artists from the Works Progress Administration era; that's when President Roosevelt had the brains and guts to put unemployed artists, writers, and actors to work. I remembered one mural, *The Evolution of Music*, painted by Lucienne Bloch in 1938. Kids didn't graffiti the murals much, maybe just a scribbled signature or something small, because if any of those murals were ruined, the kids who had done it would be hunted down by the rule of the pack. Screwing with the murals would be like somebody who killed the mockingbird when all it was trying to do was sing—even us city kids could see the talent that went into those paintings. In this case, the school's administration hoped the murals would instill, by osmosis, some culture into our uncouth asses.

These were also important core forming years. I learned how to cut classes, how to roll doobies, how to sing doo-wop in the subway (fantastic reverb)—shit was happening. I was fourteen when I went to high school, having skipped eighth grade and taking my first year of high school (ninth grade) in junior high, which is a New York tradition.

On my first day of high school there was a pit in my stomach that's normal when you're starting something new. It was no surprise what school I'd go to; each neighborhood had its preordained scholastic path or schools you'd attend unless you were wealthy and could go to private schools. My mom and dad had gone to George Washington, as did my brother, so there was history there. My brother had graduated some four years prior, and he had made a name for himself in the school band and was recognized for his virtuosity playing drums. So my first move was to try to endear myself to the orchestra/band teacher. The man not only ran the official school orchestra that played at assemblies and sporting events but also had an elective band for kids who were serious about music and were good at it.

When I introduced myself he said, "Okay, you're going to be the new school drummer because your brother was a drummer, and he was phenomenal." I was able to buy myself a couple of weeks with the band by playing so softly I practically couldn't be heard. Eventually, however, the teacher caught on; it didn't take him very long to figure out there was a vast space between the apple and the tree!

He said, "How about trumpets?"

I said, "No, I don't think so."

"Anything? Piano?" I told him I took five years of piano lessons but couldn't even play chopsticks. "What's the matter with you?"

"Practice—could never do it." That was it, I thought, blowing my last chance to be a musician as my family expected me to be. I was clueless, though, on how this balloon-bursting letdown would introduce me to another art that was then so entirely outside my radar. I remember how this place gave me one of those life-changing opportunities we don't get too often.

Once I got the message that family connections wouldn't let me fake my way into the band, I knew it was time to stand and deliver. I began a mad dash to find a way to contribute, to distinguish myself from the pack. I knew I was not going to win any points with "talkmanship" because I was always a wreck when it came to talking to girls; the low self-esteem just basically exacerbated whatever shot I had at turning on the charm. I was a man in search of a place to fit in. Some said that with my size, I could be a human blockade or a lineman for the football team. But a year earlier a star football player died on the field from what we now know as "sudden death" or heart failure, causing the school to scrap the entire football program the year I entered high school. I hated football anyway. The school had a baseball team, but back then it was kind of ragtag and nothing worth aspiring to. So I gave the swimming team a shot, and with the modest skills I had acquired during summers at the family urban country club, I actually made it. I was happy to become an undervalued member of the swimming team because at least I was on a varsity team. I was second string, or maybe third string, if all the great kids showed up on the same day. But I practiced really hard, got into really good shape, and dug being a part of something.

That's another thing I thank my dad for—that is, making sure we were passably athletic at all sports. He joined and paid for a membership to a new place called the Fieldstone Baths and Tennis Club in the Bronx. It was built under a cross-section of elevated subway trains near Van Cortland Park that was noisy as all shit. Yet we spent family times there from Memorial Day to Labor Day, and I would go on my own a lot to swim in the Olympic-size pool. I became a fairly decent swimmer, at least good enough to make a team.

When I was in my second year of high school, then a junior, I made the tryouts and was again on the swim team. However, it wasn't long after the swim season started when one day during practice the coach blew his whistle. All of us guys in the water with our swim caps and goggles stopped and treaded water or held on to the side a minute to see what the coach wanted. Who could have guessed that the very tall, very skinny man standing next to the swimming coach would redirect my flight path to the very one I find myself on to this day?

This mysterious man standing there was a very well-dressed gentleman, like a Brooks Brothers window manikin (or today we'd say he was right out of *GQ*). He was a striking contrast to our swimming coach, a hard-core jock, with his classic cardigan sweater with the holes in it. Just then my coach pointed in my direction. I looked back, hoping to see that there were guys behind me. But no. The coach blew the whistle again, then shouted, "Perlman, out of the pool."

"What'd I do?"

"Just get out of the pool."

When I went over to him, still dripping wet, I asked again what I did.

"Nothing. You're going with this guy."

"Who is he?" I didn't even look at the man next to the coach, as if he wasn't there.

"He's the drama coach, and you're going to audition for the school play."

"What if I don't want to go?"

"You don't have any choice—you're going. They had thirty-five girls show up for the school play to audition and no boys, so they're looking for boys."

"Why me?"

"'Cuz maybe you could do the drama department a little more good than you're doing the swimming team."

"What if I don't get a part?"

"You'll come back and be a red-shirt swimmer for the rest of your life."

I knew that meant I'd never get into the water during a tournament.

When I finally turned to look and acknowledge the drama teacher, he gave me a half-ass polite smile. "Get dressed. I'll be waiting with other students who are also trying out for the play. Go to classroom number [so and so], in the corridor near the theater. You'll be doing a reading."

I had no idea what a reading was, but I showered, packed my gym bag, strung it over my shoulder, and went with my curly hair still half-wet. I liked the camaraderie of being part of the swimming team and thought I was coming back. I remember saying to some of the guys that I'd see them in an hour or so. I never felt that anything was going to come of this "reading." I just thought I was going to audition like the guy asked me to and then maybe even have time that same day to show up and catch the end of swim practice.

But fucking circles—they come at you when you least expect it. Life has this giant Jules Vernesque smoke machine, run by some great magical forces in the universe that blows rings at you. When I smoked cigars, if alone and sitting back, it was cool and meditative sometimes to watch the exhaled smoke rings I could make. Some were nearly perfect circles before wobbling into misshaped Os and then dissipating. Opportunity is like that. See that perfect ring and take the leap and jump through it. Head first, hands pointed above your head to make yourself like an arrow, as if plunging into the pool at the clang of the start bell. Seize that next opportunity that comes your way. Give it an honest try and your best shot. That's how the idea of being an actor even entered my consciousness as something I could do.

The audition was in a classroom. The drama teacher sat at a desk a few rows back from the front. There were two or three of us at the head of the classroom, holding sheets of paper we were just handed. At first I wasn't really enthusiastic about it, but I also didn't want to stink up the joint; I came all this way, so I decided to do the best I could. I wasn't trying to get the part; I was just thinking about rising to the challenge of taking this text and reading it well. In theater I later learned this is called a "cold read," though, glancing through the pages, I could see that this piece was entertaining and written to be spoken with feeling.

So I gave it a shot and noticed the acting teacher apparently liking what he was hearing. He then asked me to read the lines of another character. As I did I noticed he got a glint in his eye and a sort of a self-satisfied smirk on his face. It seemed whatever I was doing in regard to reading the text and trying to make something out of it was hitting its mark.

I didn't go back to the swim team practice that afternoon. We were told to check a bulletin board outside the classroom where the audition took place the following day. The results were there first thing the next morning, and to my utter amazement my name was listed there as the lead actor. It was kind of like, *whoa*—not only was I not expecting to be in the play, but I certainly didn't think I was star material. For that moment I was feeling pretty good, fantasizing that I was the lead, like in the movies my dad and I watched. I was Gary Cooper, or the fuckin' Duke, first time out of the gate. But I didn't want to make too much of it because, I said to myself, *This has got to be a mistake.* I'm not primed for this; I'm not trained for this. I wasn't even aware of what I was reading when I was reading it. But by the same token it was a small boost in self-esteem and a little bit of an internal "Fucking A—Yes!"

I went back to the swim coach and told him that it turned out that I got a part in this play and asked him what he wanted me to do. "I don't wanna leave the team," I said.

"Let's just say that you're leaving temporarily so when this play is done, if you want to come back, I'll take you back."

As I sit here now I can't for the life of me remember the name of the swim coach, but he's surely one of those people we all meet in life who you can't help wanting to thank. Years later I realized I didn't get the part in the play because of my brother's artistic reputation; instead, I think the drama teacher probably went around asking other teachers if they knew kids with a certain disposition that might make them good for theater. My MO was being a cut-up, a class clown, and, as I mentioned, making people laugh was my main defense mechanism against a world that always stood ready to ostracize me, or so I thought. When that whistle blew, my name was the only one called. The coach obviously saw something in me, some sort of spark that may have been something that could be used outside the pool. So he threw out his own Hail Mary and a from-the-gut guess, but he hit the mark, because it worked out and changed my life. I wish I could thank that muthafucka because he's responsible for everything. That was an amazing call on his part. I never went back to the swim team.

I was cast as Peterbono in a play called *Thieves' Carnival* by French playwright Jean Anouilh. It was a very stylized comedy full of French farce about a bunch of conmen and salesmen who hoodwinked and scammed customers. Peterbono clearly was the guy in charge, the grand poobah running this merry band of scam artists. It was over-the-top theatrics, meant to be humorous, but in reality it was quite a stylistically ambitious play for a high school drama teacher to pull off, given the bunch of amateurs he had to work with.

Rehearsals started right away. I didn't know any of the other kids. There were a few who had been long aspiring to be actors or ac-tresses, but most were like me—first timers. So we were all on equal footing, but I was immediately comfortable in this new subculture, a mini-society, a society within a society. Theater was a haven for a lot of people who felt very much like me internally. We were a bunch who couldn't get shit right in life. But in the darkness of the stage, where you couldn't see into the first row because the footlights are blinding you, you get into this private little world where you are able to create order from chaos. It made us misfits feel as if we were finally in some sort of strange control, finally getting something right.

Within the first week I was welcomed into a community of people who were exactly like me: freaks, outcasts, low self-esteem, kids who didn't really fit in and were wearing the same two left shoes I had been wearing my entire life. I had finally found the group of people I was most safe with. This is a very specific, strange world of like-minded people. When the group rehearses diligently for weeks you develop an intimacy and a unique bond. It was like going home. It was like after trying on fifty jackets, you finally found one that fit. I had found my own level of community. I no longer felt like a loser. In fact, I felt like the one-eyed man in the kingdom of the blind. I felt like the fucking Hunchback of Notre Dame when they made him king of the freaks because he's the ugliest—even though I was the ugliest, I was still okay. The beginnings of peace replaced that awkward restlessness. There were enough peaceful moments that were strung together from being in that community of people and knowing that I could fail, that I could be loved and appreciated, that I could fall on my face and everybody would say, "Oh, yeah, but look at that effort, man." All this out of the unexpected happenstance of getting yanked off the swimming team and showing up for a reading. I felt this way from the moment it happened. Later I realized that I'm one of the lucky ones who actually found his niche in the world, doing what I was meant to be doing, with the people I was meant to be doing it with.

The rehearsal process took about four or five weeks prior to opening night. It consisted of this string of epiphanies. It was like some state of grace in which I was forever in a state of discovery. I would learn ten new things about acting in a day and ten more the next day. I was a big sponge. I developed a much deeper connection to my fellow actors than I ever had on the swim team. I had to count on the other members in a troupe for timing, as there are no cuts or retakes in live theater. I learned from that first experience that the better the ensemble is, with dedicated people around you, the better the chance that you will do good. If you say your line and the other guy's not responding, you're fucked. The whole play starts stinking and then you die.

As my career progressed I worked with a lot of actors who thought just the opposite. There are a lot of really big-name stars who I've worked with who prefer to work with people who are mediocre, believing it will make them look better. Not only could they be any more wrong, but it's also a corrupt and narcissistic way of calling attention to yourself. My experience is that in acting, whether it is in a movie or theater—though far more important in theater because it's a spontaneous art form—the acting process is very interdependent on a lot of people. The higher the level of the ensemble, the higher the level each of the players are going to work or be called upon to give and dig out of themselves—it will only make all look better. Surrounding yourself with enthused people makes executing the project easier, and everybody's work is going to be better.

In retrospect it was also a boon and another one of those positive serendipitous circumstances that I happened to have a teacher by the name of Kenneth Goldsberry as the school's theater director during high school. He was the first homosexual I ever met, and in no way do I mean that derogatorily. In those days being openly gay was perilous to your career and even physically dangerous. He had the guts to attempt to train us to pull off a very difficult kind of theater. He was a tall, thin man, always dressed impeccably. When he was young he had his crack at working in professional theater. From what I understood, he never acted but did a lot of jobs in theater in costume departments and scenic design.

Nevertheless, theater was his life. He was encouraging as opposed to criticizing, which was really an excellent foundation for setting the groundwork for a positive experience. Now if he had been a prick who was yelling at everybody, I could've easily gotten turned off and quit acting. He also had a phenomenal temperament. He never raised his voice, never became angry or frustrated with people. Mr. Goldsberry had a lot of patience, and he had a huge amount of appreciation every time you brought in something that was fresh and really worked. He gave us this kind of a laboratory to expand our dreams. It was like this creative prayer in which he engaged us, a prayer that if we all worked hard to get this right and put more and more time into it until we were the best possible, then he assured us that our chances of performing a good play were pretty good.

By about November of that year, after weeks of rehearsals and costume dry runs, we were finally ready for opening night. We had four shows scheduled: Thursday, Friday, Saturday, and Sunday. I remember standing behind the curtain opening night, with the rumor that the audience was packed with a thousand people or more. What I experienced moments before my entry was the same I still experience today. There's a measurable amount of what's known as stage fright or nervousness. No matter how much I rehearse, no matter how good I know I am, I'm terrified that something is going to go wrong. I'm terrified that I'm going to stink; I'm scared that I'm going to forget something I was supposed to do. But those fears, generally, at least 85 percent of them, leave the moment I walk out on stage. Yet during those moments leading up to the performance, I am simply terrified. To this day I am.

Once I walk on stage, I go into "Go Mode." I tell myself, *We rehearsed this, we all know what to do, so let's just do it.* The minute I get the fear out of my head and get into the action of the moment, a lot of the anxiety melts away. Then I start to feel the exchange take place between me, the other actors, and the audience. I wait a minute and hear the audience really quiet down out there. I realize they're really listening to me; they're actually waiting to hear the next thing I'll say or see the next thing I do. Even though I can't see the audience due to the brightness of the stage lights, I can feel them listening. And an exchange begins to take place. And suddenly I'm having a conversation with a thousand people that I am in total control over. It's trippy. It's cool. It's like an aphrodisiac. For I have entered into the realm of collective consciousness, the highest and most sophisticated of all human interactions—I get hooked. As if I've taken a substance. It's like sex, like hitting a baseball with the fat part of the bat and watching it sail four hundred–plus feet.

Even though I was still a virgin both in theater and in bed at that point, I now compare that feeling I experienced in the first play to sex. I couldn't get enough of it. It was like a hot knife through butter. And when I do that with a troupe of other players, I've just created a bond between the cast and the ensemble that is palpable, quantifiable, indescribable, and definitely something I want more of. Acting, for me, instantly became habit forming.

After our four-night run I absolutely couldn't wait to experience those moments on the stage again, and again, and again. The minute that play was over I said, "Okay, Mr. Goldsberry, what's the next play?"

The performances went better than any expected. Everybody genuinely liked it and had a good time. It was all positive comments from kids I met in the hallways, even some of my old swimmates, which was like getting rave reviews. Our production even got written up in the school paper with great things to say about it. It was all good; it was win, win, win.

I became a member of the Goldsberry troupe. Whatever play he was doing, I was in it. I ended up doing *Carousel* and *The Crucible* for him. There was also another theater director that did other plays, which I was also in. It can't remember all of them, but I went from one play to another. This became my afterschool and in-school obsession, so much so it became my distinctiveness—Ron and the drama department were synonymous.

Goldsberry thought I had talent and handpicked me and another dude named Arthur Mulford to be his protégés. For the next two and a half years, Artie and I alternated playing leads in every play done at GW. It became a given; we were like the Hope and Crosby of George Washington High School. Because of this strange but meaningful anointing, Artie Mulford became my first best friend from outside the circle of kids growing up. Artie was an OG (outstanding gangster), a tough Irish kid from the Heights with a no-bullshit demeanor and rugged good looks. As a leading man, he was a natural. And as a best bud, he had everything it took to gain my ultimate respect and trust. Plus, he was drop-dead funny, not to mention the fact that he was the other straight kid invited into this exotic world of Goldsberry's to absorb, for the first time in our respective lives, a glimpse into the real inner workings of the New York Theater. On more than one occasion Ken invited us to his very elegant brownstone in Chelsea, where he lived with his partner who worked at Brooks-Van Horn, the most prestigious costume house to all Broadway Theater. He was a very legit guy and also piss elegant—I mean fuckin' piss elegant—but both were theater people to the core. They would have us to their house and give us Heights bums a real look at the finer things in life. We were taught what forks and spoons to use in a formal dining setting. We were used to a spoon that you just rinsed off in the sink; now we were seeing an army of silverware on either side of the plate. I remember first thinking, *Why the fuck would anyone need so many utensils for one meal?* But we learned how to use them in order. Goldsberry and his partner served this food we couldn't pronounce, but it was incredible. Not bad at all for a couple of Oscar Mayer frank aficionados. All of a sudden I'm eating Paella Valenciana and getting a glimpse of this whole subculture theatrical New York universe. I might as well have been on another planet!

Another buddy of mine, named Spencer Schwartz, and I even went off on our own to try a stand-up comic routine, mimicking the comic deities we worshipped. We called ourselves "Stewart and Perry" because we thought Schwartz and Perlman were a little too ethnic for the times. Back then gays kept to themselves and a lot of Jews and Italians changed their names. We rehearsed by getting up at a school dance, for example, and doing a ten- to fifteen-minute routine. Most of our material was stolen from everybody, from Henny Youngman to George Carlin. Stewart was the straight man à la Dean Martin; I was the clown, like Jerry. We tried that for a while and actually started getting some gigs in local discotheques. Some of the joints were a bit dubious, though. One night we were performing in a club off Arthur Avenue in the Bronx. It was a pretty rough part of town, with a lot of gangbangers and a lot of unequivocal types. Somebody in the audience heckled us after I made a comment that was taken as disrespectful. The entire back row got up en masse and started for the stage. Stewart and I saw this and freaked, knowing these guys would have us for fucking dinner and hang our huevos out to dry. We quickly exited, literally stage left, and found a backdoor. We hightailed it north for a few blocks and got a taxi. That was the last stand-up we ever did.

But I didn't give up comedy. Believe me, there is no small amount of energy expended into developing one's identity as a clown, as somebody who basically did anything for a laugh. My dad used to say, "You'd break your fuckin' leg to get a laugh." He was serious. He couldn't believe it, the lengths I would go. But the comedy thing could have its drawbacks. I remember there was this one sweet, adorable, beautiful girl. She had a smile that lit up the whole goddamn world. I had a major, major crush on her. But I was a mess when it came to knowing what to say to her and how to go about it. My best pickup line was, "Are you gonna eat that?"

So one time we were sitting in the cafeteria, and this beauty is at our table. It's Monday, and I've just kind of set the high school on its ass with this play I was in. The performance I gave particularly was all the buzz. There was all this "Perlman's cool" around school. I felt like I was in the zone. So I figure now was the time to make the move.

I said to her, "How would you like to go out on a date?"

Immediately she starts busting into a wild laughter. "You almost had me," she said.

It only took me a second to read the tea leaves: she thought I was doing my clown routine. I turned to my pal sitting to my left and said, "That's it, man. I'm fuckin' moving to Detroit. No one knows me there. I'm changing my name, and I'm starting over, because this whole clown thing—I ain't ever getting laid."

My family went to that opening night of my first play and a few other times over the years. My dad and mom were very receptive, and they were really tickled that I was actually decent. They were both very encouraging from that moment forward. But my brother wasn't so down with the whole theatrical thing I was doing. He was this young jazz musician, too cool for school. I asked him if he liked my performance.

"Yeah, it wasn't so bad. But I personally wouldn't be caught dead doing that shit. In costumes, the makeup, and shit like that. But go ahead, man . . . do your thing! Whatever."

While all this good stuff was going on for me in high school our home was becoming like a volcano starting to shoot out plumes. Until it abruptly blew. That year my brother turned eighteen and finally got his cabaret card, which meant he was a professional musician, allowed to play at better-paying venues where alcohol was served. He was in huge demand in the city because he had so much talent, but getting that card was the beginning and end of everything for him.

My brother hit a brick wall during the summer before my senior year. He was working in the Catskills at one of the better hotels up there. He'd come down to the city or go really anywhere a band hired him to play at a club or a big gig. That's how musicians made a living, and many still do. Then I see there's this sudden major drama going down in the background at my house. No one wanted to tell me exactly what happened, but I knew it had to be something bad. I finally found out my brother had what was being called a "behavioral incident." It was serious enough to have him picked up immediately from the Concord Hotel and brought home to figure out what the fuck was wrong with him. My father went up there to pick him up and brings him home.

Once back at our place—I remember like a scene out of a movie—my brother is standing in the kitchen, looking really weird and rambling. He's just saying whatever, free associating, making no sense. My mother is in the far corner with her hands to her mouth in disbelief. My dad's trying to reason with him. He grabs my brother by the shoulders and makes my brother look at his face. But my brother has a kind of angry, hostile tone to his rambling. He pulls away from my father's hold and nearly squares off, with his clinched fists at his side. My brother's tone escalates to confrontational. This was freaking my father out because he thought Les was being disrespectful. My father raised his hand to slap his face, but he held it there aloft. Dad then turned, deeply exhaled, and sat down in a kitchen chair, his hands laid out flat on the table, though I could see them slightly trembling. My father stared out the window as my brother rambled on. Although we had no idea what was wrong, as it was not easy to diagnose back then, what actually happened was that my brother started to have what are now known as manic depressive episodes. This was the very first one.

No one could understand how he got it. There was no mental illness in the family line, as my father would say. He couldn't understand what was wrong or how to fix my brother. Years later my brother told me he had taken some acid while up in the Catskills. One of the other musicians and Les dropped some home-brewed LSD, and both had nightmarish trips that lasted for twelve or more hours. Once you're tripping, you can't untrip at will. So if you're having a bad trip, you are fucked. I'm not certain this is the thing that truly kicked off my brother's manic depression. He had been a candidate for it, with or without the acid trip, but whatever happened on that acid trip triggered some sort of a chemical imbalance in him that he never recovered from.

The next day my mother convinced my father to have my brother hospitalized. I don't know whether they even had a term for manic depression in the late sixties, but they anesthetized him with Thorazine, which is a horse tranquilizer. They prescribed huge amounts of the drug to calm him into a state until he was zombietized. After two days of being in the hospital he looked like Jack Nicholson at the end of *One Flew Over the Cuckoo's Nest*. He had no fuckin' life in his eyes. It was a very sad thing to watch.

They then put him on lithium as well and told my folks he needed therapy. He was released after about two months of lockdown. When he came home he was tranquil, to say the least, because he was so sedated. Yet he lost his edge, his creativity, the thing that made him the genius musician he was. To this day I think of Les as a pure talent and myself as the charlatan. I really think I got by on a very thin set of skills, whereas with Les, he was really touched by some major muses. The heartbreaking part was that he had these demons that overwhelmed his phenomenal talents, such that we never got a chance to see the genius shine through. That's the real tragedy.

It's a double-edged sword, this artistic genius, as is the disease he had. He knew he needed the meds, but he eventually refused to take them. He said he couldn't play drums when he was on the drugs. Like most who suffer from the disease, my brother just said, "Fuck this." He felt so good in the upside of manic depression that he simply believed other people just didn't understand. All that free associating to the manic is empowering, and they feel phenomenally brilliant. When my dad or anybody said, "You're outta control. You need to take the damn medication," my brother would laugh and say, "What are you talking about? This is the best I've felt in my whole fuckin' life." That's the trouble with the manic side of manic depression—you feel fuckin' fantastic!

The family was rocked considerably. My brother had numerous outbreaks, with at least another eight serious enough to require further hospitalization. All of it took a horrible, horrible toll on my dad. First of all, my dad kept saying there was no such thing as mental illness in our ancestry, so it couldn't have been that. There was always this kind of tension between him and my brother. Maybe because my brother was the first and a trailblazer; they'd been butting heads since Les was a kid. There's often a dynamic like that between the first-born son and a father. The tension grew until one of the ugliest things I witnessed between my father and brother happened. My brother was rambling about some semicoherent nonsense that also had phases in it in which he put my dad down and mocked him. My father lost it and starting swinging at Les. He yelled with each punch, "You can't fuckin' talk to me like that!"

My brother just looked at him like, "Fuck you." He didn't seem to even feel it. It was ugly. I didn't get in the middle of it, but I remember thinking Dad was wrong. Les needed hugs, fucking real help. But neither my dad nor I knew how to reach the old Les. Where was the person who was his son? Where did my big brother I knew go? My father believed he could find the solution to anything by putting hard work and effort into it. But this?

My mother tried her best, but she didn't have the resources. None of them had the resources. None of them understood anything. My mom was worried for my dad then because clearly she'd never seen him like this. We had never seen him get into a situation in which he didn't know what to do. He was a very capable guy. He'd been in the Army; he'd seen it all. He served during wartime. He came up on the streets of New York. This was a guy who always prided himself on knowing what to do. And then he gets into a situation in which he's completely fucking helpless. And everything he's trying backfires on him. He didn't know how to deal with Les. It killed him that he didn't know how to save his own blood, his son. The stress of it could have had something to do with what eventually caused his fatal heart attack two years later. I'll never know.

I suddenly realized how the stress at home that last year had made me immerse myself into theater and the drama department even more. It was such a relief to become absorbed into a character, making believe I was someone else, someone with a different life. Yet there was no discernible cause and effect that I brought to school or performances. My love of theater didn't need anything to enhance it or any external torment and suffering to expand it, but obviously I welcomed having theater to get a reprieve from the discontent and sadness that filled our apartment.

As I mentioned, the emotional stuff in life surely can be used in a performance to help give a character an authenticity. As for me, there's no magical Zen thing; there's no switch you can flick on. The transformative process of becoming the character is a result of the performance. Even if I am escaping reality, I try to tap into emotions that have to do with the human condition, those things we all go through, the sufferings and the joys. That's what the theater is. That's what movies are. That's what all of the arts are, that, if done right, are reflections of the human condition. Even painting: the great painters are capturing truth. Was it Jean-Luc Godard who said, "Cinema is truth twenty-four frames a second"? That's what it is, and it's hard to know it when you see it in real life because the continuum of time doesn't allow for that. You're too busy living. But when you're creating art, you're basing the whole exercise on some exploration of facets of the human condition. And in getting the performance to the point at which it's sublime, you're coming closer to perfection than you could ever come in real life.

I became addicted to creating, trying to figure out how to present that human condition either in a play or in a movie. You get a script, and when you decide you're going to do it and you have a role to play, then you need to figure out the execution of it. It's a riddle. You have to absorb the character's traits and motivations into your own psyche and make sense of them and personalize them. Then you come back with your own version of a seamless telling of that. That's the performance. So it is a very technical thing because it begins when you read something and acquire an intellectual understanding of it. Then, little by little, you hope it seeps its way down through your fucking dick, your balls, your calves, and your toes, and then you can physicalize it.

It's the human condition that the playwright or the screenwriter is trying to shed light on. The great plays are the ones that have the most to say about who we are and who we aren't, what our limitations are, what our weaknesses and our strengths are, and what heroism looks like. It shows us what self-sacrifice looks like, what devotion looks like, what loyalty looks like. These are all things that started out with the Greeks and the plays they wrote. And nobody got it better, by the way. Nobody. To this day. Nobody got it fucking better than the Greeks. From Socrates, Euripides, Aristotle—none ever wrote more insight-fully about the human condition than they did. Everything that we do, in all of our performing arts, are variations on shit that they came up with nearly four thousand years ago.

I remember understanding this in a new way the very first time I went to a Broadway play. Even though the theater district was 130 blocks south of where we lived, it might as well have been on the moon, 'cuz my old man just couldn't afford it. After a rich aunt and uncle from Long Island came to see one of my high school perfor-mances, they invited me to join them to see *Fiddler on the Roof.* It was thrilling. I remember every fuckin' move, every line, and every song.

Fiddler on the Roof is a perfect example of how great art can tap into that human condition I'm referring to. Who would think a story about a Jewish man with five daughters would be a sellable tale? But we love it. Why? We share his desires to keep his family together; we identify with his struggles and joys. These are ancient feelings we shared from the first time we banded together as humans and buried them in what Carl Jung called our shared consciousness. This is what the Greek dramatists understood. We relate to the play's depictions of how outside forces sweep into our lives and how we cope. Because the writer, choreographer, lyricist, directors, cast, set designers, and many more all came together to tap into the human condition, the play turned into a legacy. For ten years it was the longest-running play on Broadway, until *Grease* knocked it from its throne. It still remains the sixteenth-longest in Broadway history. The play is still being produced, and I'd bet that some high school or college troupe is rehearsing it somewhere right now. That's how powerful and noble the arts can be: oftentimes many of us don't know why we think a certain movie is great, but it is because it manages to capture and speak to the very things that make us human.

Even though the home life was going south, my parents still insisted I go to college. They didn't care what I studied. For that generation, just going to college was the goal. They believed it would give us a chance to break the poverty cycle we were stuck in. Yet getting into college wasn't as easy as I thought. It wasn't for lack of schools or being accepted. I made it into two, in fact, but, again, I nearly blew it. Unchecked, I can make myself my own worst enemy. Shit, who of us can say otherwise? But when it came to either letting my flaws keep me from college and drama or doing something about it, my decision was rapid and decisive. No school, no more theater? It wasn't going to go that way for me.

(CHAPTER 4)

Grinding Machine

During my senior year of high school, in between the trips to the hospital to see my brother, my parents were very much on top of me about applying to college. They harped about application deadlines. Both grew up during the Depression, and neither had college educations. To that generation it was imperative that a child go to college, almost as if that was the guaranteed magic carpet ride to a life of happiness, kinda like on the *Donna Reed Show* or *Father Knows Best*. So I had to go, no matter what. It didn't matter what the fuck I studied; I just needed to get the fuckin' degree. But because we didn't have any money, the notion of applying to a college that specialized in theater—by that time the die was fully cast—seemed a waste of time unless I was going to get a full ride. My parents couldn't afford to send me. Full stop!

I tried to apply for scholarships at some Ivy League schools, but nothing promising panned out. Let's not forget I was working off a 2.7 high school grade point average, a reality that completely ruled out any possibility for the Einstein Scholarship. I started focusing on schools within New York's city-university system. Every borough had one, and back then they were free, so if the numbers added up, you were eligible to go to whatever one was in your borough: there was CCNY in Manhattan, Hunter College in the Bronx, Hunter College campus in

Manhattan, Brooklyn College, Queens College, and Staten Island College, all making up CUNY, the City University of New York. These schools required a $150 registration fee, and that was it—now it can be six grand per year for New York residents. The schools were for lower- to middle-class families like mine. So my little 2.7 GPA was just enough to get me in—not to CCNY, but I got into York College in Queens.

After a little uncustomary tap dance on the part of my old man, I managed to get my acceptance switched over to another campus of Hunter College that was renamed Lehman College in the Bronx on 204th Street. It did have a theater department, but there was no word on whether it was any good. I figured, "Hey, I'll be in college, it's liberal arts. Whatever little education I can get from the place would be better than nothing. I'll find a way to join the drama club." That's where, for a second time and shrouded in circumstances mysteriously absurd, life was about to take another profound turn, once again sending me on the trajectory I remain on to this day. For it was there, at this dinky little last-chance saloon of a college in the Bronx, that I met a man who I can only describe as the Carl Jung of theater literature. This man was about to shape my place in theater in a way completely separate from my earlier encounter. Talk about the unplanned miracle—this man would awaken and solidify my entire aesthetic. But I digress . . .

To get into a CUNY college, it was required to take a physical at the end of your senior year of high school. I flunked mine. I was 310 pounds. I had high blood pressure and salt in my urine, all of which might not have been so bad were I an eighty-seven-year-old Jew. But I was seventeen. Not good. In short, I was admitted to Lehman College, but the caveat was that I had to remediate these two health issues, or no entry. The salt in the urine was something that demanded attention because it was off the beaten path for a kid my age, and it was something that required a very special treatment. I was put on a sodium-free diet. It wasn't just putting down the salt shaker but also included a list of nearly everything I normally ate. You don't realize how many foods naturally have salt in them until you have to go on this fuckin' diet. Virtually everything has salt in it. At least everything that provided me with a reason to live! I had to eat stuff that was either processed without salt or naturally contained no sodium content. The only condiment that had any zip to it I was allowed to use was mustard. Oh yeah, onions, curiously enough, also contained no salt. To this day I eat mustard and onions on everything, from my fucking cereal in the morning to my muthafuckin' hot fudge sundae at night! It's the only thing that made the food I was allowed not to taste like cardboard. My Jewish mom who encouraged me through my childhood to eat "healthy-size" portions now realized that I needed to do this to get into college. She did everything in her power not to fuck that up. She threw aside her selfish need to watch me eat and be happy in order to see me pass this physical. Dear old Mom!

It became an exercise in discipline on everybody's part, because it really required all of us to start eating differently. I stuck to it to the decimal point and never once cheated. I only had two months, from the last weeks of June to the end of August, to affect this thing. The final result was that I lost ninety-five pounds in nine weeks. A lot of interesting things take place when, for the first time in your life, you have a goal. You have to sacrifice a lot of the things you love in order to achieve it. You have to exert, for the first time, some real willpower. And you find out a little about yourself. You ask yourself, *Am I made to do this? Do I have what it takes to do this?* That was the first time I ever had any real demands put on me in which I had to rise to an occasion that was seriously outside my comfort zone.

By the time September rolled around and I retook the physical to start Lehman, my health was dandy. What I found most odd was that it was not only a physical change but was also a change in persona. I saw myself differently in the mirror and was looked at differently by the world at large. That marked the beginnings of the turning away from that kid with the low self-esteem. From that moment forth anybody who met me, especially in college who didn't know me before, would have looked at me really askance and gone, "Fuck you talking about? Fat kid?" There was no way for the outside world to understand what I was feeling on the inside because, well, once you're fat—I don't give a shit if you now weigh forty-five fucking pounds—you always think of yourself as fat. Weird, I know.

> To demonstrate, during my senior year of high school, when I was 310 pounds, we did a production of *Carousel* by Rogers and Hammerstein, which is one of their iconic musicals. I played Enoch Snow, this fat, jolly character whom everybody loves. When I became a freshman at Lehman College around nine months later and had lost the ninety-five pounds, we did the same play, except I played Jigger Craigin, who is the bad guy, the lean, nasty, mean motherfucker. That was a transformation that sparked a palpable change in self-perception.

It's an interesting thing that to this day I've never come close to being that heavy again. The most I've ever allowed myself to get to was about 255 pounds, but I'll get back quickly to around 205 to 210, which is what I call my fighting weight. I still have a thing with food; it's my number-one vice. I still eat at least one piece of chocolate every day. I remember for *City of Lost Children* I opened the movie shirtless as a street performer who broke chains with his chest. I had to get into the shape of my life! It was nothing but egg whites, chicken breasts, and broccoli for, like, five months. Then I got to Paris to start filming, and they had gotten me a flat above the best chocolatier in Europe. So now I start obsessing over how much chicken breast I gotta give up so I can have my pound of the good shit every fuckin' day. At any rate, it's a very fucking fundamental part of me, being fat. It's just one of those conditions you resign yourself to.

Many years later during therapy, in my obsession to change this perception, I was introduced to what, in Jungian terms, was called the "Shadow." It's powerful when you identify the Shadow in yourself. Everybody has one. Most people spend their lives running from it. What you really want to do is the opposite. To be truly happy and at peace, you need to embrace that kid who you once were. He's still there, so take care of him as if he were your own child, as if you're his parent. You'd love that kid and nurture him, wouldn't you?

That was probably one of the most game-changing things I did, to come to terms with that fat kid who had been the source of so much discomfort and unease. All you need to really do is just fucking love him. And know that that's your fingerprint—that's what separates you from the crowd. And there's gold in them there hills if you just know how to make peace with it. This once self-destructive image, with all its flaws, can instead become something you see as a bright, shining asset. If you start beating up on yourself, with internal talk like, "You're a loser, it will never work out, you don't deserve this . . . ," stop your fucking brain in its tracks. You can't help the thought that crosses your mind, but you do have the power to change it with a new and more positive one. When I think of myself as that kid everybody made fun of, I know his pain better than anyone and, instead, I treat that boy right. As sure as I am of this being the fastest route to find true self-acceptance, that lesson took another twenty years for me to learn.

But during college I was ready and had that swagger that only eighteen- and nineteen-year-olds can have. You know when you thought you had it all figured out and knew how the world worked? It's a sort of nice, naïve moment to live through. The very first thing I did in college was to find the drama department.

Actually, the drama department sort of found me, because I was leaning toward doing musicals. As I already mentioned, and in my frenzy to greet my college experience by finding the very first stage on which to do my thing that I possibly could, at the beginning of my freshman year I did *Carousel* with the school's Musical Theater Society. So, fresh off that little experiment, I was walking down one of the corridors at Lehman in the speech and theater building. Now, the classrooms at Lehman have two entrances, one in the front and one in the back. So as I was passing the back of one of these classrooms I heard someone shout from inside, "Hey Goldberg!" For obvious reasons, I kept walking. As I passed the front entrance to the very same classroom I heard, once again, only much louder, "HEY! GOLDBERG!" Well, it didn't take me long to realize I was the only person in said hallway, so I peeked into the room where this shouting is coming from.

And there was this rather dubious-looking teacher in front of this quite full classroom filled with eager participants.

"Excuse me, were you referring to me?" I asked.

"Yeah, you—Goldberg."

"I think you might be making a mistake," I said. "My name's Perlman."

To which he said, "Goldberg, Perlman, who gives a fuck—you act, right?" And before I could respond, he came back, "You did that musical with those musical types, right? Why don'tcha come do some *real* theater with some real serious theater types?!" And then he said—again I was given no shot at responding—"Auditions are today at three. Be there, Goldberg!"

Who could say no?

I started being in productions from the beginning. The theater department was under a professor named Ralph Arzoomanian. (His real name is Raffi, and we remain friends to this day.) The son of Armenian immigrants, having grown up in Rhode Island, he was the most colorful guy I ever met. Period. But not only was he vibrant; he was a fucking genius and an amazing teacher. I took every fucking class he taught in college. He had this incredible way of taking us from discussions of the Greeks all the way to Sam Beckett. The way Ralph taught the class, there was no fat on the bone. Every single playwright he chose to explore exemplified a movement, an epoch, an era. I diligently studied the works of Aeschylus, Sophocles, Euripides, and some of the Roman playwrights, followed by Shakespeare, Molière, Racine, and then Ibsen, Chekhov, and Bertolt Brecht—so by the time I was finished, I had really absorbed the entire history of the genius of theatrical literature. I knew the Aristotelian definition of tragedy and comedy and why Shakespeare got the joke better than any of 'em. I walked away knowing the effect all these geniuses had on the pages of theatrical literature and why theater offered such a profound understanding of the human condition, equally important as the philosophy of Nietzsche, Schopenhauer, Kant, Freud, Jung—you name it. Fuck, Sam Beckett alone encapsulated to poetry the useless, tragic, funny, mysterious morass we call life as much as fifteen Einsteins did for physics.

All this genius was wrapped up into four years and presented by what can only be described as the Damon Runyon of Ivy League. Ralph came from the seedier streets of Providence, Rhode Island, one of the toughest towns on the eastern seaboard. His folks had nothing but pride and a great work ethic to pass down. Once he discovered his love for the theater, he managed to get himself a first-class education, ending up in the famed writer's workshop at the University of Iowa along with Vonnegut, Edward Albee, and a couple of other guys you might not have heard of. Anyway, to say the least, he knew his shit. His teaching style, however . . .

Every other word out of Ralph's mouth was fuck. Or motherfuck. Or cocksucker. Fuck you, you cocksuckin' muthafucka, what the fuck . . . well, you get the idea. Whereas every other professor was wearing the herringbone jacket with the leather patches on the sleeve, Ralph's uniform consisted of Levi's, white converse sneakers, a white T-shirt in spring (a long-sleeve sports shirt in the colder months), and a set of binoculars that hung around his neck. The binoculars were there 'cuz every day, the minute his teaching duties were done, he bolted to either Aqueduct or Belmont racetracks to catch as much of the afternoon card as he could. Ralph was an itinerant, degenerate horseplayer, and a damn fine handicapper at that, a rather complex skill, which he tried to pass on to me. But alas, anything requiring even the slightest of math skills, and I was hopeless. I did enjoy accompanying him to the track, though. He always sat in the most expensive part of the clubhouse and only bet long shots, which made for as much excitement as one could bear. "Fuck it," he'd say. "I like to play the fuckin' horses!" Hey, who was I to fuckin' argue?!

I really wanted to get into his head because this fucking guy was brilliant, a bona fide iconoclast. He was completely different from anybody. He rubbed the whole staff the wrong way. He made everyone uneasy, 'cuz in a world where people were trying to curry favor to further their careers, Ralph thumbed his nose at all pretense, thus symbolizing the hypocrisy of it all—fearlessly, to make things worse.

I'm at the point now at which my position as an actor is very, very different. My enthusiasm to be an actor and the motivation behind it is more in line with my devotion to the literature of it and the nature of storytelling, as opposed to what started it all: the high of performing it. Storytelling started from the time we could speak. The earliest of humankind gathered in damp caves to tell stories of their lives. It's apparently a genetic need we have as a species to tell and hear stories. That's what it's about for me now. It's as much about why we need it, why we make films and tell stories, as it is an essential means of reasserting our humanity. That's what it's evolved into for me, and it all started with this guy who I met in college, this Arzoomanian, this chance meeting that turned into something profoundly divine!

I had a great first year of school. As a freshman in college, though, I remember thinking, *Damn, girls are actually looking at me in a different way.* Who knows, maybe this was my Detroit, my new beginning, in my new skinny jeans. I soon met Linda, my first steady girlfriend. We went the whole sixties route together: we shacked up, lived together, set up house, and had a dog and three cats in a little apartment in the Bronx. I met her because she was designing costumes for the school plays, so when, one day—it mighta been around the same time she was measuring my inseam—we suddenly clicked. And that was that.

That first year I acted in two plays during the first semester and another two in the second. Ralph always directed one of the four because there were three or four other theater professors, each doing one. But what I quickly learned from Ralph was that acting was not just about getting my jollies off and digging audience applause. I developed a different perspective, one of "Holy shit! I get to act out the character created by these genius playwrights." The great ones created a reality that moved us, instructed us. They hit the bull's eye that all great art achieves. If something appeals to our collective conscious-ness—the things we have in common as humans, the same thing that joined us going back to the cavemen sitting around the fires telling tales—then it's a hit, a marvel, a work of art appreciated by all. What nobler thing could you do on this planet than participate in anything that tries to perform so realistically that it touches the nerve of all who witness it? If high school was the awakening to the magical element of the theater, then college and, in particular, Ralph gave it depth, gravitas, universality.

That year I was cast as the lead, Sky Masterson, in a production of *Guys and Dolls*. I remember it was on a Thursday, the opening night, when my whole family came to see it. Afterward they gave me the typical family "atta boy" kudos, which I was pleased to get. But the next night, as I'm leaving the theater, I see my dad standing in the alley near the backstage door.

I said, "Pops, what are you doing here? I'm really sorry but I was planning on going out tonight with a bunch of the cast."

"No," he said, "I'm not here for that. You go out with your friends. I just came by to check something out. Go have some fun, I'll see ya back at the house." And then he split. I didn't know what he meant "check something out" until the next day, when we were in the car together, and he lowered the radio.

"You know, kid, you gotta do this."

"I gotta do what?"

"This acting thing. You got no choice. You gotta do this! You got this thing that only some get. It ain't like you *should* do this—you *gotta*! So don't let anyone ever tell you otherwise!"

He then turned the radio back up. But in that moment it was like a wax seal on a document. My father gave me permission—permission to follow my goal, to perform. And don't think for a minute there weren't times when the universe was more than giving me signals to chuck the shit. Don't think I wouldn't get tested down to the very core. Don't think when the bank account was on empty and the phone hadn't rung in two years I didn't think to say, "Fuck this, old man, and your fucking advice! This is nuts!" But I never did. 'Cuz when my dad said those words he had a look about him. That order was sacrosanct. In fact, it wasn't an order at all . . . it was a blessing. And within a few months, just like that, he was gone. As if it was some holy, sacred deathbed wish. Give the shit up? Sheeeeeeit!

During the first year Ralph found that he happened to get a good bunch of us kids in the troupe who wanted more than what the school was willing to give. He started to bring in some of his downtown friends, some of his ex-real theater-type people. He brought in a guy named Arlen Digitale, a hopeful downtown director who was always on the cusp of big things but needed to subsidize his income with a little light teaching. Arlen saw without looking too hard that my passion for the stage was more than a passing college tryst. So he hooked me up the following summer with a PA gig working with some real players on some new plays they were trying out of town. As soon as classes were over in June I started hanging with this theater troupe as they rehearsed in the Village before taking it to the Provincetown Playhouse.

I'd never really hung out in the village. I was a Washington Heights and Bronx kid. But suddenly I'm downtown for the first time, hanging out on Bleecker Street, right in the middle of where the whole Beat generation was converging. I started meeting all these people who are like Actor's Studio people, who were really poor but really starry eyed and totally into what they were doing. I started to get exposed to this horrific life—these people had nothing but holes in their shirts and sweaters and were struggling to put spare change together to pay the rent, but they were doing it—and suddenly I wanted to be a part of this special breed more than anything else. We ultimately went up to the Provincetown playhouse and then down to Stockbridge to mount these two brand-new plays by up-and-coming writers.

It was the biggest, best party I ever went to and a summer that could never be duplicated. Here I am in Provincetown, Massachusetts, right on the fuckin' beach. I mean suckers saved up all fuckin' year to spend two measly weeks vacationing on that beach we've taken over for free. And I got every fuckin' Actors Studio muthafucka who's right on the cusp of greatness comin' up from NYC for a few free days on the beach to get out of the hot, smelly city—and whatever free weed they could inhale. We even rented fishing boats when nobody had a dime to his name. (How we pulled that one off remains a mystery to this day.) I went tuna fishing with no rods or reels with actors Lane Smith and Jamie Sanchez, with Lane, the country boy, leaning over the rail of the bow, calling out, "Tuuuuunaaaaaa," coaxing the fish to jump in the boat the way he'd call pigs into a barn. It was crazy. It was simply the best time. Then we moved down to Stockbridge, rubbing elbows with Eugene Ionesco, who was there for the world premiere of his newest masterwork. I'm chillin' with William Penn because it was his hometown and he was . . . well, we were all just totally chillin'. And then, sure enough, one day I'm walkin' out of the famed Alice's Restaurant having had lunch, and what do I see—my girlfriend, Linda, and my cousin Kenny, together. And I go, "What the fuck? . . ."

Didja hear about the optometrist who fell into the lens-grinding machine and made a spectacle of himself?!
—Bert Perlman, 1919–1969

(CHAPTER 5)

Forever-ness

The week of my dad's funeral, or the traditional weeklong Shiva that Jews "sit" after a death, as I mentioned earlier, is when you bring out all the photos of family life. It was a week of intense polarities, part of me wanted to crawl into a dark cave and just listen as my inner voices struggled to find direction; but the part of me that knew better knew my Mom needed me. And with my brother also having moved out years earlier, I wanted to make sure she was okay. It was the kind of challenge I had never experienced before, with no one there but myself to orchestrate how each moment of the day would go. And all the while the struggle with the eeriness of it provided me with just enough activity so as to prevent me from dwelling on the obvious; the apartment was silent, no music, no dad. The smell of dad's old clothes mixed with the souring fragrances of all the flowers that had been sent during the Shiva. It was just on the verge of being too much.

That week you bring out all the photos of family life. My childhood was wedged into these plastic album pages and in shoeboxes filled with Kodak three-by-fives or older black-and-whites, the ancient-looking, sepia-colored kind with those wavy corrugated edges. But like all photos, there's a long list of events and unbelievable coincidental situations that led up to the moment when you stood still and said, "cheese!"

EASY STREET (THE HARD WAY)

That's what I was looking at—the unseen area and space that no photo can ever really capture. For me, it seemed like I was prematurely urged to start to piece together everything. I had to—my old man had just died, and I knew it was my duty to take the reins, like the heroes in the Westerns my dad and I loved to watch. I was gonna need every bit of the strength and manliness I saw in those movies we watched together, especially now that we lost our lead actor. I was gonna be the one who leapt onto the team of runaway horses to *whoa* them down in order to bring some stability to this rocking stagecoach of our family life.

We didn't have hundreds of people show up that week. To the world, it wasn't like losing a head of state, even if to me it was more paramount than that. It was a very small, intimate group, as I mentioned: family members, neighbors, my mom's coworkers from the county clerk's office, and my dad's peers, who were then mostly TV repair guys and fellow teachers. By that time my dad had long hung up the dream of being a professional musician, and I had never met the people from that era. He had been a TV repairman ever since my brother and I were young kids. In the last days he taught television electronics in a vocational high school, the kind of school where they sent kids unable to make it anywhere else, already deemed longshots and marginalized, pigeonholed to either learning a trade or becoming career criminals. In those days those schools were one step away from being sent to a locked-down reform school. He used to tell his class straight up, "This is like the last-chance saloon, you know what I mean? You don't make it here, you ain't going to make it anywhere."

The night before my old man's first day as a substitute teacher at Chelsea Vocational he came to my bedroom when I was just about to sleep and asked to borrow my baseball bat—I had a prized Louisville Slugger that he had managed to get a couple of Yankees to sign.

I heard him opening the chest at the foot of my bed. "Can I take your bat with me to school?"

I said, "Sure, I guess. Why not?" I thought he was teaching electronics, but I knew my dad well enough that he must've had something up his sleeve.

When he came back that night we were having our regular family supper, which was always at six o'clock on the dot, when he talked about his first day as a teacher.

"I walked into class and said my name's Mr. Perlman. Anybody comes within thirty feet of me I start swinging this fuckin' thing. The whole class looks at me in shock, like I'm an escapee from the loony bin. But I'm keeping a straight face until they realize, 'Holy shit, this dude's fuckin' with us.'"

From that point on my dad won those kids over, and he eventually became the most popular teacher at the school. I only wish he had found this calling earlier in life, because this was clearly what he was born to do—be a big brother, to be somebody who, through love, understanding, and patience, was able to redirect misguided energies. I'm pretty sure there's no higher calling than that!

Irving, Dad's older brother, like everybody from my father's side, had all tried to be musicians. He had worked hard to be a professional violinist; my dad's sister, Aunt Mildred, a professional singer, and another uncle played the accordion, until the hard knocks of the creative life made all eventually throw in their towels. Nevertheless, at every dinner party at my house or at another relative's place, after we ate, boom: all these fucking instruments would come out of the woodwork, and the whole night would be a fantastic escape from the ordinary. I loved those times. People were singing; people were playing. People were telling jokes; people were getting drunk. The booze was flowing, and I began to become addicted to ways of removing myself from the mundane, which I found to be really deadly. I dreaded routine, the sameness of breakfast, lunch, and dinner. Every day was deadening to me, and there was nothing to aspire to; nothing about it had any kind of color to it—it was just drab, drab gray.

"The Perlman curse," I said. Those were words my father used. My father was citing the fact that very few in the male Perlman line ever lived past fifty—Uncle Irving and I are the only exceptions. Everybody on my father's side tended to die young. My dad's dad didn't make it past fifty. My dad didn't make it past fifty. It was kind of a curse on all the Perlman men. Hell, my brother didn't even make thirty-nine. I mean, fuck, this shit was so palpable, I remember when I was in my forty-ninth year I got so nuts that every month I was buying another quarter-million dollars' worth of life insurance. Even my wife started lookin' at me like maybe I was worth more dead than alive. But Irving's story inspired me deeply about how life sometimes makes you throw the dice, whether you want to or not, and in the most dramatic way. He was supposed to be dead when he was twenty-one because he had an inoperable tumor where his spine met his brain, and nobody wanted to touch it. The last doctor he went to said, "So what's everybody telling you?"

"Everybody is telling me I got three to six months to live."

The doc said, "If you do nothing, that's right. So then, why don't I try to take it off, and if you die on the operating table, well, then, you lost three to six months of your life. This is the only chance you got, and by the way, I'm not guaranteeing you anything, but who knows." So Irving got the operation and lived until his eighties, thus being the first to break the deadly Perlman curse.

During Shiva I talked with my uncle about when Dad got sick a couple of years ago. I remember it was a scene right out of Spencer Tracey in *Boy's Town*. Dad was in this big ward in Columbia Presbyterian Hospital, and I went to visit him at around 5:45 in the afternoon. So you know how the light is at that time of the day. (In cinema I later learned that little sliver of time was called "magic hour" and one every cameraman wants to capture because . . . well, it's magical!) So he's in this huge ward, the size of a half a football field, and his bed was all the way on the other end, right by the window. There's this streaming sunlight, late afternoon sunlight, coming in, and it's backlighting this sort of tableau, and I know I'm kind of walking toward the bed, but all I see are shapes. I see about thirty figures all sitting around someone propped up in a bed. As I get closer and closer to this beautiful image I notice that this crowd is all young Puerto Rican and tough Irish kids sitting around my dad. His class had come to visit him, you know, in the hospital, and that was the moment when I realized I wasn't the only one who thought of my dad as angelic. The look on every one of those kid's faces—and these were tough kids, man—I mean, these kids really, really loved Dad.

The only grandmother I knew was on my mom's side, my dad's parents having died long before I could remember. My father's family was third- or fourth-generation Jewish Americans, originally from Hungary, but my mom's mother barely escaped Poland just as all the Nazi shit started to hit the fan. She fled with three daughters, leaving her husband to come meet them later. Two of the girls died before she made it safely to New York City. That's where she had my mother and my mother's baby sister, Natalie. And although my grandmother wasn't a particularly religious person when she was in Poland, because of the whole debacle of being ethnically threatened and shot at and her children dying simply because they were Jewish, she found religion when she got to the United States. Imagine losing your flesh and blood, your little daughters, to some insane global hatred? She became more and more religious as she got older. She was the reason why my parents insisted I get bar mitzvahed and all that stuff. My mom was not particularly religious, and my dad, although a true humanist, was a self-declared agnostic; he had a palpable disdain for anything religious. But out of respect for my grandmother, everybody kind of wanted me to go through the motions, which is what I did. And that's all because she was such a great lady and commanded true respect.

I hung around with Mom for the few weeks before school started, but soon after I returned I suddenly felt like I existed in a surreal world, partially because one of the strangest things I ever experienced occurred. And it happened every night while I slept. Prior to this I never really had an ability to remember my dreams, but that suddenly changed dramatically. It happened for one full year after my father died, for 365 days exactly. Then it stopped, and I haven't been able to remember dreams more than in snippets ever since. But that year, every night when I went to sleep, from the first moment until I woke up, I experienced these vivid, Technicolor dreams. They were as if presented by Cecile B. DeMille; they were Cinemascope, Cinerama, flamboyant, and bizarre. There were also some Hitchcockian moments to them. There was a lot of flying and soaring and falling off rooftops.

The only constant in all these varied dreams was my dad. He was the star and overbearing presence during each of these nights. In all the dream scenes it was me and my dad going through sometimes very surreal, sometimes very mundane situations, though all of it can only be described as truly cinematic and epic. The longer this happened and the longer I realized these dreams were going to keep occurring, the more I knew this must be important and that I must pay attention. Because it was lasting for so long and it was such a departure from anything I ever experienced before, I didn't know if it would ever stop happening. These visitations, which are how I began to view these dreams, seemed to be coming out of some very primal need on my part. It felt good after a while, and I saw it as a way to steal back a little of the time with my dad that had been stolen from me.

I sensed there was a sort of mysticism, for lack of a better word, to the exchanges my dad and I had in these dreams. I was not a bystander in these dreams, and a lot was asked of me and being shown to me. Some of the dreams were explicitly instructional, whereas others were violent and unsettling. Some had some really horrific things happen; some were very languid and pastoral. There was this incredible cornucopia of experience that felt so real and more vivid than anything that was happening to me in my waking hours. I began to understand something intensely special was transpiring. I was getting this glimpse of some other space outside the materialist world of time and the brick-and-mortar world we know. There were happenings that were unexplainable, as if coming from another unseeable level. They were meant to be funky and weird, but they were way bigger than I was fully able to comprehend. It seemed clear that there were other forces in the universe that were more than the pragmatism view that my dad raised me to believe. These forces I saw in these dreams were unexplainable, ever-present and omniscient, and larger than the universe.

In a strange way, when that year ended, I had my first personal relationship with a higher being. And even though the person who was the star of these dreams was a proclaimed agnostic and maybe an atheist, he was my guide to these mysterious forces, forces that man called God to begin with. I was able to regard Dad's passing as a gift and a loss. He gave me the gift of knowing that he was going to maintain a place right next to me forever. He showed there were other powers that allowed his spirit to live on. And although I retained a disdain for all things religious, I began to create my own version of a deity.

I never talked to anyone about these dreams or my beliefs before. So let me admit here that I do pray, every day, anywhere from two to eight times a day. I have this deity that I purposefully allow to remain unde-fined and ethereal. And yet I know He sees all and knows all. Punto. Pe-riod. It came as a result of my dad's loss. This was not a drug-induced experience that gave me a gate to another door of perception—type of horseshit, with all that astral plane stuff; instead, I got an uncompli-cated and simplified understanding of a being that was grander than I could imagine. Later I realized something like this doesn't happen often or to too many people. It must've been akin to what inspired writers of texts such as the Bible and other religious dogma to attempt to explain. But the experience is such that words can't describe it and in fact only screw it up and regurgitate it into dogma. I also knew my higher power didn't need to be worshipped or given lip service or pros-elytizing for, that I did not need to convert anyone. It's a personal rela-tionship and needed no church to validate it. The more I realized this, the more I saw how the chance people who came into my path were not so coincidental, Ralph Arzoomanian being one of them.

I finished college after doing numerous productions, though my maturity level changed after the death of my father, his dream world visitations, and from Ralph's enthusiasm for art. Eventually I under-stood a performance was a means to express a playwright's point of view. I tried to understand what it is he's writing about and why, his modality, and what he's capturing. When I took the focus off of me and put it onto the character itself, then I was really cooking. I men-tioned Hemingway before: guys like him, the iconic legendary writers in literature, every single thing they wrote got me to say, "Were you tripping on acid when you wrote this? This is fucking awesome. Where did this come from, and how did you pull it off?" You know, you could spend a year just analyzing *Waiting for Godot* as an existential sort of document. Forget about the fact that it's entertaining and funny.

In the last years of college, in addition to the school productions, a bunch of us in the troupe formed a little ensemble to write and perform sketch comedy. It's called blackout sketch comedy, like what you see on *Saturday Night Live*. Our impromptu production was fairly good as far as the mad-cap, funny kind of quasi-barbillion genre of comedy goes. We went around and performed at old age homes, underprivileged high schools, and hole-in-the-wall clubs—we had a ball. I was just experimenting, trying to find where I could fit in the performing arts and who I was as a performer. Mostly what came natural to me was comedy.

I lost touch with the girls of our blackout troupe, but one of the guys, Joel Brooks, is still here, like me, banging it out as an actor in Hollywood. He's one of the most talented guys I ever met. Joel made a career as an actor, and if you check out his IMDb entry, you'll see he's got a very long string of credits. But why Joel and I decided to go to graduate school together at the University of Minnesota was for another reason, something other than theater. By the end of my senior year I had turned into a wanted man. I needed to get out of Dodge because the law enforcement department of the City of New York was looking for my ass. I needed to go on the lam, and in a hurry.

It started after my dad gave me that first car of mine toward the end of freshman year. I was doing plays and getting home between 11:30 to a quarter to midnight every night. I was living in the Bronx, where there was absolutely no parking at all, ever, so I pretty much double-parked for the entire last three years of college. In turn, I accumulated $7,536 in parking tickets. It might as well been $750,000, because when you don't have a dollar, $7,500 is a fortune. What happened in NYC back then is that if you didn't pay the $35 ticket, it became a $65 ticket, which became a $90 ticket, which capped off at $130. At a certain point you are deemed a "scoff-law." Then they treat you as if you are running a drug cartel, and they can put one of these things on your tire, the boot, so your car is immobilized. (Now I think they just tow the car and you can't get it back until you pay.) But they can stop you at a red light and put you upside a wall and make you spread your fuckin' legs like ya just killed Grandma!

Initially I simply ignored the accumulating tickets, but I then began to see the seriousness of the results of my double-parking ways. In my mind, I was basically a fugitive from the law because of fucking parking tickets. There was not a moving violation among the lot. No speeding tickets, no plowing through red lights, nothing as sexy as that—just double parking. I felt like Al Capone when they got him for tax evasion. At the end of senior year I started to wonder how I was going to address this snag. Everybody in my troupe was figuring out what their next move was going to be once June came around and our college days of having that safety net was about to be pulled out from under us. You graduate from college; it's time to make the move. Being a scofflaw in the biggest city in the world—and with me smoking copious amounts of weed—I got a little paranoid. I saw myself being carted off to county jail, and I never took myself for a guy who'd do well in prison. I always liked tossing my own salads.

The decision to go to graduate school was sealed by the parking ticket dilemma and was fueled by me wondering if I was indeed ready to jump off the cliff. In truth, I didn't relish the thought of segueing into the starving life of a beginning actor. I saw a glimpse of their lives, as I mentioned, while I was a PA in Provincetown and Stockbridge. I saw what a shitty quality of life they had (except for the occasionally crazy parties). It was a heavy price to make a living as a working actor in New York, but that's what it took. Although I wore bell bottoms and had a semi-Afro, I wasn't ready to be that bohemian. Don't get me wrong: I was no bourgeois either, but I did like the idea of having shit in my refrigerator at two in the morning when I was stoned and had the munchies. Primal needs. Need I say more?

Joel and I noticed this flyer on a bulletin board in the drama department locker room that the University of Minnesota was offering a full ride to get a master's degree in fine arts, with an apprenticeship to Guthrie Theatre, which was, at that time, the premiere reparatory company in North America. It was called the Bush Fellowship. My best buddy, Joel Brooks, and I applied and were called. Neither Joel nor I was awarded the fellowship. I was, however, invited to attend the university on a partial scholarship because of my financial situation—my dad having just passed away and my mom having limited resources. I decided to take the offer because I figured, hey, no self-respecting New York cop would look for me over a couple of parking tickets in fucking Minnesota! Joel agreed with my nonlogic, and the plan began to take shape.

My girlfriend, Linda, who had also graduated college but wasn't ready for grad school, encouraged me to go. But she wanted to come along. I told her that I didn't know if that was a good idea.

"It's cheaper to stay in the dorm. And I might not even stay there that long . . . it all depends," I said.

She put her arms around my waist and hugged me. "Come on," she said, "let's commit to this."

So we did. We loaded our crap up into an eighteen-foot rental truck and drove out there with our dog and three cats. We rented a beautiful house in the country. It was very scenic, very peaceful, and very much *not* like New York. Within a month of setting up house together, I told Linda I had to leave. We had been emotionally separating slowly since the latter part of college. She was from Upstate New York originally, and she mentioned she'd like to go back to live there one day. I think she had had enough of the New York City experience for this lifetime. I wanted to sow my wild oats and thought it would be much better to tell her up front that I wanted out rather than sneaking around and cheating on her. We didn't argue. I moved into a cold-water flat, a rat-hole efficiency, in an area called "Dinky Town" near the downtown campus.

Although we both knew it was best for the both of us, it was tough and not pleasant. It was the first time I ever had to separate from someone I was very close to. I had not yet experienced the pain or the spoils of a relationship when it ends or transitions into something else. Linda stayed in the house and did fine for herself. She still lives probably within a mile of that house we first rented in 1971. Who knows? Maybe our paths crossed for that reason, because she always seemed so comfortable there.

I looked upon my adventure to the Midwest with curiosity. When you grow up in New York or in Los Angeles you can develop a stilted view that everywhere else in the country is uncool. I wanted to learn what folks, real American Midwest folks, felt and thought—what their process was and how they moved through life. I wanted to use this opportunity to look at being an American through a different lens.

The University of Minnesota is a top-ten school. It's filled with resources and has huge operating budgets, an amazing sports program, and a highly regarded drama department. Minneapolis was as culturally vibrant a city as any city I've ever been in. There was also lots of money in the Twin Cities. The rich, with time on their hands, donated substantially to make the city have the best galleries, the best art museums. The Guthrie Theatre had a modernist style and an interior with circular seating, rising concentrically from the stage, for an audience of more than eleven hundred. I had some really cool professors there, but there were no Ralphs. There weren't even guys who were a fraction as dynamic and unique and interesting as Ralph. I tried them all because part of the reason why I decided to extend the educational direction in theater wasn't solely because of parking tickets. Ralph had lit a fire under me; I wanted to find out if there were other people who were going to blow my mind and turn me on to unbelievable ways of thinking about the dramatic arts.

I had a very tough time finding anybody who liked or accepted me in my first six months on campus. I didn't think I was particularly hard to get along with or that big of an asshole, but I saw there was this miniresentment about having a bona fide New Yorker in their midst. It seemed the Twin Cities wanted to emulate New York culturally and was determined to show me that being from the Apple wasn't "all that"!

But as much as I loved the place and the people in it, I never thought I would stay there once finished. Joel only lasted a year and went back to New York City to begin his acting career. I thought about going with him, but I stayed and wanted to finish what I started. I remember one dinner, when the lead actors in the production were invited to a dinner held for the sponsors of the Guthrie. I was among the glitterati of Minnesota, as well as professors—guys who were brilliant educators, sophisticated, well-read, well-traveled PhDs—when a discussion about Watergate came to the floor. This was an incredibly dramatic event in the political history of the United States: a president got caught blatantly putting his middle finger up to law and order. I listened to the conversation in utter amazement.

They were saying, "There's no way in the world Nixon could've done that." "He's our president, right or wrong." "Presidents are completely above this kind of suspicion. Why don't they just leave him alone?"

I was thinking as a New Yorker, saying to myself, "What a schmuck Nixon was for getting caught. He was running the greatest country in the world, surrounded by the brightest and the best, and he goes and gets involved with a bunch of fucking losers."

I had to bite my tongue that entire dinner, because I almost shouted, "Of course, he's guilty, every fucking politician is fucking guilty . . . it's just that the smart ones never get caught!" When you grow up in New York, where I came from, you just understood that nearly everybody is shady, meaning everybody's got an angle, especially the guys who run for office. Everybody's doing something for a whole set of reasons that's different from the set of reasons they said they're doing them for.

In the summer of '72, between my first and second year at the University of Minnesota, before Joel split back East, we decided to drive to San Francisco. We wanted to get a glimpse of the very hip, very celebrated Haight-Ashbury. We'd never been out West, and it was our Jack Kerouac *On the Road* moment. We drove through Nebraska, Colorado, and Utah. The moment we hit the Rockies . . . well, it was like I was tripping. My whole life's experiences never provided me with anything that could compare to the majesty of what I was seeing with my own eyes. I was taken aback by the grandly insane beauty of America.

Standing below those mountains and looking up as they soar to the clouds in this black massiveness and are crowned with brilliantly white snow crowns—it is incredibly humbling, tremendously moving.

When we finally hit San Francisco we fell into the whole hippie world, sleeping on people's floors and couches and wearing tie-dyed clothes. We worked as day laborers to get enough money to eat and get high at night. We did some rehearsals and got to see the inside view of the kind of experimental theater that was happening out there before we drove back to Minnesota. Joel left right off for New York that same night we arrived back. Overall, it was a cool trip, one you could only do when you're young.

Even though I was kind of a fish out of water in the Midwest, in truth the people there were super-nice. I had a great time and made a lot of really good friends who I still have to this day. Although no Ralphs, I got to meet some phenomenal people and encouraging and nurturing teachers. And although I learned next to nothing, I did get a master's in fine fucking arts—whatever the fuck that means. (I have that diploma covering up a hole that I punched into the wall in my bathroom, so it wasn't completely useless.) As soon as I graduated I headed back to New York City. I showed up with this rather large dog I had adopted from a shelter in Minneapolis, and this didn't exactly make my re-entry to New York all that smooth.

After I bald-tired my way back to New York City, I had no place to stay. Lots of friends offered a-few-days places to crash, but I wore out my welcome everywhere. Once, I slept on a friend's couch, and when I came home at the end of the day, my dog had eaten the guy's couch and a few chairs. So my return to New York was an inch short of triumphant.

And now a guest appearance from the professor . . .

As often happens in life, my first encounter with Ron Perlman was accidental and, in the wash of time, serendipitous. I was teaching a class in theater at Hunter College in the Bronx (now Herbert Lehman

College) when I saw him walk by in the adjacent hall. I didn't know him well, but I had heard that he participated in some of the campus musicals. As he strolled by I left the classroom and called out, "Goldberg!" He continued walking away, and I made another attempt, "Yeah, you! Goldberg!" He turned, looked at me, pointed to himself, and mimed, "You mean me?" I said, "Yeah you, Goldberg. I need to speak with you." It was as necessary as it was an inelegant introduction for both of us. The theater division was having trouble casting for A Midsummer Night's Dream, and I used that occasion to urge him to try out for the play and help out a colleague of mine. Somewhere in there I got Ron's name straight and held on to it for dear life for the next fifty-plus years.

Well, he did try out for the play, was cast as the lead "mechanical," and was outstanding. In the ensuing months he took academic classes with me in Play Analysis, History of the Theater, and so on, and about a year later I cast him as the lead character, Max, in Harold Pinter's Homecoming. I have to add that I also cast Joel Brooks as his son Teddy, and I never had a better tandem of actors in all the years I directed at that college. Ron was a revelation in that part. First of all, the character of Max is not only a colorful and complex character; he is also the generator within the play. He's similar to a basketball star who improves the play of everyone around him. Ron proved to me with that production that he could drive a play from the center out and keep it moving. And I've seen him execute that dynamic in all his professional work. It is a singular ability that is generous as well as rare.

I was never nuts about encouraging my student actors to make it a profession. While an active playwright I saw too many instances of actors in and out of my New York productions having an extremely tough go of it. Case in point: I was directing a play of my own Off Broadway, The Moths, and I made it a point to have Ron and Joel attend to the open calls and early rehearsals. But the open calls were my imperative because the actors came "out of the cold" as it were, uninvited and usually miscast for the roles for which they were auditioning, not to mention here and there physically worse for wear. But Ron was determined to stay the course, so when the next semester came around he was off to the U. of Minnesota for graduate study in theater. I recall him telling me after he graduated that he was well prepared for the academic requirements at Minnesota as a result of his studies at Hunter. Although I was thrilled with his acting as a young man, I was more than thrilled with his development as a student in the subject matter dealing with literature, history, theory, and the like. He was a straight-A student with me in all those areas, and there's no doubt in my mind that the intelligence that informed all his acting roles was one of his stronger attributes. I also take great satisfaction in having introduced him to horse racing and good cigars. There were times after his studies were over when he would secure a box of Punch cigars for me from a store in Greenwich Village. He and his sidekick, Burton Levy, who I loved dearly, would get me the cigars when I so prompted. I believe Burton is mentioned in this book, and I'll leave it to Ron to describe the essence of that relationship, but I will say this: for years and years Burton would call me and speak of nothing but Ron, and I mean on and on. I loved it.

When a young guy is going to college, everything he takes in gets magnified. Ron has told me more than once that I taught him a lot that he eventually used in his career. But he has to know that I basically put things out there and it was his intelligence and innate talent that pulled it together and made use of it on a practical level. But if I can be given credit for the cigars he uses as a prop, I'm more than content. It was one of the best things in Hellboy. Every puff he took gave me a definite charge.

There is an area in which he excels that few are aware of: his ability to direct plays. Years ago he took it upon himself to direct a couple of readings of my plays in NYC. Neither of the two plays is chip-shot, and one of them is unproduced for two reasons. One, not many venues have wanted to produce it, and two, I'm not confident that there are a lot of directors out there who could handle it. The reading Ron directed was sensible, extremely competent, and a revelation to me. I would trust him with any play I've written, case closed. Again, there's no substitute for intelligence and talent, and when you throw in a quart of sensibility you've got the whole bag. And Ron has that versatility. I once watched him act the role of an Amish father whose child was murdered by a bunch of vandals throwing stones. As a Jewish kid from the Bronx, he couldn't be more unlike the character he played, and yet he gave a brilliant, understated, yet piercing performance. I kept waiting for the cigar, but unfortunately the Amish don't smoke, so I was out of luck. Cigar or no cigar, I was thrilled. There's not much in the repertory he can't do. I used to tell my students that if you can act in a Restoration play, you can pretty much do any style that exists. I've never seen Ron do Restoration, but there isn't a doubt in my mind he can't pull it off.

At this point he's done a lot of films and television, and most of it has been readily available to the public. There's no need for me to go over all that. I was there at the beginning, loved witnessing the middle, and am curious to see how his career takes shape and evolves. And yes, it will evolve. Oh, and I love him.

—*Ralph Arzoomanian*

(CHAPTER 6)

Godfather

After sleeping on people's couches, with my dog fucking up all over the place, throwing up, chewing up everything from sneakers to couch legs, I rapidly pissed away whatever goodwill I had left. I was losing friends. They didn't answer my calls or want to speak to me again. I was having second thoughts about whether leaving Minnesota had been a good idea. I mean, I was at least getting laid in Minnesota. Yes, you heard me right! And with *women*! I know this sounds irrelevant, but to a young man at that age, only breathing was more important.

In Minnesota, however, I knew, as culturally vibrant as the Twin Cities were, I could only go so far in theater. In New York the sky was the limit. There was no ceiling. In fact, there was no place you couldn't go. Shit, if your imagination was big enough and the chips fell where you wanted them to fall. . . . Despite the difficult settling process, I needed to be in New York to begin my quest to become a professional actor. I was finally ready to no longer be running from it; I was finally ready to run toward something.

The people of the real heartland of America were, for the most part, upfront, solid folk, yet I needed to be back in my hometown, the land of corruption and cynicism. I don't mean this to come across as a condemnation, but it's true and part of what makes NYC the most unhypocritical place on earth. You know the code, you know the rules.

In the Midwest I once gave the ticket guy at a ballgame $20, and he started to hand back change. I said, "No, that's for you."

"Sir, the ticket is fifteen-fifty."

"No, no, I'm asking you to give me a better ticket."

"Oh no, I can't do that." I realized at that moment I was in the wrong fuckin' town, because if you do that shit at Yankee Stadium, you're going to be sitting right behind the dugout. It may not be $20 anymore, but that's what it was when I was a kid—now it's $100 or whatever—but people know what grass looks like and it's fucking the way fucking business is done in New York.

As for the parking tickets that awaited me, the bureaucratic side of New York City was dead serious. While I was at the University of Minnesota the Parking Violations Bureau was better than the Canadian fucking Mounted Police or Scotland fucking Yard, and it must've operated under the same slogan: "We always get our man." They didn't know I was in Minnesota, so instead they found my next of kin, which happened to be my poor mom in Washington Heights. They kept sending her harassing letters. They wanted to know where this Ron Perlman was so he could write them a nearly $8,000 check. They sent more and more letters and even called her and said they were going to put me in jail. I didn't know about this while it was happening, but it was sad. My mom pleaded, "Please, don't hurt my boy." And she wrote them a check for $7,500 and change. (I expect to be all paid up with her a week from next Tuesday. I'm kidding. That's a joke. And thank you, Mom, for letting me be a free man upon my homecoming.)

What saved me from my first few weeks in NYC living the life of an unwelcomed squatter was the return to the city of my best friend, Burton Levy. He had visited me a few times in Minnesota, but of late he had been in Upstate New York trying to put together one of his many business deals. This guy became my Medici, my "sponsor of the arts" during the next five years while I pursued acting. I met Burton in college. I noticed him hanging around the theater. He had this kind of fascination with theater and saw it as a way to make money if you were able to produce a hit or make a film. His curiosity turned into something of a friendship between us, which burgeoned into something that will never be replaced again, an incredible bond we developed. Burton was the first guy I ever met who taught me what a stand-up guy is supposed to look like. He's the first guy I ever met who taught me what it means to have someone's back. It's more than just the phrase, "I got your back." He taught me what that was supposed to actually look like and that it was something people mean when they say it. I'll tell you something, at sixty-three years old, that's pretty fucking rare. Because I've heard a lot of people say it but have seen very few people mean it. Burton meant it, and it was the other way around as well.

Burton had been a real character in Lehman College. Whereas most kids made ends meet by bussing tables, driving cabs, or working as camp counselors, Burton got a job as a concrete inspector. This was a fairly important position in the New York construction scene. No building got green lit in New York if it didn't have concrete samples that passed certain standards. Burton was one of a handful of guys who were certified at either putting the kibosh on or giving the go-ahead to huge jobs. There might be ten concrete trucks waiting in line to pour a foundation, and all were on hold until Burton gave the thumbs up or down. Talk about sleeping with the fishes—there were an awful lot of people with an awful lot at stake riding on his decisions. It wasn't the safest job, but Burton knew how to walk that tightrope.

Subsequently he was the only guy I knew on campus who had his own money from a good-paying job. It wasn't family money or inheritance money; he had money that he was pulling in on his own. There was a kind of exoticness to him that made me think, "Maybe this is a guy I need to get to know better." It turned out—and I say this without exaggeration—that Burton Levy was the toughest Jew I have ever come across in my whole fuckin' life. He grew up in Yonkers, in one place not mentioned too often in the book *Where Famous Jews Came From*. Burton got to be tough the hard way—on the mean streets of one of the toughest little suburbs of New York City.

I remember one night when Burton, another friend of ours, and I went out to have a drink at this bar in Yonkers. Burton was kind of a controversial figure up there because he was one of these guys who told you how it was and didn't make any bones about it. He had a lot of friends, but he also had a lot of enemies. So we walk into this one bar, and as we walk in a guy on his left and a guy on his right both punch him on the chin at the same time. It was like it was choreographed. It was like Busby Berkeley. Because Burton was blindsided and didn't see it coming, it was the one and only time I ever saw him go down to one knee. As he was going down to the ground after being cold-cocked, somebody came up from behind and hit him over the back of the head with a bar stool.

My other friend and I started to jump in, but Burton put his hand up and said, "No." That crack on the head with the barstool seriously pissed him off and only woke him up more. Burton was built like a bull, with calves the size of Montana and a neck the size of New Jersey. I watched Burton single-handedly beat the piss out of probably eighteen guys at once. He was a little disheveled when done, but he insisted we stay nonetheless. We sat at the bar and had a drink. He just wanted to let them know there was no question of who was the toughest muthafucka in that place. After he gave a fuckin' sizeable tip, held down by our empty scotch glasses on the bar, he stood and casually straightened out his clothes' creases and brushed off his clothes—and then we left.

That was my best friend, Burton Levy, and eventually the godfather to my children. While in college Burton and I often went with Professor Ralph to the track. Burton also had a little taste for horseplay, and like me, he liked Ralph's point of view about culture and the world. Burton and I started smoking good cigars and drinking the finest scotch. We went to Madison Square Garden and watched Muhammad Ali fight, and then Jerry Quarry fight, with Burton somehow always managing to get ringside tickets. All of a sudden Burton showed me how you could actually demand stuff out of life rather than have a backseat and just take whatever shit fell off the back of the truck. It was an empowering period for me: I didn't have to accept borderline poverty as my family had been resigned to for generations. Burton and I dreamed together, me wanting to be an actor, with Burton thinking he might become a theater impresario and raise enough capital to make a difference in the theater scene.

Burton Levy, who was my very first and always will be my one and only lifelong best friend. And when I say best friend, he's been gone since the year 2000, so for fourteen years now, I've been without him. He's still my best friend—he'll never be replaced. I really don't float the word around very much; I actually think there can be only one best. Burton never married, even if he had short-term things with a lot of different women. Although not the marrying kind, he loved kids. As the godfather to my children, he showered them with every single thing a godfather is supposed to shower a kid with. From gifts to ideas to "You can come to me if your father or your mom does something really fucking stupid—I'm your haven." He became this shining symbol of safety for them, for both of my kids. Even though we lost him when my daughter was sixteen and my son, ten, to this day they've never had a figure in their lives who's come close to the space that Burton occupied. He had a horrific time toward the end, and he died horribly and very young at fifty-two years old. He was an example of somebody who was too big for his own limitations. He was one of those stars that burn out the brightest and the fastest.

Burton became my "sponsor of the arts" within a month of my return to the city. He had gone to Woodstock, an Upstate New York hippie town, and struck a deal to become partners with an older guy who owned an exotic jewelry / handmade handbag store on the corner of Eighth Street and McDougal, right in the middle of the hippest street in the hippest part of NYC. The guy was getting older and had nobody to leave the store to, so he took Burton's offer so he could phase himself out. And because I needed a little income and wasn't exactly knockin' 'em dead in my quest to take the New York theater by storm, Burton enlisted me as a part timer.

The store did great from the beginning, and I made enough to rent my first broom closet–size apartment in the Village. It was so small— are you ready for some small jokes? "It was so small, you had to go outside to change your mind." "It was so small, you couldn't laugh 'Ha-ha'—you had to laugh 'ho-ho.'" "It was so small, you put your key in the lock, turn the key, and you rearranged the furniture." That's how fucking small this fucking place was. But hey, the store paid handsomely for Burton to keep indulging in his expensive habits and paid for me to keep my lights on while I pursued theater.

I had been a professional student for the last eighteen years. Suddenly I found myself in the cold, hard world, needing to figure out quickly how to get work as an actor, and I began to plant some flags in the ground. I had no agents. I had no credits other than academic, which meant nothing. I basically started flat-footed and inert. I relied on two publications; one was called *Show Business* and the other, *Backstage*. I think *Show Business* folded, but *Backstage* is still around. These publications listed auditions a little bit for Broadway, a little bit for Off Broadway, but mostly for free shit, which was Off-Off Broadway. These publications would come out once a week, and I would circle every audition I could possibly go to. And that's what I did. I did a lot of auditioning for Off-Off Broadway plays. Every once in awhile I would see an open call for a Broadway play, and I'd go to those as well. That marked the beginnings of me auditioning for musicals with a particularly mediocre voice and getting three bars into the audition and hearing somebody in the middle of this darkened theater go, "Thank you! Next." That same thing, or the equivalent, happened for at least three hundred plays I auditioned for. It's 99 percent rejection, and 1 percent of the time someone would say, "Yeah, come do this play," but it was always for free. I was just good enough to not get paid. It seemed as if I was running in place as fast as I could while getting absolutely nowhere.

Here's the dynamics of what actors have to do to break in. If it's an open call, they post what time to be at the theater. Because they are seeing people who are unrepresented, without appointments, you need to get there really, really early. It's first come, first serve. You might need to be there at ten in the morning, and you don't get your chance to be seen until 4:30 in the afternoon. At least one hundred, maybe two or three hundred show up. Most of the time you stand outside the theater in a line that snakes along the sidewalk and around the block. If it was the middle of winter, they might put you in a big room or cram the hopefuls into the lobby—it's called "a cattle call" for a reason. But you went and took a chance because you have to run out every single ground ball and go after every long shot. I did auditions for *Evita*, *Hair*, and whatever was playing in the seventies. Most of the open cattle calls were for musicals. Rarely were open calls for a straight play. For that, you had to be sent to the audition by somebody who had vetted you and signed you as a client. You needed a bona fide agent, but I didn't have an agent the first three years I was in New York. The plan was to throw shit against the wall and hope that something would stick. I always stayed busy with Off-Off Broadway plays. They paid nothing unless the piece was being played out of town, and then at least you'd get a fuckin' dump of a room and food money.

You could not have a straight job with set hours if you wanted to become an actor. Auditions could be anytime and for however long it took. Same for rehearsals. That's why many aspiring thespians wait tables, bartend, or have jobs with somewhat flexible hours. And that's why Burton and his store became my "sponsor of the arts." I might go on these out-of-town runs for a week or for three months, but when I came back Burton always welcomed me with open arms. He gave me enough of a salary to get groceries and keep my lights on in my apartment. My place was a ten-minute walk to work, close to the subway entrance, and the best setup I could've wanted. Burton was encouraging, and on top of it, we still talked about how we'd break into theater or cinema in big ways as we did in school. I didn't have to drive a taxi or bus tables, thanks to Burton.

At this time Joe Papp became a big star in New York and in all of theater. He went from doing this neighborhood shit, going from doing *Hamlet* in underprivileged neighborhoods in Brooklyn, the Bronx, Queens, the Lower East Side, or Alphabet City, to Elizabethan plays in the summertime in Central Park. Suddenly the mayor of New York gave him this amazing fucking building on Layette Street for a $1 a year. It was the former Astor Library converted by the city into a theater. He called it the Public Theater, and it is, to this day *the* most important laboratory for new plays and playwrights in all the country. That was Papp's rent—a buck. So Joe Papp becomes the impresario who Burton and I had been talking about becoming ourselves. We saw it was possible for someone to culturally capture the imagination of the most important city in the world and then become somebody who physically changes the landscape of and how theater is talked about in that city. This only stoked our dream to a greater degree. It became like, "Here it is. This is the guy doing exactly what we're talking about doing." I am, in fact, still kindling this dream, as you'll see when I talk about Wing and a Prayer.

The rebellion of the sixties transformed into the golden era of the seventies when incredible stuff was happening in theater and cinema. In 1972 *The Godfather Part I* was released, and that, for my money, is the greatest movie ever made, for a variety of reasons. But the main reason is that, unlike the two *Godfather* movies that followed, which are perfectly great, this one had a historic, high-water-mark performance by one of the most significant figures in film history, Marlon Brando. He was always good, but there were three times when he was exceptional, when serious students of the art of acting like myself couldn't begin to dissect and deconstruct how he did what he did because there was just too much magic involved. One of those three performances was Vito Corleone, in *The Godfather*.

The other films this magic came through was in *On the Waterfront* and *Streetcar*. Those are the three times when he really let loose. Having worked with Marlon and been up close and personal in the little bit of time I had with him on the set of *The Island of Doctor Moreau,* I got a rare chance to really observe him. Like so many actors of my generation, I had such an obsession with the guy and such an incredible unquenchable thirst to get a glimmer of where that kind of genius comes from. But Marlon never wanted to talk about the craft. He talked about politics, about religion, about child rearing, but the unwritten law was that the minute you ever asked him a question about acting, you were excommunicated. And if you knew that unwritten law, you knew not to ever go there. And because that's the only thing I ever gave a shit about, I just didn't have much to interact with him about. So most of my time spent with him was in observance. And the one thing I was able to observe about him—and this is not just true of him but also of a couple of other geniuses—was the inexplicable need to never be pinned down.

If you ask any actor who lived after 1950, there's Marlon, and then there's everybody else. No one—*no one*—will disagree with that. A couple of the old-time guys might make fun of him because he mumbled and he scratched himself and he was self-indulgent. If they had studied him like I did, even they would have marveled at the depth he was able and willing to plumb. He bottled that magic in *The Godfather*, when Francis Ford Coppola made a perfect film from beginning to end, not just in terms of storytelling but also in cinematography, music, production design, and performances. Every single actor in that movie—most of whom were obscure, including Pacino, James Caan, Robert Duvall, Richard Castellano, Abe Vigoda (the guy who played "Fish" on the television show *Barney Miller*)—all became movie stars as a result of appearing in that one movie. That's how much of a game-changer that film was. John Cazale, Lenny Montana, Al Lettieri, Diane Keaton, Talia Shire—every single actor who appeared in that movie did a different kind of work from what they had ever done before or would ever do again. So there was something; it was a promontory. It was like Mount Olympus in terms of what it achieved as a movie and the visceral way that it affects you from beginning to end. You can never really put it into words because when you try to explain the story, the dynamic, and understand it intellectually, what is missing is the feeling that you get (or don't get) when you watch it.

Human condition. That's what made this movie one of the greatest events in cinematic history, because the movie got that on film. It comes from Brando's unbelievable performance and his transformation into Vito Corleone. He captured, as the patriarch of his mob family, a range of emotions—vulnerability, ruthlessness, and intense loyalty, sense of family, of being responsible for the greater good, of moral compass. All these things wrapped up in one character that was also so Italian that you could believe he landed on Ellis Island and pulled himself up by his bootstraps from nothing with only a kind of sense of direction.

The seventies were an extremely exciting period for movies because the work of Coppola, Martin Scorsese, Brian De Palma, Hal Ashby, to name a few, came as close as we had in decades to producing a new golden era in cinema. It was if they had absorbed what was magical about the first forty years of movies, starting in the twenties, thirties, forties, and fifties. These guys were spewing back in a lens what was paved for them by the John Fords, the George Stevenses, the George Cukors, the Preston Sturgesses, the Frank Capras, the Alfred Hitchcocks. What Brando and Elia Kazan did in *On the Waterfront* can be marked as a departure point in the entire way storytelling is done on film. Yes, there's plot; yes, there's story; yes, there's a lot of the other things that all movies had. But there's one thing that no other movie had prior to that: this kind of neighborhood behavioral, very primal feel that you get as a result of what the actors were trying to do. Brando, Clift, and Dean were America's answer to Constantin Stanislavski's famed "method acting." Kazan showed you in living black and white and, every once in a while, in living color how much deeper storytelling can go.

As good as the seventies were—my absolute favorite era in movie history—truly the golden age of cinema was the thirties and forties. Then it was simple storytelling and big personalities. Those filmmakers surrounded themselves with authors like Hemingway, Faulkner, Odets, and Earnest Lehman—the greatest writers in film history were doing their thing in the thirties and forties. That was an exploration of the human condition in all of its grandeur. In spades. And it was looked at from every angle and in such a way that, even as they were incredibly entertaining, they were also so much more. Those movies were instructive: every single thing I learned about what kind of man I wanted to be didn't come from going to school or from hanging out in the neighborhood; a lot of it came from watching the way Bogie handled the situation, the way Duke walked through some trouble, the look that overcame Gary Cooper as he made a decision, how Tyrone Power figured his way out of a situation, what kind of crap Clark Gable had on his heels when he wanted to charm his way in and out of stuff. Watching those movies taught me that kind of character-building shit.

But as much grandeur as that era engendered—and I could go on and on—the personalities were truly fucking stellar. We had Gable, Tracy, Cagney, Cary, Eddie G., Bogey, the Coop, Jimmy Stewart, and the Duke . . . and the women: Myrna Loy, Stanwyck, Jean Arthur, Hepburn, Crawford, and, of course, Bette Davis, who, in my opinion, was probably the greatest actress of all time, pound-for-pound. The personalities were vast and magnetic and compelling and so much larger than life that you just couldn't take your eyes off of them. So when you meld amazing writing with these kinds of personalities, told through the lens of these incredible auteurs, you have a study of the human condition as important a chronicle as any other.

The seventies was when all these guys were coming up, such as Paul Newman, Robert Redford, George Roy Hill, Sean Connery, Michael Caine, Pacino, and De Niro. All of these guys were born of the seventies, and it's as important a period in cinema as there ever was. But the jewel in the crown was and always will be *The Godfather Part I*. The other thing about the *Godfather* was an identity awareness I got from being a New Yorker that I didn't find in Minneapolis. I saw the *Godfather* while still out there, and it became another reason why I had to come home. I went on to pay to see that movie about twenty times—I just couldn't get enough of it. It captured that unhypocritical aspect I discussed. Here was a New York crime family who was doing, in reality, bad shit, and yet we cheered for them. I always identified with Italians. I actually went on record before, in some interview, describing myself as an Italian mistakenly born as a Jew. While I was growing up most of the kids I didn't know thought I was an Italian from the way I carried myself. That's why I begged for the role in *Drive*, in which I played a Jew who is parading as an Italian gangster. That was fuckin' fun. I want to live in Italy some day. I want to die there and be buried there. I want to spend my final years there because that place is the embodiment of the fact that everything is corrupt. But with the Italians, they're not trying to hide anything—it's blatant; it's just part of a deal. Even marriage is built in with a mistress. It's like, "Yeah, I'm going to marry you because you're beautiful, and I love you and I will take care of and provide for you fuckin' forever, but there's gonna be a deal on the side. *Kapeesh?*" That kind of antithesis of hypocrisy—even if I don't agree with it or if I do—resonates with me. I'd rather get that kind of muthafuckin' truth than the typical two-faced, agenda-driven bullshit-type of people you mostly gotta deal with.

But that was New York, with all this great stuff happening in theater and cinema. It kept me on the long lines at cattle calls, stomping my feet to keep warm and eating a candy bar as my fuckin' lunch. It got me to show up for audition after audition, acting in whatever play that would have me, never stopping, because I wanted to be in. I wanted to contribute to this great art that was being made right in front of me. It finally happened though, three years later, when I got my first lucky break.

(CHAPTER 7)

Just Good Enough
to Not Get Paid

After nearly three years of acting for free in Off-Off Broadway shows, toward the end of 1975 and in the beginning 1976 two events occurred that pretty much changed everything. The first happened at Burton's store. One day in late autumn two girls walk into the store—both attractive, but one killer attractive. Like hamina, hamina attractive. "Need any help?" I went right into my best Gable-kind of charm. But it was probably more like Pepé Le Pew, with my over-the-top eagerness.

"No, we're just browsing," she said, but even that standard answer—to me anyway—seemed to have an irresistible coquettishness to it. Well, after about five minutes of scintillatingly awkward small talk, the killa chick zeroed in on one of my favorite pair of earrings. I gave her the price, she said she'd take them, and we finalized the sale. Then, just as they were walking out the door, that same hottie turned and asked, as if an afterthought, "By the way, are you hiring right now?"

"Are you asking for yourself?" I shot back.

"Yeah, maybe just something part time."

I didn't wait a second, forgetting I had no authority to hire anyone. "How soon can you start?"

"Oh, anytime really." She had the warmest, most delicious half-smile I'd ever laid eyes on.

"How 'bout tomorrow? Can you come in the morning, say eleven o'clock?"

"That's fine. See you tomorrow." And off she went. A moment of sheer and unabashed reverie was suddenly and decidedly replaced by the sobering realization of, *Holy shit, I just hired someone*, when I was the lowliest employee in the joint. I immediately turned to Burton, who was looking at me like I just escaped from some nuthouse.

"I just fucked up, right?"

"Yeah, you did, but . . . it's cool. I'll fire her tomorrow night. Meaning ya got one day to close the fuckin' deal."

I couldn't wait for eleven o'clock the next morning to come. This was, far and away, *the* most beautiful girl I'd ever laid eyes on. The next morning came, as did my fantasy paramour. We spent the next seven hours replacing attempts at nonchalantness with quibbling and jabbing. Yes, love was definitely in the air. At quittin' time I looked up at Burton with my saddest puppy dog eyes, silently begging him *not* to fire her. He complied; the governor had granted a stay.

This little courting dance went on for about four months—quibbling, jabbing, getting her time in my life miraculously extended, all much to Burton's chagrin but with the tacit resignation that only a best friend could muster. Four months—that's how long it took me to man up and ask this chick on a proper date. With February 14 fast approaching, I realized if I let one more holiday go by I'm DOA. So I screw up my courage, throw back some Binaca, and blurt out, "Whuddya doin' Valentine's Day?"

"I'm not sure," she said, again with the coquette routine.

To which I said, "Yes you are. You're goin' out with me. Like on a date 'n shit!"

Our first date went pretty good, if ya know what I mean. Her name was Opal Stone, and she's now been by my side for thirty-eight years.

Gave me two of the coolest kids in the universe. Opal Stone from Montego Bay, Jamaica. The most beautiful girl I ever saw. Still is!

More or less around the same time my courtship was going on I got my other break when I went to an open call at La MaMa Experimental Theatre Club, one of the true groundbreaking avant-garde symbols of the times that were a-changin'. The guy directing the play was Tom O'Horgan, who was already a legend in New York, having directed *Hair*, *Lenny*, and *Jesus Christ, Superstar*, so this was definitely a cut above the average bill of fare that had been my steady diet. Plus, this was to be the North American premiere of a play by Fernando Arrabal, a renegade Spanish expressionist writer of note known for his anarchistic ravings.

Tom O'Horgan was the force behind one of the most experimental and controversial theatrical experiences of the day, emblematic of the tearing down of all the old traditional edifices. He did this play on the Lower East Side that had people getting naked, glorifying the drug culture, the hippie movement, and free love and singing about the Age of Aquarius. That play was *Hair*, which eventually made its way to Broadway, setting box office records. So now Tom was stepping back to his roots, coming back to the East Village, the original scene of the crime, to mount this insane work of theater of the absurd. The play was *The Architect and the Emperor of Assyria*.

It just finished a run at the National Theater in England that starred Anthony Hopkins as the emperor and Jim Dale as the architect. It got checkered reviews and was deemed a bit too experimental, but a lot of eyes were on O'Horgan to see whether he could put this one in his magical bottle and shake out another hit. There were probably a few hundred people there auditioning for two parts, as it was a two-character play. After I did my audition in the morning I was pulled aside and asked to come back in the afternoon. In the afternoon there were fifty of us auditioning. After that, I was asked to wait around for a final callback to take place that evening—it was down to about twenty of us.

The next day I got a call that I got cast as the emperor, the same role Hopkins had played. There were actually four actors hired due to the fact that the play was simply too arduous for one cast to carry, so responsibilities would be split into two rotating casts. Now it was simply a matter of seeing what chemistry led to which pairing. And even though we're supposed to be alternating with one another and nobody's really any better than anybody else, as we get closer and closer to the opening I realize that the other guy is the A guy and I'm B. He was slated to do the first performances, the first preview, and the first opening night, whereas I was going to do the second preview and the second night after opening.

It was a very long, really overly written, very verbose play that took about three and a half hours to perform with only two characters. No matter how fucking interesting it is, it's a play that was fucking difficult to keep an audience engaged in and was really begging for them to lose their train of thought. And sure enough, the A cast goes on for the first preview. My partner, Lazaro Perez, who was the B architect, and I were in the audience, and we're watching this thing, and it's a fucking disaster. It runs like four hours and twenty minutes, and you could tell that there are the rumblings of an all-out rebellion happening in the theater—nobody wants to be there, nobody can believe their eyes; it's just bad taste and horribly executed.

Apparently shortly after that there was a big pow-wow, and the powers decided to hold off this North American premier for a few more days. That opening night can make or break a play because it's reviewed by the *New York Times* and every other important periodical, and, as I said, everyone was expecting magic from O'Horgan. So the heat was most definitely on. Finally we get word that Laz and I are now slated to do another preview before the official world premiere. I was aware that Laz didn't have a whole lotta faith in me, 'cuz all the while he thought he should be on the A team, with the winners. And frankly, who could blame him? But after the debacle of the first preview nobody knew what the fuck to think.

As coincidence would have it, one night while I'm out walkin' my dog in the Village, I happen to run into Laz. I could see he was really uneasy about doing a play that had already proved to be problematic and, worse, with the wild-card partner that was me. I said, "You don't know me really good, and I don't know you really good, but fuck it . . . let me go buy a bottle of wine and we go over to my place and hang out?"

So we go over to my apartment, and after we chill for awhile I tell him I know how to make this play work.

"Nobody can make this fuckin' thing work," he said.

"I know how to make the play work, but you got to stay with me, you got to trust me, and you've got to stick with me."

"Why would I do that? What the fuck are you going to do?"

"I'm going to go so fast, nobody's gonna know what hit 'em! The problem with this play—it's verbal diarrhea. But if we do it fast enough, the audience will never have a chance to catch up, and we'll have them. It's the only fuckin' way."

"I guess, man. What else is there? I'll follow you. I'll do whatever you want. What choice do I have?"

With Laz following my lead and keeping up with me, we turned what took four hours and twenty minutes a few nights ago into a running time of about two hours and thirty minutes, and doing so by following the same script, not cutting one word. We went like fuckin' crazy men! We got a standing ovation at the end because we never gave the audience a minute to realize what a piece of overblown shit they were watching.

Afterward Ellen Stuart, the head of La MaMa, comes to the dressing room and makes the announcement that now Ron and Laz are going to be the A team and are going to do the opening night—critics' night. The world premiere, baby! The day before the opening they bring in the playwright. Fernando meets with me and Laz and gives us about an hour's worth of cuts.

I said to him, "Fernando, did you just come up with these cuts?"

"No," he said in his thick Castilian accent, "I've had these cuts for the last ten years."

"Were you always meaning to give these to us?"

"Yes, I was always going to give them to you. But I just wanted to hear my masterpiece one last time as I lovingly wrote it!"

I wanted to fucking kill him.

Now, I had an eighteen-page monologue right in the middle of this thing where the other character leaves the stage and it's just me for eighteen pages. You know how hard it is to memorize eighteen single-spaced pages? And it had to be performed like a magic act so the audience would never catch on that what they were watching wasn't all that good. Well, once again, if you did it fast enough, the audience wouldn't know what hit 'em.

So we opened. We get amazing reviews. We get a bona fide rave review from Clive Barnes, the number-one reviewer for the *New York Times*. He wrote a half-page homage to these unknowns Ron Perlman, Lazaro Perez, and Tom O'Horgan. Barnes compares it to the Anthony Hopkins production and discusses why Hopkins's emperor fell short while mine didn't.

The play became the next "in thing," and all the artistic hipsters of New York came flooding in to see it. For the first time in the history of my life I felt like I was in something that people wanted to see, and one of the reasons they wanted to see it was because of what I was doing. That was the beginning of literally everything: it got me calls from about four or five New York agents. It got me my very first trip to Europe, as Laz and I were asked to tour the play all over Holland, Belgium, and Germany. From that play I got my first agent, was able to join the actor's equity union, and was finally fuckin' able to have bragging rights to having done a production in New York that made a little bit of noise. Easy Street—am I right, baby?!

Like I said, while all this is going down, I'm fuckin' head-over-heels in fuckin' love. Opal and I began to cohabitate about three months after our Valentine's dinner. We got a place together over on Twelfth Street, just off Eighth Avenue, which, believe it or not, we managed to hold onto for thirty-six years. Opal had come up to New York from Jamaica when she was about five. So she always had identified herself as a New Yorker. In the early going I kept waiting for her to tell me she had had enough of the bohemian lifestyle, that she was gonna go back to the 175 dudes that were constantly circling her, most of whom were like heavyweight New York sports stars.

But we both genuinely enjoyed spending time in each other's company, and this click was immediate; it happened from that first dinner date when we stopped playing games and let our pretenses down. She ended up being a really good old lady for a guy like me. It was very, very clear I could have gone through life with nothing. There was nothing to indicate that I was ever going to be successful financially as an actor. And she made no pretenses that she didn't know this was so deeply entrenched in my DNA that it was something I was going to have to pursue, good or bad, whatever it brought. She was game. She seemed to be ready to go all the way and take whatever came, and this was also something that always remained somewhat of a surprise to me. When *The Emperor and the Architect* went on the tour of Europe, which took me away for about two months, she was exactly the same when I came home. That was the first time I realized she was capable of being the same chick when I came home as when I left. Nothing changed; she didn't feel threatened by me being gone. She kind of almost felt relieved that I got a chance to flex my muscles as an actor and go out and discover new lands, conquer new domains. And it's been the same ever since.

After I returned from Europe I wanted to find an agent with clout. I then got a very intriguing message from a Richard Astor, an agent with some very well-known clients. He wanted to meet to talk about the idea of working together. I went up to his office in Midtown, in the Forties, and, never having been inside of an agent's building before, there was a kind of mystical aura to the entire event. Astor was this very elegant homosexual, the gayest of the gayest men I've ever met, with this Tennessee Williams and William F. Buckley combined kind of wit.

We're sitting in his office when he leans back in his high-back swivel chair and says, "I have a piece of very bad news for you."

"Um, you asked me to come here. We just met. Why would you want to ruin a perfect, unformed relationship?"

Astor said, "I think it's rather important for you to understand this, and what I'm about to say I don't say with any joy at all, but you should resign yourself to the notion that you're not going to get any work until you're forty."

I was twenty-six at the time. "Wait a minute."

"I'm not done yet," he said. "You're not going to even begin to get any work until you're forty, but you're not going to hit your stride until you're almost fifty."

I'm sitting there, dumbfounded. "Why do you say that?"

"Your aura. There is nothing youthful about your talents or your style of working or your aura as an artist. What you do doesn't fit into this young frame of yours, so you're going to have to wait until you're completely mature and become a middle-aged man before your talent catches up with your persona and your persona catches up with your talent."

I felt like I was sitting in front of a fuckin' oracle. I said, "That's the most depressing thing you could've possibly said to me."

I stand, and he asks, "Do you want to sign with me or not?"

"Why would I want to sign with you? You're telling me right now you can't get me a fuckin' job for fourteen years."

"Well, there's always a possibility. I'm really good at what I do. If I were you, I'd sign with me and we'll take our chances."

So I signed, but as time went by, nothing changed. I was really not getting any good auditions. Occasionally he would get me into meetings with movers and shakers in Manhattan, but it never led to anything. Ultimately I said to Richard, "Look, you very well may be right in your prediction, but I don't have time to wait. The way you're representing me seems to be as if you're absolutely set on this notion of yours that all I'm doing right now is marinating. I really need to work and need money to feed myself."

I then signed with these two beautiful ladies, older ladies who fuckin' adored me, Pat Baldwin and Shirley Scully. They seemed to be really, really fan girls; they seemed like family, always rooting for me to do well. It was irresistible to not be a part of their world, and we ate dinners together, partied together, went on vacation together—we really became close, and they became like adopted aunts.

But they too kept running into problems getting me work. It's so much easier on everybody if you're a recognizable type, so they were constantly trying to figure out how to market me. Casting directors would say we heard Perlman can act, but does he play teachers? Does he play accountants? Can he be a cop? Or is he a better gangster?

Here I was, this guy who was basing everything on this chameleon-like approach to acting in which I can play whatever you cast me as, when people preferred to plug me in as an entity, a specific type, a niche. I started to wonder, *Holy shit, this motherfucker Richard Astor—as farfetched as it was—he might be fuckin' right.*

People were saying to me, "You're just not commercial. You're not Proctor and Gamble. You're not the guy next door. We can't put you in a commercial. We can't put you in a box."

It went along like that for a few years, and it was very frustrating. I acted in stuff that hardly paid and spent an awful lot of time making money by selling jewelry and handbags on Eighth Street and McDougal with my dear friend Burton Levy. Then, in 1979, I get a call from Shirley and Pat. They were all excited with good news: "There's something going around right now that we submitted you for and they actually want to meet you." I was listening. "It's not just a meeting like it usually is with a casting director—the filmmaker *himself* wants to meet you."

I said, "Well, what is it?"

"It's very odd. It's this caveman movie. But . . ."

"Hold on. Are you shitting me?" The image that came into my head was the movie *One Million BC* with Victor Mature and Virginia Mayo. That was a low-budget thing in which they wore these leopard skins, carried clubs outta Vic Tanny's gym, and spoke broken English. I'm saying to myself, *Fuck me, this is where I'm going in this fucking business? Fucking cavemen movies with bad fucking eye makeup? I mean, Jesus Christ, this is what I went to fucking graduate school for?*

(CHAPTER 8)

My Cave or Yours?

"It's for a movie!"

My agents Pat and Shirley tried to convince me to go to a meeting they set up for what I thought was some crapola of a caveman flick. I had only always done theater, and this was my first movie experience. "Ron, you got to get serious about this. We don't get many shots at movies. In fact, we don't get *any*! Would it hurt to just go to the meeting?"

So I sat down for an interview with this very handsome French guy. In fact, everything about him was handsome. His big, salt-and-pepper colored hair-do was perfectly handsome, and he was wearing designer jeans that were obviously dry cleaned, 'cuz I'd never seen dungarees that had a crease in 'em—handsome! He was wearing a white, furry cashmere sweater wrapped around his shoulders and tied in the front. In addition, he had this thick French accent, which, all in all, made me think this dude was clearly a trust fund baby wanting to dabble in film as a little hobby.

I was ready to fuckin' bolt, thinking, *Holy shit, man, if I had Daddy's money, I'm pretty sure I wouldn't use it to make a fucking caveman movie.* Ten seconds into the meeting I think, *Fuck this, this is a big waste of time,* so I decided to start playin' with the dude—ya know, just for my own edification and enjoyment.

He had a notepad in front of him and was holding a very handsome pen (can't remember if it was a Mont Blanc, but I do know it was handsome!). "What is your name?"

"Are you fucking kidding me? Don't you have a piece of paper there with my fucking name on it? I'm Tony fucking Curtis."

Obviously he was going through some sort of checklist. "Have you been trained? What is your training?" He looked up and seemed a little puzzled, but he kept going.

"Well, I'm housebroken and I can fetch the newspaper from outside the front door in the morning, but every once in awhile I make a mistake and drink out of the toilet bowl."

This went on for like twenty minutes, with him seeming unruffled with my total blasé disrespect. In fact, I was being *such* an asshole that I thought I'd get him to say, "Let's step outside and settle this." I was convinced this way-too-handsome dude and his little caveman project were wasting everybody's time. After a bit he started looking at me with some sort of a weird fascination. It seemed the more disrespectful I was, the more fascinated he became. At the end of the meeting he stood and shook my hand. "That was fascinating—you are fascinating. I'm going to see you and your fascinating self again."

"You'll pardon me if that news doesn't quite fill me with joy, but if I had a nickel for every fucking guy that ever said that to me . . ."

"No, you'll see. I'm going to surprise you. You'll see me again." And sure enough, about two months later I got a message from my agents that this very handsome guy was coming back to New York and I'd been invited to attend a two-day session in a dance studio for an audition. I was told that each day might be four or more hours, and I was to wear loose-fitting clothes. It all sounded a bit fuckin' odd but hey . . . handsome, rich kids with movie money, ya know?

I didn't know how odd it was until I showed up at the studio and saw about thirty-five or forty of the strangest-looking dudes ever assembled in one room. Did you ever see the movie *Nightmare Alley*? It starred Tyrone Power but also had about one hundred real-life sideshow acts and carnival characters in it to add authenticity. This is what this fucking casting call looked like. There was one guy who was eight and a half feet tall whose head was the size of a peanut. Another guy was a certified hunchback, with one eye looking up and the other looking down. Some other poor fucker had one arm growing out of his left hip and another one growing out of the back of his head. The whole room was filled with the freakiest, most gnarled, most scary people I've ever seen. It didn't make me feel all that good about myself, knowing this was my niche.

There were a couple of bright spots, though. Danny Devito was there. That's where we met. He was like me—just a guy starting out, auditioning for whatever. But, even though I love him and we're friends to this day, he is really a unique-looking man. I admire him 'cuz he also said "fuck it" and made what he was given work for him. Danny, luckily, didn't get the part, which in turn made him available to do *One Flew Over the Cuckoo's Nest* and then *Taxi*. Sometimes life has a way of working out. Also at the audition was an old acquaintance of mine from back in the La MaMa days, Nameer El-Kadi. Although we hadn't become that close back in the day, he was in one of the casts of *The Architect and the Emperor of Assyria* when they, by popular demand, remounted it a year later. Little did I know of the "excellent adventure" he and I were about to embark upon.

The first day of the studio session was an orientation on how cavemen were supposed to move. They brought in these internationally acclaimed mimes to teach us movement. You know the guys who make a living on the street pulling rope that's not there or opening an imaginary window and climbing through it? The whole first day was this kind of orientation with regard to body movement that was to be employed in depicting a species not yet fully formed. The second day had more of the same but culminated with individual improvisations. The idea was to see how we would portray prehistoric behavior. The handsome French guy with the beautifully handsome cashmere sweater wrapped beautifully and handsomely around his shoulders with the jeans with the crease in them was there for both days, keenly observing everything.

For the improvisation we were told to act as if we had discovered something we'd never seen before and explore it. Each hopeful was given a few minutes to do his take. So I walked in as a caveman, slightly bent over and my arms swinging sort of ape-like. I chose to discover an imaginary tennis ball. I rolled around on it, I kicked it, and I batted at it. I was into my deal for about a minute when the French guy stopped me.

"There are two things I want you to know," he said. "Number one, I told you I'd see you again, and number two, I'm even going to see you at least once more after this."

I said, "Jesus Christ, I appreciate you trying to be nice and everything but, I mean, stop with the smoke blowing!"

"Come here for a second. You really don't believe me, do you? Here are my notes. You see that? No one has done an improvisation that has gotten four stars except for you. I'm going to see you again, and it's probably going to be in Europe."

"Right, see you in Europe. Maybe we could do a spot of shopping at Harrod's!"

"I know you think I'm full of shit. I know you don't believe anything I say, but I'm telling you I'm going to see you again."

Well, about a month went by, and I was playing softball in Central Park one afternoon when an actor friend I know stopped when he saw me and came over to chat.

"Wow, Perl, you gotta be blown away."

"About what?"

"About the fact that you're on the shortlist for that caveman movie. In fact, it's sounding like you're gonna get the offer. That's the word around town—that you're going to get the offer."

"Well, I guess that's cool and all, but sorry, dude, if I seem underwhelmed over a fucking caveman movie for some ultra-handsome, rich French guy."

"Dude, do you know who that rich French guy is?" I just stared back at him. "That's *Jean-Jacques Annaud*. He just won the Academy Award for best foreign film. He's one of the most celebrated, sought-after filmmakers on the planet right now, and his next movie is going to be the most serious look anybody's ever taken at what life was like eighty thousand years ago. And you, ya big dope, you're up for one of the leads."

"Are you shitting me?" For the first time, suddenly I'm nervous.

I got my glove and bat and bailed out of the game to go find the nearest pay phone. I called my agents—they told me it was true. And I started playing the tape back in my head. And all I know was I abused the shit outta this poor French dude.

"I'm hearing I'm on a short list for one of the leads! How's that possible? I wasn't very nice to the guy!"

"No, the director loves you. In fact, whatever you did, he can't get enough of it. He thinks you're terrific and loves the idea of you being in this movie! You are on the shortlist for one more audition." It turns out that Annaud had been on a thirty-two-city tour to find the perfect cast for his movie *Quest for Fire*, a big studio movie, green-lit by Alan Ladd Jr., who was running 20th Century Fox at the time.

About a week later I got a call from Annaud's staff telling me that I needed to fly to London. They flew me first class and put me up in this phenomenal hotel. In London we did a few days more of mime improvisation training, but this time it was a smaller group assembled. When we were all done no one was told anything aside from "Thank you for coming. You'll hear from us soon." We were just all herded to the production office to pick up our per diem cash and our ticket home.

When I made my way to the production office there was a very friendly secretary there who gave me my money. I thanked her and asked, "By the way, this is my first time in London. Do you know any good restaurants in the area?"

"You should eat someplace really, really special," she said. "I like this place called Mr. Chow."

"Okay, but why should I eat someplace special?"

"Because you should be celebrating."

"And why is that, if ya don't mind me being too nosey?"

She got up and led me by the hand to another room where there was a big board listing the final cast. The second name up there was mine, and that was when I found out, *Holy shit, I got the second lead in a major production for 20th fucking Century fucking Fox*, a character named Amoukar in the motion picture *Quest for Fire*. To be directed by the incredibly handsome, incredibly respected Jean-Jacques Annaud! You bet I went to Mr. Chow, even if it was all by myself. That's how the seventies ended and the eighties started for me. This was not only my first movie; this was also my first movie audition. As I mentioned, my agents had a hard time getting me auditions for movie roles because there was nothing they could figure out to plug me into. I wasn't really a cop because I was a bit of a hippie. I wasn't really a teacher, because I wasn't nerdy enough. I just fell in between the cracks of pretty much everything you could possibly think of. How ironic that the only thing I could really trade off of was this quasi-Neanderthal bone structure of mine with the prominent brow and the deep-set eyes. Weird, right?

Once I was back in the States I was told to stand by because production was scheduled to start soon. But what happened next sounds like one of those good news–bad news jokes. The good news is, hey, I've got the lead in this movie. The bad news is that just as we are about to begin production the Screen Actors Guild called a strike, preventing all American actors from going to work on American-produced films and television. The absurdity was that during a thirty-two-city search for the cast of *Quest*, Annaud managed to cast nothing but Americans for the four leading roles. This was a big 20th Century Fox film, and you can't really shoot around a union. The union goes on strike for the first time in twenty-one years just as I'm about to have my movie debut, and we spend the next four months fielding phone calls. "Is the movie still on? Is it off?" "It's off. Yeah, they're scrapping it." "No, it's on again."

Jean-Jacques had already spent three years and probably around $6 million in preproduction, which was a huge amount of money at that time. He had a lot of skin in the game. He did everything he could to keep it going. But the forces at 20th Century Fox cannot make the movie with American actors because American actors are on strike, and American actors can't cross the picket line. It quickly became a massive clusterfuck.

My newest dear friend, Everett McGill, and my old friend Nameer El-Kadi had also been cast in the movie, and during this time we did some informal rehearsals, but mostly just to keep close to one another to keep from going buggy. About two months went by, and I got a call from Everett at 5:20 one evening: "Hey Perl, I got bad news for you. It's off, but this time it's for real. It's done. They can't figure out how to do it. Fox has tried everything possible to figure out a way around the strike. Nobody knows when the strike's gonna be over. They were supposed to start shooting in Iceland. They blew that location because they lost the window, because it was starting to get way too cold in Iceland and way too dark way too early."

"Fuck! So close, and yet so far." There I was, not only getting my first movie but I was also going to be the lead. It was going to be with 20th Century Fox, and it was going to be a-fucking-mazing, with an Academy Award–winning director to boot. Who was handsome! God-dammit, man, what fucking luck. I looked up at the clock and said, "Okay, it's 5:30. If I get on the D train right now, I can be at Yankee Stadium by 7:15 to make the night game." They were playing Oakland.

I had $100 to my name. General admission seats were like eight bucks, so I gave the guy at the ticket window the eight dollars and then I pushed in another $30 and told the guy that's for him. Like I said before, he knew exactly what I wanted without saying a word, and I wound up with the best seats I've ever had—on field-level, between first base and home plate.

I was all fucking by myself after just getting the worst piece of news I'd ever gotten in my short professional career. Maybe the worst piece of news I'll ever get as a professional. And the beer guy came by. They have these trays of beer in plastic cups covered with cellophane. The tray probably held thirty beers, and I saw only one beer missing. I signaled for him to come over. "How much is that?"

"Two-fifty."

I said, "No. Not one. How much is the whole fucking tray? How much for that?" He says, "The whole thing? You think I'm a fucking Einstein or something? I don't know how much it is."

"What could it be? Fifty to sixty dollars?"

He said, "Gimme fifty and it's yours." I paid him for this big tray and told him to start passing out the beer to everyone sitting around me, saving one for myself. By the seventh inning I had about forty-five new friends and two dozen phone numbers. I was the most popular guy at the game. The worst night of my life turned into the most fun I've ever had at a ballgame. The Yankees routed. They hit about seven home runs. Oscar Gamble hit two all by himself. They were on fire that night. It was just win-win-win. It was a magical night, 'cuz I basically decided to meet adversity by just pissing right in its face.

Sure enough, two days later, I got a call. The movie was on again. They figured out a way to resurrect it. It's funky, it's weird, but we were doing it. And it was 100 percent go. At that moment I learned that if a negative thing comes at you, bombard it with positive. That night when Everett called I thought, *Fuck this. I'm not gonna give in to how absolutely abjectly depressed I should be right now. I'm just going to go celebrate.* And because of that, everything turned positive again. In my head I didn't accept that the movie was dead, and somehow, once again, the fuckin' universe came up big!

20th Century Fox pulled off an incredible feat of backstairs maneuvering and handed the movie off to a Canadian company to produce, with the understanding that once the movie was finished and in the can, the movie would revert back to 20th Century Fox for worldwide distribution. But that the movie was going to be produced, for all intents and purposes, as a Canadian film. So it was a foreign film, which meant that American actors could work on it. And the Screen Actors Guild agreed that those conditions were fine. They signed off on it and they let us go. Instead of going to the original first location of Iceland, we started in Scotland. We did three weeks there and then segued to Africa at the end of November of 1980 and spent five weeks there. And then we went on a break for about four months, to wait for it to get warm enough in Canada to finish the movie. We had another month and a half to two months to go, shooting in Canada. If you're working on a Canadian film, you are obligated to shoot a huge percentage of it in Canada. So that's why we had to do that.

Once in Scotland it was clear before the first scene was shot that this certainly was not *One Million Years BC*. We realized we were doing something that had an incredible amount of integrity to it. Annaud brought in Anthony Burgess, who wrote *A Clockwork Orange*, to create a glossary of prehistoric words for us. Aside from being a giant in the fiction world, Burgess was a teacher of linguistics at Oxford University. Then Annaud brought in Desmond Morris, the man who wrote *Man Watching* and one of the most highly regarded anthropologists of his day, as a consultant. He taught us the behavioral ticks that most likely characterized humans of eighty thousand years ago. During that epoch mankind was almost Homo sapiens, but not quite. There were still elements of chimp behavior and chimp movements. We were not fully upright, but we were almost upright. Desmond Morris gave us the template for movement as well as behavioral traits. That began to explain all those long, tedious mime sessions to find that perfect intersection of prehistoric and modern man. Annaud was making the quintessential evolution movie, with the best team he could assemble.

So the guy I wrote off as a handsome French trust fund baby, once on set, was as serious as a fucking heart attack. But this newly formed lovefest was about to get a major test. Jean-Jacques's notion was that he needed to make the shooting conditions as brutal and uncompromising and unpleasant physically as anyone could imagine. He wanted us to be in the same environment humans had eighty thousand years ago. The conditions he put us in were flat-out punishing.

Even if Jean-Jacque is now one of my dearest friends on this earth and one of the true and abiding benevolent angels in my life, back then it only took a week into shooting before the handsome, dashing Frenchman and I butted heads. Big time. Allow me to set the stage . . .

CHAPTER 9

Wanna Set the Night on Fire . . .

Quest for Fire pinpointed a moment in time, some eighty thousand years ago, when conditions existed in the evolution process to make possible the major strides leading up to the final modernization of mankind. The film was set somewhere around the Pyrenees, where, just to the north, due to rugged climate and tough topography, the tribe's development was a bit stultified, whereas tribes to the south enjoyed the luxuries of more languid, temperate climes and, thus, easy living, which in turn allowed them to develop at a slightly quicker pace. So the basic conceit of the film is that the northern tribes, one of which our three heroes call home, regarded fire as a possession—you either had it, or you didn't. Whereas the southern tribes had already discovered the secret, one that has since been passed down to Boy Scout troops the world over: the ability to start one's own fire.

The film opens with a furious attack on our heroes' tribe, thus causing the loss of their most precious resource, fire, and a circumstance that critically threatens their very survival. The three fiercest warriors are chosen to go on a journey to find more. The clock is obviously ticking, as the longer this quest takes, the more compromised their loved ones back at the cave become. So they travel south, desperate to save the day.

As for the making of *Quest*, the honeymoon that had character-ized everything leading up to the start of principal photography was about to take a major and dramatic turn. The peace-love-brotherhood environment that marked the preproduction process, what with the dinners, the parties, the gatherings, and the words and gestures of en-couragement, were about to be replaced with, "Holy shit, lemme just get the fuck outta here alive!" For as we were to learn, from the very first day of shooting Jean-Jacque's notion of recreating the hardships of a group of men with no modern-day comforts was to completely and irrevocably remove all semblance of comfort, thereby leaving us with a set of circumstances that were as *un*comfortable as was hu-manly possible. He wasn't satisfied with creating just the illusion of hardship; he wanted actual hardship itself. So he went out of his way to make sure we were just completely victimized by the elements. He truly believed the poignancy of the story was how the environmen-tal elements were always going to be the thing that won the day be-cause mankind was not yet equipped to be the master of his own fate: humankind's early destiny was decided not by him, but for him. The harnessing and creating of fire was to be *the* primary discovery that ul-timately allowed us to survive as a species, and the locations he chose for the film were picked to duplicate the harshest conditions possible.

The benchmark of this film was that we were always kind of in the middle of nowhere. We had to use locations that had never been civilized, that had never been built upon, and had no signs of twentieth-century comforts—no electrical lines, no homes. It made for incredible imagery, but it was brutal for us. It was the most un-comfortable film—to date—that I have ever been on. Everett McGill and I both ended up with frostbite on our hands and feet. Nameer El-Kadi, who remains one of my dearest of friends to this day, says he's fine, but I think he's bullshitting me. We were barefoot and walking through frozen tundra, we had to run through fields of three-foot-tall heather that had literally turned into icicles, and we had to stand in streams that were 33 degrees Fahrenheit, just at the point at which they're ready to freeze. For most of the film we were in the middle of nowhere. We didn't have tents, dressing rooms, or Winnebagos we could go to for warmth. We would get finished with a take and be completely compromised, shivering and out of our minds. The only thing that kept us warm were the wardrobe girls who wrapped us in these huge blankets and sleeping bags, as we stomped our feet and blew into our hands to keep the circulation going. My lasting gift from that, my very first movie, was that whenever it's the slightest bit cold, I lose feeling in my fingers and toes. Glamorous Hollywood, am I right?

So cut to the first sequence we're going to shoot. We were in a barren freezing area of Scotland during November. The sequence has our group walking along when we find a little stream and stop to take a drink. We've been on the quest for weeks and weeks and weeks to find fire, but to no avail. We're hungry and pissed off, and all of a sudden we see two saber-toothed tigers stalking us. Turns out they were even hungrier than we were! The script dictates that we haul ass and start running. We're running, the tigers are running, and this sequence builds up to this frenzy until you see, off in the distance, this one sole tree, like a miniature, midget fucking tree, slightly larger than a toothpick, with about seventeen leaves on it, and that's all there is separating us and certain death. We run and we run and we run, and we make it to the tree.

The script had us hauling ass up this tree as high as possible so as to prevent the tigers from having us for lunch. So we're up the tree, the tigers are on the ground trying to outwait us, and we gotta survive for three days on seventeen leaves. Okay good, okay fine, sounds easy enough, right?

That sequence was rather complex and scheduled to be a three-day shoot. After four hours in the makeup chair we were ready to begin at seven in the morning. Our group, now in costume, does the establishing shot with us running in the frozen three-foot heather; that was the *first* thing to get my attention. I realized I'm hauling barefoot through plants that had literally turned into ice sculptures or actual stalagmites.

They were cutting right through my feet, and we were being asked to run at twenty-five miles an hour because we've got these fucking tigers on our tails.

So right off the bat, the Perl is in "what the fuck?!" mode. But hey, let's just get through this, 'cuz it's bound to get easier—it has to! After we get all the running shit down and make it to the tree, my man Nameer was the first to climb to the top in a snap, and even big, lumbering Everett managed to get up just enough to make it look plausible. What they—and I—hadn't realized is that this Jew from New York had never climbed a fuckin' tree in his life. The only thing I ever climbed was when I once jumped over the fence of the schoolyard so I could play ball because it was locked on Veteran's Day or some shit. I didn't know shit about climbing shit, trees especially. So we spent the entire first day with me not being able to pull myself up into this puny, little muthafucka!

We spent half of the second day attempting to do the same. It wasn't working. We broke for lunch, and they finally sent out a team of carpenters to put pegs in the back of the fucking tree so I could have something to fucking hold on to. Meanwhile Jean-Jacques Annaud is so fucking pissed off at me because now he is on his second day and has somehow managed to be two days behind shooting, and that's costing him serious money. On *day two*! Yes, that's right: after two days of filming we're already two days behind, and he's blaming me, this fat Jew from New York who can't fucking climb a tree for this whole behind-schedule fucking debacle. Finally, at the end of two days, I've gotten up in the tree, and we now have to do in one day—in order to get back on schedule—what we were supposed to do in three.

That night, after shooting, everybody from the crew was in the dining room at the hotel. I noticed that Jean-Jacques refused to make eye contact with me and, when he did see me, just turned away in absolute avoidance. He was so fucking pissed off, he looked like if he had a gun, he'd fucking shoot me. 'Cuz I am now the bane of his existence. After all, 20th Century Fox was already sending communiqués to Scotland saying, "You better get your fucking shit together son, 'cuz we're fucking pulling the plug on this whole thing." Annaud, rightfully so, had nobody to blame but this fucking fuckup who couldn't climb a muthafucking tree.

So he wouldn't look at me, huh? Well, screw this, I thought, and I walked up to his table as he was having coffee at the end of dinner and said, "Can we talk?"

"I do not think that is a good idea!"

"Really?"

"No! I'm so mad at you. I may kill you right now. So, please, do yourself a favor, and do me a favor, and walk the fuck away."

I didn't budge. "I really feel as though it's important that you and I come to some sort of an arrangement. Because obviously what's happened these first two days is not good for anybody!"

"You think so?!" He started yelling and screaming. "Look! It's not my fault you can't climb a fucking tree." He started attacking me to the point at which he was completely not interested in engaging on any rational level. You could tell that the pressure he was under was so palpable, it didn't compare to anything I'd ever experienced before. I had never been on a movie before, and I never realized what's at stake and how expensive every shooting day is. And when you get behind a day, especially on a movie like that, in which you only have these locations for a limited amount of time—if you don't stay on schedule, disaster lurks just around the corner.

Yes, it was partly my fault, but what I wanted to tell him was that if he had planned this differently and had taken into account his actor's needs and enabled him to give a performance rather than be challenged into doing difficult physical tasks in a compromised state, it would all go smoother. I wanted to communicate to him that if you just figure out a way to empower me to play this character in a way in which I'm actually in control of the elements rather than the elements being in control of me, I can maybe give a performance, and then everything would work out way better than you can imagine. I started to explain that to him. But he was having none of it and instead was looking to make a quick exit and leave me to my own miserable misery.

I said, "Hey! Hang on! You yelled, now it's my turn!" Remember, I've never been on a movie before. Here I was yelling at the director, and people were turning their heads in the dining room, going, "Oh shit . . . Perlman . . . oh my God, he's about to be on the next plane back to fucking New York. They're gonna dropkick his ass for sure."

Jean-Jacque stopped and listened as I explained that if an actor is completely compromised by the elements and all he's thinking about is his own survival, you're just going to. get a guy thinking about his own survival, not a performance.

He then said, "Do you think that I'm going to pull up a chair and sit back waiting for you to do whatever it is you are going to do, when all you've done for the last two days is completely fuck me and my movie?"

"Jean-Jacques, do yourself a favor and get yourself a fucking chair!" And I walked out.

Jean-Jacques and I did not speak for the next three weeks. Well, that is not entirely true: we spoke, especially him to me in order to describe the day's work. But there was a palpable tension. On that third day of shooting the first sequence, we were up in the tree, doing all these scenes—this interaction between us and the tigers, us eating leaves out of sheer desperation, the ultimate departure of the tigers, and our eventual dismounting of the tree. So it's a lot of stuff on that third day in order to make up for the time we had lost. Well, not only did we get it all in the can by four o'clock in the afternoon, but we also had enough time to do this beautiful improvisation that was not even in the script but was phenomenal because we caught the most beautiful light of the day, with us exiting the tree and playing out the relief of having escaped with our lives. There was a palpable sense of relief from both the crew and the cast because, just like that, we were back on schedule. I had stayed up very late the night before figuring out what I needed to do to give the performance. I had just dared Annaud, and I knew if I didn't deliver something akin to a miracle, I was toast. I knew that. And on that third day the tide got turned, and frenzy was replaced by order. And calm. And from that moment on, there was an obsessive determination on my part to prove my theory that with a modicum of concern for safety and well-being, mixed with copious amounts of planning and homework, a detailed, nuanced performance could be given that would include but not be overpowered by the elements. And with that, there began a subtle evolving into the dynamic of my once-contentious relationship with Jean-Jacques.

Then, about three weeks into filming, when we're finishing this one location, we got to this other scene. And suddenly something remarkable happened. As we got ready to rehearse the scene for the crew to watch, instead of staging the scene and designating camera angles, Jean-Jacques said, "Everybody take a seat. Let's see what the actors are going to do." And I froze for a moment: let's see what *the actors* are going to do! Holy shit! That's the first time he ever said that. And we improvised the scene, and he said, "Wow, that's very nice. Okay, let's just shoot it. We'll put one camera over here. We'll put one camera over there . . ." And for the rest of the movie that's how it went: instead of directing a scene before he got a chance to see what we were gonna do, he actually watched what we were gonna do, and then, if he saw something that needed clarification or a different interpretation, he would give us notes and we would all be on the same page. But when he said nothing and we just went into shooting mode, that meant he was happy. And, as they say in France, the *rules of the game* were forever changed.

When we finally finished shooting our first leg in Scotland, Jean-Jacques and I had slowly and fantastically evolved into becoming the best of friends. This complete and amazing trust evolved between the two of us. There was now a division of labor. He realized that he didn't have to do everything; he could let the actors do the acting, he could do the directing, and we can both be on the same page and both be making the same movie. And his transformation happened right in front of our eyes. I've now done three films with Jean-Jacques Annaud, and there's no one on the planet—he's tied with Guillermo—who has given me greater roles, respect, adoration, and love. He's as close to being a family member as anyone I've met along the way. And I think we both believe we are so close to one another because we started off so rocky. But at the end of the day he's an incredibly fair-minded guy and talented guy. He's just a brilliant, brilliant, brilliant man. A tried and true genius. But he knew what he wanted and, prior to that, had never imagined he could give over to the actor and the actor could supply not only what he was looking for but also maybe even something he hadn't even imagined! I like to think there was a huge learning curve for both of us. I know there was one for me, because I came away from that experience believing it's the director's job to drive you to the point at which you can do nothing other than bring your A Game.

You can hate a director for that or you can love and admire a director for that because he's actually pulling the best out of you. And it was with Jean-Jacques, on that movie, that I learned this. But I also watched him discover that the actor has spent a lot more time thinking about how to pull off this moment than even the director has because that's his job. So to participate in this evolution of bringing together two different artistries to paint one picture . . . well, I can't speak for Jean-Jacques, but there is a satisfaction to that convergence that rivals even the greatest of sensations. And the more detailed and bold the choices I was making, the more vivid the mutual wavelength we entered became, thus making him able to augment it, to vary it, to enhance it, and merge it into his vision for the rest of the picture. Jean-Jacques has just turned out to be one of the most sensational, magnificent, generous people I've met in all my travels. And as you will see, this was only the beginning of what would turn out to be one of the richest relationships of my lifetime.

After Scotland we went to Nairobi. The location was a two-and-a-half-hour drive from the nearest anything, right in the middle of Tsavo National Park. It wasn't until we arrived there that we were told there were no telephones—hell, the computer hadn't been invented yet, nor had the cell phone, so forget about worrying about a signal. There weren't even any land lines. No telegraphs, fax machines, coke dispensers—nada! There was simply no way to communicate back to civilization. For five weeks! And they didn't tell us that until we arrived there. So we got really paranoid that our families were going to wonder what the fuck happened to us. Anyway, we not only get through it, but Africa proved to yield the singular most unique experience of my life—spiritual even, like going back as close to the Garden of Eden as exists on this earth. And I discovered that the more intense the elements and conditions of a movie set are, the deeper the bond that forges within the family who is the cast and crew. For these are memories that remain as vivid to me as if they just occurred.

The African section of filming took us right up to the Christmas holiday, which traditionally means that the company would break for two weeks and resume right after New Year. But in the case of this rejiggered production of *Quest*, our next location for the final section of filming needed to be Canada. And because it was simply too cold to shoot in Northern Ontario until at least the end of March, we were all about to disperse for around three and a half months.

So there I was, riding on this huge crest of starring for 20th Century Fox, a major studio, in an extremely esoteric production that's going to leave me with nothing less than some really serious bragging rights. And I was feeling good. I was on a high, and I had a few bucks in my pocket. I'm living a little bit, well, not real large, but enough to fly Opal to meet me in London and spend two weeks traveling the UK and then France.

I'm so close with Jean-Jacques by this point that we even went to visit him and spent a couple of nights with him at his country house just outside of Paris. Opal and I have this magical vacation together. Once we were back in the States in about early February I said to her, "Fuck it. Let's get married."

"What?"

"Let's get married, and let's do it on Valentine's Day, 'cuz that's five years to the day from our first date. So it'll be an easy anniversary to remember."

She said, "How does one get married on Valentine's Day when nothing has been planned and it's February 11?"

"I just want to fucking elope. I just want to get the blessing of your mom and my mom, take my best pal Burton and your favorite sister or two, go up to some fucking justice of the peace, and come home, married. 'Cuz all it is, is an extension of what we've already been doing. We've metaphorically been married anyway for five years."

"Well, you crazy-ass motherfucker, okay, YES! Absolutely." And so I got the Yellow Pages out for justices of the peace, and there was only one listing. It was in Spring Valley, which is just on the other side of the Tappan Zee Bridge up in Westchester County, but it was supposed to be a chapel with a scenic view of New York's skyline.

I called the pastor, or whatever the fuck he's called, to book an appointment, and he said, "Well, I'm very busy on Valentine's Day, but I can slip you in between 1:30 and 2 o'clock." We drove up there—it's fucking freezing. My best buddy, Burton, along with Burton's girlfriend and Opal's sisters, Janice and Sharon, came along to watch us get hitched. Once there, it wasn't so glamorous or quaint; the guy simply performed services on his front lawn in this suburban neighborhood. Fuck, we coulda been in Akron.

I said, "Not for nuthin, but didn't it say view of the New York skyline in your ad?"

"No, you can see it," he said, "but you have to get on the roof, and if you hold on to the antennae and lean out as far as you can, you can actually see the skyline of New York. Trust me—it's gorgeous!"

Well anyway, metaphorically at least, we had this very kind of bucolic country version of this elopement that was as romantic as I possibly could have made it, given the fact that we didn't even leave time for blood tests and all the other shit you gotta do to get a marriage license. We just made it in by the skin of our teeth so we could make the Valentine's Day date. But at the time I was romantic enough to say that this was important: I want to do this on Valentine's Day. What the fuck good is a holiday like that if you can't commit to the one you love? I also like the symmetry of getting married five years to the date, like the circles I talked about. Because, shit, marriage is really a fucking big casino. It's not for the faint of heart, and whatever good omen I could put into it, I wanted to do.

About a month later I went up to Owen Sound in northern Ontario. It's about a hundred miles due north of Toronto. It was a magnificent location, just a stone's throw from Lake Ontario. The Great Lakes are like fucking oceans. Freezing my ass off, freezing my kishkes off, and shooting the beginning and the end of *Quest for Fire*. All of the stuff that was to depict our tribal life was to be shot at these cave locations. There was the film's opening, during which we depicted this epic battle between our tribe and that of a warring neighbor and in which our fire is lost. And then there is the film's end, which consists of our triumphant return, complete with fire back in its cage. And to my surprise and delight, Jean-Jacques had decided to use one of the changes at the end of the script that one time, months before, I had offered him when he was in New York before shooting began.

The end of the movie consisted of a montage of various vignettes of our hero's tribe now that, through the miracle of fire, life has regained its stability and has, indeed, been advanced. My suggestion to Jean-Jacques was that this little visual exploration include the sitting around the campfire and the regaling of the stories of our quest, almost as if this discovery brought with it the dawn of storytelling, as if the telling of these stories, these sagas, these adventures, were part of our DNA, thus making us more human, and that the story should be like the first fish story ever told—you know, like when you catch a four-pound fish but by the time you tell your buddies about it, that fish is sixteen pounds. Jean-Jacques included that moment in the montage, with the story being told by none other than yours truly. My mom and I were so proud!

Literature is nothing more than the expansion of storytelling. Storytelling is obviously the impulse to chronicle something you've been through in order to give it its due, to have a catharsis. Like, "Holy crap, I've been through this experience, and it was a life-or-death experience, and I made it through, so there's a huge amount to be learned from it. Aside from this adrenaline rush, it had to be the most instructive moment a man can have. And I absolutely need to chronicle that not only to make note of it for myself but also to assert the fact that I've been here, that I have done this and I have had this experience. But perhaps by chronicling it I can share this experience with the people who immediately surround me and then expand the notion of community through a shared experience, forming what is at the root of our collective consciousness.

Tapping into this ancient collective consciousness is what drives me to perfect my passion as a filmmaker. Once I became aware of the fact that everybody's looking for the reason we're all here, I understood the purpose of what storytelling, literature, theater, and, thus, film is all about. The reason we're here is to talk about what we did. And if you talk about what you did in a way in which it resonates with every other person who's ever been here before or is ever going to be here again, no matter what their race, creed, ethnic background, ability to speak or not speak language, well, then you've left a mark. It resonates on such a level that it's completely universal. That is collective consciousness, and as close as we can all come to that—that's what we strive for in making movies. And that's the meaning of life. It's to know you're not in this alone, that there are a gazillion of us who have come and gone and who feel the same things you're feeling, and in knowing this comes solace, peace, a degree of resignation. That no matter what it is I'm going through, I'm not the first one, and I'm not gonna be the last.

Quest for Fire was released in February 1982. In its first year it grossed $20 million, a lot for the time. It got great reviews and was well received, eventually winning an Oscar for best makeup. While waiting for it to come out, I was pumped and ready for the next major project, but as was to become a pattern I could not begin to imagine, it led to nothing. Even as it was playing in theaters, with all this wonderful noise about it and with many reviewers positively mentioning my performance, I started to get this unsettling feeling. It wasn't as if there were a dozen new caveman movies waiting to be made— where do I go from here? 'Cuz certainly the phone ain't ringing off the hook with life-altering offers! Not only would the next few years bring about more of what I'd been through before, but now there was also an added element: I was creeping closer to the edge of this black hole, just like my brother, a hole in which only one of us was to barely make it out alive.

CHAPTER 10

Get a Real Job

Prior to the release of *Quest* the buzz was great. Everyone expected the movie to do well, and 20th Century Fox was reasonably sure they had a hit on their hands, which they did, although a modest one. I believed I had just finished a dramatic touchstone in my career and certainly one that would be a life-changer for me. At long last my enduring dream, a life on "Easy Street," was moments away from becoming a reality. The film, after all, was for a major studio. It was made by an Academy Award–winning director, with the most distinguished people on the scene, including, as I mentioned, Anthony Burgess, Desmond Morris, and Claude Agostini, the DP (director of photography), who was an award-winning camera man. The insiders were heralding my performance before the public even got a glimpse, and all this was leading up to me acquiring my first Hollywood agent, a development that only furthered my conviction that my time had finally arrived.

Coming back to "normal" life, even if I didn't have to deal with freezing my ass off anymore, took some adjustment. I didn't make enough money from the role to dramatically change anything financially. I still needed to pay the rent month by month, keep the phone and electricity on, and take my new bride out to an occasional dinner, or whatever. Fuck, I had hoped something would've immediately emanated right then and there from the experience, but it didn't. There was part of my ego that made it very difficult for me to square up the fact that I needed to go back to the same day job I had before I had left. Back to selling handbags and jewelry on Eighth Street and MacDougal at Burton's place. He welcomed me, of course, but to me it was like going back to him with my tail between my legs. It was, "Yeah, I'm a movie actor but I still need a fuckin' day gig for an hourly wage." What ensued wasn't a total downer because, as the months rolled closer to *Quest's* release, there were more and more positive vibes coming my way, enough to make me believe that, upon premiere, new doors would fling open.

About three months before the film came out they started showing it around at special screenings in Hollywood. One guy, a classy, brash agent by the name of Robert Littman watched it and thought this would be my breakout film. Bobby was as colorful a guy as I've ever met in this business. He was a British Jew who talked at the top of his voice at all times of the day and night, was a wellspring of stories, and as magnificent a natural raconteur as I had ever met (only topped by my dad and Ralph Arzoomanian). It was about eight o'clock in the evening, and I remember sitting down in my New York apartment to make myself a drink when my phone rings. I hear this guy just yelling and screaming at the top of his voice: "IS THIS RON PERLMAN?!"

"Uh, yes it is. Who's calling?"

"YOU DON'T KNOW ME, BUT I'M YOUR NEXT AGENT."

I had to hold the phone a few inches from my ear so as to protect myself from injury. I said, "Congratulations. You couldn't have picked a nicer guy."

"MY NAME IS ROBERT LITTMAN, AND I REPRESENT SIX ACTORS."

And I said, "Oh, I guess business is slow?"

He finally tones down his volume: "No, I have six, I don't need any more."

"Who are they, just out of curiosity?"

"Alan Bates, James Coburn, Gene Wilder, Elizabeth Montgomery," and he names one more icon of the day, I can't remember who. And then there's this awkward pause after he names the fifth one, and he says, "Oh, I forgot, my sixth one died."

"Sorry to hear that. Who was he?"

"Lee J. Cobb." And I said, "So you're calling me because you have an opening?"

"They told me you were funny, but I didn't expect you to be . . . well, funny. I'm calling because I want you to sign with me. I'm coming to New York right now. Where are you?"

"I'm in my house, in my tighty whities, pouring myself a nice cocktail."

"Well, I can't get there that quickly. I'm in Hollywood."

He flew in the next day, and we went out for dinner at some fancy place with a lot of showbiz people at the other tables. I could see from the moment we entered the joint that the guy knew everybody and everybody knew him. He was definitely seriously connected to all of my heroes and icons, and on a first-name basis. So I took the bit and worked out an arrangement with Pat and Shirley for them to be my New York agents while Littman would represent me in Hollywood. He told me I would need to come out to Hollywood so he could introduce me around so as to start building the myth. Once he was back in LA he'd call and ask when I was coming out so he could work his magic. I wanted to go, but I was reticent because . . . well, I didn't have any fuckin' money. I didn't have the extra cash I needed to pay for the plane ticket or a hotel room.

"Yeah, I'll be out there," and I kept putting it off, and putting it off.

Eventually the official press tour for the film happened. We did talk shows; we did the *LA Times*, *New York Times*, CBS *Evening News*; we did Letterman (this was when he had his original show on NBC after Carson). We're doing all kinds of press, and we're going from place to place in limousines. That's the first time I'd ever been in a limousine in my life. When they sent us out to the West Coast for a week or so I met up with Littman, and he brought me to parties hosted or attended by celebrities every night. I was at Jimmy Caan's house one night, Alan Ladd Jr.'s house the next night. I'm just partying with nothing but people who keep my mouth agape for the entire seven days I was there. At the time there was an executive chef at a place called Spago, which was kind of like this parking lot they had converted to a restaurant, and it became *the* quintessential Hollywood hangout. I was eating lunch every day there, doing press interviews from there. Orson Welles was coming and going, Kirk Douglas was coming and going, and Jack Lemmon was coming and going. I mean, I suddenly felt as though the Earth had shifted under my feet, and . . . well, I'm for sure not in Kansas anymore, Toto. I was buying into what everyone was telling me: I was surely among this next wave of the new celebrated generation of actors.

That was where my head was at opening night. But as the weeks went by I slowly began to see that all of it was leading to nothing: no calls, no roles, no offers. This crescendo is quickly followed by the blackest hole I've ever been in. I began to seriously wonder what was in store for me. Clearly, cause and effect meant nothing. If you do A, B, C, and D in the movie industry, it doesn't necessarily mean that it's going to lead to E, F, G, and H. Whereas maybe in other industries it would, but this particular business there are other forces at work. In reality, even as I sat in a theater one night a few weeks later and watched the film once again by myself, I came to understand that *Quest* was a one-off. My performance was the creation of a very, very esoteric, specific kind of behavior, completely covered up by makeup and costume, such that the acting never even showed through physically, much less emotionally. It was a very abstract performance. There was no real set of clues left behind. No forensics blurting forth, "This is the guy, and we know exactly who the fuck he is and what the fuck he's gonna do to set Hollywood on its ass."

In short, I had been on the highest waves of expectation that a man could possibly be on that my life was going to change completely, patently, and for all time because I was a part of this amazing achievement, because, as I was being told, of my personal contribution to the film's success. "Your life is gonna fucking change, dude. You're about to become a movie star, son. You're gonna be rich, you're gonna be famous." Full stop! This is what I was told—actual fucking words that came out of people's fucking lips, not mine. And then . . .

When I left the theater that night it was as if I had become possessed by some dark force, almost like a del Torian demon spirit had suddenly taken over my mind. Everything began to seem pointless. Opal tried to cushion the blow by telling me something else would come, but this depression was so personal and so profound that I was immune to consolation, and to this day neither Opal nor, indeed, any living person knows how far I fell and to what degree. What I am about to describe has never been told. And it all happened while fucking *Quest for Fire* was still in the fucking theaters.

What I'm telling you is that for a kid who came from the background that I came from, who had nothing, who never had any reason to really imagine that he would ever be able to depart dramatically from the die that was originally cast on the whole Perlman thing—to have this in front of me, dangling this carrot, it was seductive. It played tricks with my mind, and I began to buy into the belief that I'm going to wake up and my life is going to be different. I was going to be living in a fucking penthouse and fielding phone calls from agents, producers—hell, studio heads. I was going to be choosing what fucking movie I was gonna be doing next. I was gonna be deciding whether I want to work with the Bette Davises of the day. More importantly, I was going to be able to finally do something significant with my acting—to create and contribute whatever I could to our culture. I was gonna make a difference, a mark. There was all kinds of fucking weird shit rollin' around in my noggin. The fact of the matter is, nothing happened. I mean, Nothing, with a capital *Nuth*. The silence was profound. And deafening. And devastating!

I guess this darkness or demon was always there. I'm pretty sure it can't be too much of a coincidence that I lost my brother to the very thing I almost lost myself to. So maybe there was some sort of a chemical thing that went through both him and me, something we shared in common, despite what my dad believed. But what I had, I later came to understand, was clinical depression, whereas what my brother had was manic depression. Yet both are and can be killers. For me, it was a result of this nothing, or really the perception I had of it as being nothing. Whatever . . . it spiraled swiftly and was all-encompassing. I couldn't stop thinking, "How could I have been that wrong? How could I have allowed myself to be that completely bullshitted?" I was bullshitting myself; I was bullshitted by the universe at large. I bought into a whole lot of shit that a whole lot of fucking people who didn't give a shit about me were saying. It triggered this emotional descent, which, I guess, for somebody who has a sort of chemical proclivity, like the one I described, led to something that became overwhelming. And it became something that, no matter how hard I tried to grab onto it with both hands, I couldn't get a grasp. What made it even stranger was that it came at this moment that should have been the very opposite. If I've learned anything on this journey I'm on, it's that I'm in an art form ensconced in a business that is at once neither or both. But one thing is for sure: it is not for the faint of heart.

If you've never been through clinical depression before, it's just gonna sound rather academic, anemic even, like, "Come on, Perlman, you just made a fuckin' movie. It can't be that bad. You're overdramatizing all of this. Get yourself together and stop with the bullshit." And that's the way most of the world treats something that is as disturbing as this mental illness, simply because most of the world is reminded about how ill-equipped we are to deal with somebody who is in that much trouble. Depression goes through stages, but if left unchecked and not treated, this elevator ride will eventually go all the way to the bottom floor. And finally you find yourself bereft of choices, unable to figure out a way up or out, and pretty soon one overarching impulse begins winning the battle for your mind: "Kill yourself." And once you get over the shock of those words in your head, the horror of it, it begins to start sounding appealing, even possessing a strange resolve, logic. In fact, it's the *only* thing you have left that is logical. It becomes the only road to relief. As if just the planning of it provides the first solace you've felt that you can remember. And you become comfortable with it. You begin to plan it and contemplate the details of how best to do it, as if you were planning travel arrangements for a vacation. You just have to get out. O-U-T. You see the white space behind the letter *O*? You just want to crawl through that O and be out of this inescapable hurt that is this thing they call clinical depression. "How am I going to do this?" becomes the only tape playing. And if you are really, really, really depressed and you're really there, you're gonna find a way. I found a way. I had a way. And I did it.

I made sure Opal was out of the house and on a business trip. My planning took a few weeks. I knew exactly how I was going to do it: I didn't want to make too much of a mess. There was gonna be no blood, no drama. There was just going to be, "Now you see me, now you don't." That's what it was going to be.

So I did it. And it was over. Or so I thought. About twenty-four hours later I woke up. I was groggy; zoned out to the point at which I couldn't put a sentence together for the next couple of days. But I was semifunctional, and as these drugs and shit that I took began to wear off slowly but surely, I realized, "Okay, I fucked up. I didn't make it." I thought I did all the right stuff, left no room for error, but something happened. And this perfect, flawless plan was thwarted. As if some force rebuked me and said, "Not yet. You're not going anywhere."

The only reason I could have made it, after the amount of pills and alcohol and shit I took, was that somebody or something decided it wasn't my time. It certainly wasn't me making that call. It was something external. And when you're infused with the presence of this positive external force, which is so much greater than all of your efforts to the contrary, that's about as empowering a moment as you can have in your life.

These days we have a plethora of drugs one can take to ameliorate the intensity of this lack of hope, lack of direction, lack of choice. So fuck it and don't be embarrassed or feel like you can handle it yourself, because lemme tell ya something: you can't. Get fuckin' help. The negative demon is strong, and you may not be as fortunate as I was. My brother wasn't.

For me, despair eventually gave way to resolve, and resolve gave way to hope, and hope gave way to "Holy shit. I feel better than I've ever felt right now." Having actually gone right up to the white light, looked right at it, and some force in the universe turned me around, I found, with apologies to Mr. Dylan, *my direction home*. I felt more alive than I've ever felt. I'm not exaggerating when I say for the next six months I felt like Superman. Like I'm gonna fucking go through walls. That's how strong I felt. I had this positive force in me. I was saved. I was protected. I was like the only guy who survived and walked away from a major plane crash. I was here to do something big. What started as the darkest moment in my life became this surge of focus, direction, energy, and empowerment.

I wanted to change everything, and the first thing I thought of was to try to find a way to make some dough to pay the rent, 'cuz selling handbags just wasn't cutting it. I saw this TV commercial for Fugazy Continental, one of the early limo companies in New York City, advertising for drivers. Part of what they were advertising was that if you come work for them, you can be an owner/operator, setting your own hours and making the dough of your dreams. They were trying to recruit a lot of guys to jump on board and pay them a very, very hefty fee in order to have access to the amazing opportunities that being a part of Fugazy Continental entailed, or so the commercial said. I needed a job that let me set my own hours so I could continue with auditions, so I finagled my way into the company without paying anything. I was hired as an independent and was paid per fare. I had a fuckin' chauffer uniform, a hat, and the whole fuckin' get-up.

I worked for them for about a week before I realized I hated working during the day, so I said, "Can I get the car for twenty-four hours a day, and I'll bring in a second guy. He'll be my day guy, and I'll do the night?" That was when I lured my friend Nameer El-Kadi, who was the second lead in *Quest for Fire*, into joining me. And so it went, me and Nameer. Ya got the two leads in the greatest caveman movie of the last six months in our new roles as chauffeurs for this fuckin' limo company. Fuck it, though, we made the best of it, and the money they said they'd pay didn't seem bad. You drove around all types of money people, some celebs, some politicos. I was okay at it, treating it as though it were a part in a movie. Speaking of which . . .

One day I got an assignment to pick up some guy and his secretary someplace in Midtown and take him to the American Bar Association on the Upper East Side. So he got in the car—very sweet older fellow, very well mannered, very warm—and began to tell me what a thrill it is for him at his ripe old age to be treated to his first limo ride. Turned out this guy was a distinguished New York magistrate, beloved by all in the industry, and that night all his peers would be honoring him. Very exciting. And a limo to boot.

So I said to him, "Yeah, I kinda know what you mean. I just took my first limo ride a few months ago."

"Oh really? What was the occasion?" And when I told him I had starred in a movie he leaned forward and looked at me closer. "Wait a minute . . . were you in *Quest for Fire?*"

"Yeah. You really recognize me from that?" He said he knew something was weird about me the minute he stepped in the car but only finally put his finger on it. So then he said, "What's a movie star doing driving a limo?" And I told him how things don't always work out the way ya thought they might but how much I loved being in a limo too. So when money got tight I figured, "What the hell? I'll drive a limo. It can't be that much different in the front than it is in the back. You know, one year you're in the back, the next you're in the front. And that, my friend, is America to me!" The judge laughed his fuckin' ass off. When he got out he tried to give me a tip, not knowing the protocol. "Thanks, Judge, but keep it. This was the best ride I had all month!"

So I did that for about a month when the first check came in that was supposed to pay for the first weeks' fares. The dollar amount seemed off. I did the math, and it seemed like I worked my ass off. I felt like I worked 175 hours the first week, and the first check was only $230? How is it possible that I could have put in that many hours and ended up with so little? So I walked up to the cashier who fronts the paymaster, and I said, "Hey, who do I talk to about this check?"

"What's the problem?"

"It seems as though you guys shorted me a little bit." I was getting really loud.

The cashier says, "Sir, would you keep your volume down?"

"No, I won't keep the fuckin' volume down. I worked my ass off the week this check is for, and I'm supposed to get thirty-five dollars more. Not two-thirty—it's two-sixty-five! What the fuck is going on here?"

"Well, the paymaster is inside, but he's a little bit busy right now, and hold on, you can't go in there . . ."

But I already said, "Fuck it," and pushed open the door to this back room, and I held the check up in the air with my left hand and said, "Who the fuck do I speak to about this fucking check?!" I'm talking at the top of my voice. As I get halfway through the sentence, I realize I'm in a room with thirty-five guys. They all are wearing suits, but with no sports jackets, and they all have shoulder holsters on. I'm the only guy in the room that's not packin'. But some fuckin' jerk inside me keeps going. I said, "Who the fuck do I talk to about making good on this check?"

There was about ten seconds of silence, and then one guy looked around to the other guys in the room and said, "Who the fuck does he talk to about taking care of this fuckin' check?" Everybody started laughing. The guy then came over to me and put his arm around my neck, like in a mafia movie, and he said, "This kid is beautiful. I love this fuckin' kid." He looked at the check and asked how much I was shorted. He told some other guy to make the check right. He looked at his other guys and said, "For thirty-five fuckin' dollars. I love this kid. This kid has got *some* fucking brass over here. Give this kid whatever he wants."

After that, the dispatcher started throwing me these crazy good accounts. I was driving for some major players in New York—ESPN guys, CBS guys, and everyone like that. They were throwing me some really good accounts because I amused them, if ya know what I mean! For thirty bucks I was ready to get shot 175 times. I was gonna look like fucking Sonny from *The Godfather*. This was part of the new me, when I was starting to feel really, really good about myself. So the next phase of this "recovery" was to take charge of my acting career. After getting paid for a few more weeks I decide to catch a cheap red-eye to Los Angeles. Bobby Littman, my Hollywood agent, had always said I was welcome to stay with him anytime, so I took him up on his offer. Early the next morning I knocked on his door. "Listen, Bobby," I said, "I ain't got no money, so can I sleep on your couch?"

"Of course, Perlman. Come in. You don't have to sleep on my couch. I have a guest room. We'll have a marvelous time."

I basically moved in and quickly started taking over the place. I borrowed one of his cars. I made him stay up late and keep telling me stories about Hollywood and all of his buddies and pals, to the point at which after about a week and a half he came into the guest room where I was sleeping and sat on the side of the bed.

"Can I ask you a question, Perlman?"

"Sure, Bobby, anything!"

"How much longer are you going to be here?"

"Bobby, you know, I'd like to leave, but I learned from my first Hollywood agent that I shouldn't really go anywhere till he gets me a fucking job." He just looked at me. "Do you know who my first Hollywood agent is, Bobby?"

"It's me."

"It's you, Bobby. So I leave the minute you get me a fucking job."

He got on the phone and I heard him yelling, "YOU GOTTA HIRE THIS GUY. GIVE HIM ANYTHING." He came back into the bedroom and said he'd have a contract for me before the month was out and that I should go home. Instead of a horse head in his bed, Bobby got me. To this day I never did see a man more possessed!

I worked at Fugazy for about a month more, until Littman called and said I was hired to do this movie in Hollywood called *Ice Pirates*. I had to be out there right away. The film was a spoof on *Star Trek* and *Star Wars*, done in a purely comedic version. It was shit. I don't want to even talk about *Ice Pirates*, but it was a studio movie and I was heading back to Hollywood—with a paying gig. Finally the silence was silenced!

(CHAPTER 11)

Stage or Scream

While I was shooting *Ice Pirates* Opal came out to visit me. It was her first trip to Hollywood, and, I don't know, there must've been some exotic scent in the air. What I'm tryin' to say is that she got pregnant during that trip. I mean, she didn't *know* she was pregnant right away, but she sure suspected it, if ya know what I mean!: "Um, excuse me, hello, but what in the fuck do you think you're doing Mr. 'Boy, wasn't that beautiful'? We don't have the income needed to have a kid right now. HEY, I'M TALKING TO YOU!"

I said nothing. I got her in the car and drove up the winding roads above Hollywood to this spot I used to go to when I had an hour to kill. It was this magnificent lookout spot on Mulholland Drive that overlooks the entire San Fernando Valley, where you could see all the studios, *plus* Brando's house, *plus* Nicholson's, Brando's neighbor's house. I mean, this was the place to sit and dream big, son! I stopped the car just short of the cliff, rammed it in park, turned to my dearest Opal, and said, "Excuse *me*! Do you know when the right time to have a kid is? WHEN IT FUCKING HAPPENS!" I paused for dramatic effect, threw the car into reverse, and sped down the hill, never saying another word on the subject—that is, just until we found out days later that her hunch was, in actuality, true, and our firstborn was, indeed, on its merry way.

After about a week being home my prophetic Mulholland resolve started to waver a little. That high an actor is on while he's in the middle of a gig gradually started to get replaced by the same old, same old. I began thinking, "Well, once again, my career is over. The phone's not ringing, and nothing is happening." And reality was biting. I mean, it was one thing when it was just me and Opal I had to worry about; we got real good at the spaghetti-and-meatball, followed by the meatball-and-spaghetti diet. But it's another thing when you've got a baby to think about. It takes on a completely different modality. Before I even had time to panic, the phone rang, and it was my agent girls, Pat and Shirley, with a tone in their voices that actually sounded promising. "Peter Brook is in town and wants to meet you." The frame of reference jumped out at me. During the sixties and seventies Peter Brook was one of the true godheads of theater everywhere. He had written a book called *The Empty Space*, which became *the* textbook for anybody who studied theater during those decades. He had been the artistic director of the Old Vic and the Royal Shakespeare Company, where he did one iconic production after another, thus continuing to raise the bar for the work that was done at those distinguished and venerable institutions. He then eventually went off on his own and started doing very experimental stuff, and some of it was so experimental, so unconventional . . . I mean he would actually go off to a hilltop in Tibet and perform obscure versions of the classics for goats—literally, goats and animals, because there was no one else there to watch. But that wasn't the point, was it?! However, regardless of what Peter was calling to discuss, the notion of having *any* discussion with Peter Brook commanded one's undivided attention. So I gathered up my goat vaccine and off I went, titillated all the way.

I embarked over to my old stomping grounds, the La Mama Theater in the East Village, where Brook was holding his meetings. I was excited because this guy occupied such an amazing place in this incredibly pure part of my fascination with theater, in particular, and all art in general. More than just a director, he was like the high priest of theater at that time. When I sat down with him he told me he hadn't been able to get me out of his mind since he saw *Quest for Fire* and that he was inviting me to join his company. This fuckin' blew me away. Finally *Quest* ceased to be in vain—it actually did lead to something. And although what it led to wasn't something I would have ever guessed, and although it didn't lead to a prime table at Spago's, it did take me to the single-most esoteric, purely artistic avenue one could ever be invited to stroll down. He wanted to mount the classic ancient Hindu epic upon which all spirituality emanates, *The Mahabharata*, first for his theater company in Paris, the Théâtre des Bouffes du Nord, and eventually for the screen. His idea, as the original story is in eighteen volumes of Sanskrit and is the most epic story ever told, was to stage it as a trilogy, three three-hour plays. He had the brilliant French screenwriter Jean-Claude Carriere to adapt it and was offering me the role of Bhima, whose father is the god of wind and whose mother is the most beautiful mortal woman ever born to this Earth. Oh, and because the Bouffes du Nord was an experimental theater company, there was no money, or very little anyway. Oh, and I'd hafta move my newborn baby and young wife to Paris for two years.

Needless to say, it was a big honor to finally be talking with Peter Brook, who was truly a god of mine and, indeed, any other theater actor of my generation. And it came as a result of what he saw in this movie, which I thought no one had noticed at all. So right away I was incredibly seduced. "Good," he said and then suggested we go for a walk. He took me to a bookstore on the Lower East Side and bought me a copy of the *Mahabharata*, which, in its condensed version, was more than twelve hundred pages. He said, "This is a story that is really not meant to be read; it's meant to be told verbally. But if you're going to read it, this is the greatest adaptation there is. So start sinking your teeth into this, and if you are interested in continuing to talk about this, here's all my information. We would love to have you in the troupe."

I was looking at him and down at this giant fuckin' book in my hands.

Then he said, "I know this is a big decision, so while you are making it I would like to invite you to immediately become a part of the group by joining the cast for the production of *La Tragedie de Carmen* that I'm about to open at Lincoln Center. You do this while you are pondering and, in the meanwhile, you get a taste of what it's like to work with us."

So perform I did in *Carmen* at Lincoln Center, and it was a dream come true. Lincoln Center is like the Yankee Stadium of New York culture. And I was doing it for the great Peter Brook. My first performance fell on a Friday night, exactly one week after Opal was due to deliver our first kid. And God bless my dear wife for having the decency to wait till I got my first performance under my belt, because the following morning Opal went into labor. Now Saturday is a two-show day on Broadway, a Saturday afternoon matinee followed by another show in the evening. Well, I had a clause in my contract that, as I was my wife's Lamaze partner, if she went into labor, I was excused and could miss a performance. So I missed both the matinee and the evening show on Saturday. I did, however, enjoy a way better show: I watched my daughter Blake be born into the world, and the minute I held this precious child in my arms and she looked up into my eyes, I had an epiphany: I was not gonna go to France. I was gonna pursue a career in cinema in a more conventional way right here in the good ol' US of A. And even though being invited to perform at Lincoln Theater by the inimitable Peter Brook was probably the greatest compliment that could ever have been paid to me, and even though I knew this invitation represented a major circle closing for me, still, I was certain destiny lay elsewhere. Yes, what Brook had embodied and what he had evolved into equated to pure artistry, never concerned about pandering for profit or appeasing the bottom-liners. And there was and still is something inside of me that yearns for something that pure, that innocent, that unfettered.

But at the end of the day it would have required almost the devotion of a monk, to be cloistered in a world where there are no temporal limitations. Well . . . turns out I just ain't that muthafucka; I just didn't have *that* kind of devotion. Turns out all I wanted was to be a crass, commercial American actor who was going to make some fuckin' money and give this fuckin' kid a life I didn't have.

When *Carmen* finished, Opal and I felt we had a decision to make. We had an eight-month-old baby, and we both realized that the opportunities available for a New York actor to actually make a living never seemed to have my name on 'em. If you were getting paid in the Apple, you were either doing soap operas or commercials or singing and dancing your ass off on the gay white way. So we packed a couple of bags and made our way out to Hollywood—Opal, me, and eight-month-old little Blake. We chose to stay at the Highland Gardens Hotel, which is this funky-ass little efficiency apartment/hotel famous for catering to actors, singers, dancers, and musicians. The reason I knew about it was because it was where Janis Joplin had overdosed. What more perfect way to be introduced to the seedy underbelly of Hollywood? But mainly we stayed there because it was a very transient kind of place, where one was free to either commit or not. You could stay a day, a week, or for years. It was a way for us to come check out Los Angeles without getting stuck in Los Angeles, because we both had a feeling that we might hate it. Which is also why we decided to hang onto our apartment in the Apple for the time being.

We had been there less than a week when my mom called. She found my brother. He was dead from a gunshot wound to the head. I guess she got suspicious when she couldn't get him on the phone for days on end. So she went down to his pad in the Village to see what the problem was . . . fuck! What a nightmare.

I was on the next plane back to New York. I had no idea what to expect, but I knew it was gonna be ugly. I was terrified for my mom—whether she could handle a blow like this, having lost the first love of her life, my dad, at such a young age, and now this. The flight back to New York found my mind going faster than the plane. My brother, up until this last episode, had only experienced the manic side of this manic depression of his—that is, until this last one. This one found him lower than low. I had spent all day every day for the last four months talking to him, counseling him, trying to get it into his head that there were beautiful things out there waiting for him. He was not to be reached. But even I, who had been through my own version of what he was going through, never, ever thought he had the resolve to take his own life. And then he waited until I left town to do it. Sadness doesn't begin to describe what I was feeling, and what I am still feeling.

One of the hardest parts of that moment was, aside from the profound loss of my hero, my brother, was there I was with a mom who desperately needed something to believe in and something to give her a reason to not give up. And I had this brand-new child and wife and this life that I'm just about to embark on. The decision as to whether to just kind of throw that plan out the window and come back to New York, to be the rock my mom could lean on, was one of the toughest I ever had to make. Ultimately, she made it a lot easier for me, as she's always done when it comes down to me and the good of my career. She said, "No. There's nothing that gets in the way of that. I'm fine. Besides, I have Irving"—her second husband and one of the sweetest most generous of men—"I'll be good. I'll be fine. You go back and do this thing. That's what everyone would want."

So after a period of a few weeks of mourning and putting my brother's house in order and all of the things that bring the closure of the moment, I went back to the Highland Gardens to my wife and my now nine-month-old child. I started this insipid career march toward God knows what. But at least it was something I was going to commit to, even though we decided to go month-by-month, holding onto the apartment in New York because we were only going to commit to it just so far. We left the door open to come back. If LA was truly all the things we ever heard it was—vapid, one-dimensional, superficial, an idiot's delight—there was only so much of it we were gonna tolerate. We would only stay if we saw some real signs that it was gonna be a sort of utopia for me, commercially.

I did a few TV shows. I played an attorney twice, once in the TV series *MacGruder and Loud*. I played a thug twice, once in the *Fall Guy*, and for a TV show called *Split Image*, along with a few other small character roles. Everything indicated that Hollywood was every bit as terrible at figuring out what to do with this fall-through-the-cracks character actor as New York had been. Those first years were rough, and we barely scraped by. We survived from these bit parts and some inheritance dough my rich aunt left me, the one who took me to my first Broadway play, *Fiddler on the Roof*. We kept our expenses very low. We bought a cheap car, stayed in a cheap flat. We cut corners.

Then something happened toward the middle of the end of '85 that kind of changed the conversation. I read an article that said my friend Jean-Jacques Annaud had signed on to direct the adaptation of this incredibly celebrated book, *The Name of the Rose* by Umberto Eco. The book had been on the *New York Times* best-seller list so long it had broken records for the amount of consecutive weeks it had occupied first place. So there was this huge bidding war as to who was gonna be the guy to adapt the book into a film. It turned out that Jean-Jacques Annaud, who had done *Quest for Fire*, was most convincing both to the studios and to Umberto Eco, and little by little he was starting to put the pieces together to make this into a movie.

I went and bought the book and read it. The book was really hard to get into. It was almost like reading *Titus Andronicus*, in that it's so dense with characters. It's kind of a very obscure, very mysterious, fourteenth-century monastery world that had Franciscans and other Orders—to a Jew they all look alike! All told, it took me four attempts to get past the first one hundred pages. And then I finally got on a roll and started really getting into this mysterious world Eco was depicting, and it became one of the greatest books I've ever read. I noticed that there was a role in there of this hunchback, Salvatore, who spoke seven languages, but all in a jumble, not as if he was literate but more like he was too mentally challenged to understand there was a difference between one and the other, so he spoke every word of every language all at once, with a logic that was impenetrable. But he was part of this world that got swept into this order of outlaws within this strangely conflicted world of religious fervor.

The character grabbed me. He was this hunchback who was mentally challenged. He was ugly, deformed, distorted, and yet he was functional. Plus, he had an insatiable sexual appetite and was a coward of the highest order. He was this compendium of fascinating elements that made for an analysis and execution as an actor that would have been every bit akin to the fascinating challenge I had already enjoyed with Annaud in *Quest*. I became obsessed with the idea of trying to solve the puzzle that was Salvatore. It was like a Rubik's Cube, trying to line up a series of divergent attributes and mold them into a piece of humanity that, even though you'd never seen anyone like him, seemed at once organic and natural. That very exercise was why *Quest for Fire* had been so satiating, and I imagined having that identical kind of rush creating the role of Salvatore in *Name of the Rose*.

So I reached out to Jean-Jacques, and he liked the idea of me playing the part but was very discouraging because he said the production was really complicated. There was a lot of politics involved, and he needed to put me on tape to get the approval of a whole lot of people for me to win the role. Meanwhile, I'm reading things saying Sean Connery had signed on, and F. Murray Abraham had signed on. This was beginning to become more and more of an obsession for me, to become a part of this thing, 'cuz it's gonna be a real high-water mark for anybody involved.

I waited for Jean-Jacques to come to Los Angeles and then spent an afternoon with him doing improvisations in front of a video camera, trying to find some sort of essence that would lead people to believe I was the right guy to play Salvatore. We never really did. In fact, looking back on it, I think it was a pretty mediocre attempt. I don't think I had a particularly good handle on the character yet. I don't think Jean-Jacques even had a particularly good handle on what he was looking for in the character yet. We both had this unbelievable desire to see me get it, but that was pretty much the end of it. This one event that would have been the signpost I desperately was seeking, this signal that it was right to keep going, was slipping through my fingers. Fuck! Now what?

(CHAPTER 12)

Name of the Rose

Sure enough, a few months went by and I read in the paper that the role of Salvatore was awarded to Franco Franchi, who was sort of like the Red Skelton of Italy and a beloved TV personality. He was a comedian who had his own variety show. He did a lot of voices and invented a lot of characters. So I said, *Okay. Congrats Mr. F. You can't win 'em all. This was not meant to be mine*, and all that other bullshit one tells oneself when trying to play down a pretty big disappointment. So I went on with my life.

One night Opal and I . . . well, without going into too much detail, I ended up on the couch in the living room. At about five in the morning the phone rang. I fumble for it in the dark, dropping it several times. Finally: "Um, hello?" I could tell from the interference on the line that it's definitely not a local call.

"Hello. I'm looking for Ron Perlman. Hello. Hello?"

I was groggy, fucking half-asleep. Not half-asleep—fully asleep. "Who's calling?"

"My name is Anna Gross, and I'm calling from Germany. I'm calling to offer Ron Perlman . . . is this Ron?"

I said, "Keep talking."

She said, "Well, I'm calling at the behest of Jean-Jacques Annaud to offer Ron the role of Salvatore in *Name of the Rose*."

"Come on! Who is this . . . really?"

"I know you think that this is probably a joke. And I'm well aware of the fact that it's five o'clock in the morning where you are. I know this sounds too weird to be true, because I also know you know that we started production on this movie three weeks ago. But nevertheless, we are offering you the role of Salvatore in *Name of the Rose*, and the reason why we need to cut to the chase and stop with this scintillating repartee right now is because you need to be on a plane at eleven o'clock this morning if you're going to do this role. Now once again, is this Ron?"

"Okay, enough. Who the fuck is this?"

"Oh Jesus! Wait a moment. I'm putting Jean-Jacques on the phone right now so we can prove to you that we're not kidding around. But before I give him the phone I need to have your agent's phone number, because we need to strike a deal right now so you can get on the plane at eleven o'clock to be here the first thing tomorrow morning, to start shooting almost immediately."

As it turned out, she wasn't bullshitting. Jean-Jacques got on the phone, and I said, "J. J.? Is that you? What's going on?"

"So it took me a little bit of maneuvering," he said, "but what we both wanted to has come true; you are gonna be Salvatore. So get your ass over here. I gotta go. And whatever you do, just make sure you make that eleven o'clock flight."

The first thing that came to mind, I guess in my still-asleep shock, was, "Holy shit, I got dry cleaning! I got most of my good fucking clothes at the fucking dry cleaners. What time do they fucking open? Do they open in time for me to put them in my fucking suitcase?" I thought that by using the word *fucking* enough it would help me to regain consciousness. And then, sure enough, the sleepy, groggy state started getting overwhelmed by the *Holy shit, I gotta get moving state*, so I started making calls to my agent, wakin' his ass up and figuring out what in the fuck to do next. I had to pick up a copy of the script from Lynn Stalmaster, the Los Angeles casting director, before I left. They wanted me to be ready to hit the ground running the minute I landed in Germany, as shooting was to start immediately.

With all the hubbub coming from the living room, finally Opal woke up. I told her the news, and she knew by the look of sheer and utter panic in my eyes that I wasn't fucking around. Oh, and she forgave me, by the way, for what neither of us could remember what we were fighting about in the first place. I threw some shit in a bag, brushed my teeth, grabbed my passport, kissed the baby, and, *boom*, out the fuckin' door. The driver swung around to get my dry cleaning, and, *boom* again, I was on my way. The half-smile that never left my face during the whole ride to the airport belied the strangely delicious irony that played out in my mind's eye: For two and a half, three years I was thinking *Quest* was a one-off and nothing like it was ever gonna happen again. And sure enough, and with the same magician, no less, Annaud rode in like some dashing deus ex machina on a white charger to save me from oblivion and obscurity. And not only that but also hands me this jewel of a character on a silver tray and says, "This is yours." This unbelievable role was an incredible opportunity to do something requiring all of the skills I'd learned. I mean, looking back on the creation of Salvatore, it took every single fiber of my being to solve the riddle of who this character was and how to play him.

I poured over the material, going back and forth between the novel and the screenplay for the entire ten-hour flight. I was obsessively attempting to figure out how I was going to distill this character I previously described, with all his behavioral quirks, seamlessly to life. The first revelation that hit me on the plane was that the reason the audition had been so mediocre is that I didn't have the guy in me yet, that I needed a model outside of myself to draw from. I didn't know who this guy was. I didn't know what he looked like. I didn't know what he talked like. And because he was such an exotic compendium of behavioral traits, I needed to physically see a guy like that. I concluded that my search might start in an institution for the mentally challenged, just as Salvatore himself was. So I wrote down a list of things that I'm gonna need the minute I hit the ground in Germany. I wanted to see if they'd arrange for me to be taken to as many institutions as possible, in hopes of finding the seeds. I also figured out on the plane how to

Mom, Dad, and I
visiting my bro playin'
a gig at the Concord
Hotel, Catskills, New
York, circa 1964. *From
the author's personal
collection.*

My dad, immersed in what he loved most—and the way he will always be remembered!
From the author's personal collection.

The gorgeous Opal Stone and yours truly on our wedding day, February 14, 1981. *From the author's personal collection.*

FUCK! I'M MARRIED! *From the author's personal collection.*

The Godfather, Burton Levy, and his pal, Buddy. The two toughest Jews I ever knew. *From the author's personal collection.*

Throwing a little birthday party for my adopted pop, the beautiful and amazing Roy Dotrice! One of those men who are too good to be true! *From the author's personal collection.*

From *The City of Lost Children*: one thing is for certain: I'll never be in that shape again! The City of Lost Children, © *Twentieth Century Fox. All rights reserved.*

In St. Paul de Vence, in the south of France, on a break from filming *The City of Lost Children,* circa 1994. Blake and Brandon, ten and four, respectively. *From the author's personal collection.*

Salvatore, *The Name of the Rose. From the author's personal collection.*

Johner, *Alien Resurrection:* Jeunet and me, redux. Alien Resurrection, © *1997 Twentieth Century Fox. All rights reserved.*

Josiah Sanchez, *The Magnificent Seven:* taking my place among all the other Jewish cowboys? The Magnificent Seven *(TV series), © 1998 MGM Television Entertainment Inc. All rights reserved.*

Guillermo del Toro and I in a moment of off-camera love. Out of multitudes! *Photo by Bruce Talamon, © Warner Bros. Entertainment Inc. All rights reserved.*

Can you blush? Iconic moment between Snipes and me, *Blade II*. Photo by Bruce Talamon,

William H. Macy and I in *Happy Texas*: if that ain't a screen moment, I just don't know what is. *Courtesy of Miramax.*

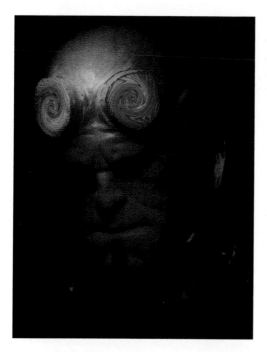

Hellboy I: where the rubber meets the road! Hellboy. © 2004 *Revolution Studios Distributions Company, LLC. Courtesy of Sony Pictures Entertainment.*

Hellboy with Liz and Manning: the adorable Selma Blair and the equally adorable Jeffrey Tambor. Hellboy. © 2004 *Revolution Studios Distributions Company, LLC. Courtesy of Sony Pictures Entertainment.*

Clay Morrow, *Sons of Anarchy*: during some of his better times.
From the author's personal collection.

Game-changers, all!! *From the author's personal collection.*

solve his jumble of languages and make sense of all the seven different languages that Salvatore used, but used without reason. So the other things I needed once in Germany were copies of the book translated into all the languages the character used. I would find everything Salvatore ever says in the book, and I was going to write down every sentence in all those languages. Then I was going to do an eeny, meeny, miny, moe, thus creating his random modality of speech.

I landed in Germany about mid-afternoon, and once there, I was taken immediately to the set, where they were already deep into shooting the movie. I said hello to my old friend Christian Slater, who is the son of another old friend, Mary Jo Slater, a casting director I had known in New York since the beginning. Finally Jean-Jacques appeared. I got a big hug and a kiss. And I said, "Jean-Jacques, I'm gonna ask these guys to provide me with a few things to make this thing happen and happen quick. Can you help me out with that?"

"Absolutely." He took me to the producers and said, "Give this man everything he wants. Except more money! That's how we lost the last guy!"

I told them I wanted to visit mental institutions, and within twenty minutes I was on my way to the first one. The place was a locked-down facility for people with Down syndrome, who, of course, back then were insensitively referred to as mongoloids. This place had patients who were distorted physically and were mentally challenged beyond the point at which they were capable of living on their own, but they were marginally functional. This, indeed, was where I found Salvatore! I watched this one guy interacting with a group, having been given a bunch of ice cream Popsicle sticks so as to create a little house or something; it was the institution's version of occupational therapy. But while he was doing it, he was touching every girl's tit that he could get his little hands on, including the nurses and all the patients. And he was just getting the biggest charge out of this, squeezing a titty and then giggling profusely over how clever he was to cop a feel. This obsessive proclivity for sexual thrills was a *huge* window into one of the completely illogical attributes Salvatore displays in the movie. And so now I was locked into this guy! As he went back to his little task of building a stick house with Popsicle sticks, all the while his eyes were darting around, seeing which titty he could snag next. That was a part of Salvatore that I needed. Suddenly I am infused with power and well-being. I am on a roll. I decided to check out one more place, a prison for the criminally insane. To say I didn't find my guy in there was an understatement. In fact, all I knew was that I needed to get the fuck out of there as quickly as possible. Aside from the open call for *Quest for Fire*, that was the sickest place I've ever been in my life.

When I went back to the set I thanked everybody for making my little tour happen. Then I got my marching orders. They told me Jean-Jacques wanted to have dinner with me that night. I checked into the hotel and waited until a driver fetched me at around nine o'clock to take me to a restaurant where J. J. was waiting.

"Good to see you, my friend."

"Same here, mon ami, same here! So, tell me, J. J., how the fuck did I get here?"

"Well, frankly you were very close to getting the role from the beginning, but because this movie is a coproduction between Germany, France, and Italy, and because each country is responsible for putting in a small modicum of money to come up with the budget, after the Italian government put in their four million, they said, 'Who are the Italian actors in there?' I said, 'We don't have one.' And they said, 'Well, what role's open?' And I tell them there are none. So they flex some muscle and said, 'Well, you either open up a role, or we take our four million dollars and go home.'"

"Ergo, Franco Franchi," I said.

"Exactement! The only role I was still figuring out was Salvatore. So I said, 'Salvatore is half-open,' and then they directed me to Franchi. So, reluctantly, I sign him on and tell him to come in for a haircut. I wanted to make him look like he had mange or something, with patches of hair missing and exposing his scalp, giving him an even more unsettling demeanor. It was a special haircut I had designed. So we made an appointment for Franchi to come in, and he doesn't show up. A week later we made another appointment. Again he is a no-show. He did this about four times, and then finally, on the day I called you, it was the day prior to when he was scheduled to do his first scene. This is after weeks and weeks of him not coming in for the haircut. So he arrives to get the haircut, when, apparently, trouble brews. They pull me from what I am doing and call me into the makeup room. They say, 'Jean-Jacques, we have a problem.' And I say, 'What's the problem?' Franco Franchi stands with the haircutting cape around his shoulders and raises his voice. 'I tella you what is de problem. If I cutta my hair . . . now, you haffa pay me double.' And I said, 'Excuse me? What did you say?' And Franchi repeats, 'You hearda me. I want twice as mucha money, and then I cutta ma hair.' I turned my back on him and said to the producer standing behind me, 'I want him off my set. He's trying to rob me, and if he's not off my set in five minutes, I'm going to go get my gun and I'm gonna start shooting at him. You got it?!' And the producer says, 'Yes J. J., I got it, but the character works tomorrow. Do you have a second choice?' And I say, 'HE IS MY SECOND CHOICE! MY FIRST CHOICE IS ASLEEP IN LOS ANGELES!' That's when you got the call at five in the morning."

"Over a fuckin' haircut. What kinda beautiful fuckin' luck is that?" I said.

The next day on the set I met Sean Connery. I couldn't believe I was in the presence of a movie star. And not only was I in the presence of a movie star, but I was in the presence of *the* movie star. Because in my mind there was everybody else, and then there was Sean. To this day I feel as though Sean Connery is the very last of the great movie stars of old, like in the mold of the guys who were around when I was a kid growing up—larger-than-life, guy-guys . . . nothing ephemeral about them. Complete masculine forces of nature. Like Gable, Gary Cooper, Spencer Tracy, Jimmy Cagney, Humphrey Bogart, Lancaster, Kirk Douglas, Jimmy Stewart, and Robert Mitchum. Sean was cut from that cloth. And there have not been any to replace him since. The closest you come these days is Clooney, but pretty much everybody else is ephemeral, everybody else is kind of like . . .

I'm not talking about a lack of talent, because there's a lot of actors out there who are incredibly talented, but what we are looking for in our leading men has changed, starting with McQueen, Newman, Redford, all of whom possessed a bedroom sort of manliness. Then that morphed into the leading men of today. But back then there was the final hold out for the fuckin' OG, fucking alpha-male thing. That was Sean fucking Connery. And so to be in his presence, the very first true, bona fide movie star I ever worked with, was indeed a gift of a very singular nature.

He seemed delighted to meet me and was so welcoming and warm: "You're that fellow who Jean-Jacques keeps talking about. He adores you. It's good to meet you. I can't wait to work on this film with you."

And so he immediately welcomed me into his world, even to the point of giving me the feeling that he was gonna have my back. Regardless of what happened, he was completely behind me playing this role. There was nothing I had to worry about. Sean was tickled that Jean-Jacques got his way in this particular thing. He was completely up on the whole story about what happened to the original guy, how he got fired, and how happy it made Jean-Jacques. He was such a fan of Jean-Jacques; he was truly one of "us."

As soon as we began shooting the same scenes together, he made me realize that he was as dependent on me giving a performance that was gonna fuel him as I was on him. I felt part of this exclusive club, even if I had that same ol' fucked up tape running in my head: "I'm not worthy." At first I was thinking I had no business being on the same set as Sean Connery, much less in the same scene as Sean Connery. Then, not long after we met, one scene was scripted in which I spit in his eye. I was hesitating . . . how do you spit in the eye of the great Sean Connery?

Sean leaned in to me and said, "You have to spit in my eye because if you don't, I won't have anything to play." And that's how I came up with the fucking balls to fucking spit in 007's eye. And you really, really gotta do it, 'cuz the only thing more terrifying than spitting in the muthafucka's eye is "take two" of spitting in the muthafucka's eye!

There were not a lot of moments in my life when I got the acting lessons I did from Sean. I remember one day I was not on the call sheet. It was going to be this very, very big, dramatic scene in which William of Baskerville, the character that Sean played, is in serious trouble. He was to be investigated by all of the Brotherhood because at one point he had been labeled a heretic, thrown out of the church, and spent a huge chunk of his life paying for this empty accusation. Now he's back, and there's this whole host of guys from this other order just laying for him. He's a Franciscan, but his rivals are desperate to finally and decisively take him down. So there is to be this kangaroo trial, and it's this big scene with probably thirty actors. Sean has some gorgeous dialogue to speak in this scene.

Because we were on location and I didn't really have anything much better to do, I went to the set that day just to observe. I watched Sean do this one moment about twelve times. It was the first time I realized the glory of language when it is loved and respected as if it were a beautiful woman you wanted voraciously, for that is how Sean caresses his every word and every syllable. I was never able to catch it by watching his movies, but being on that set with him, seeing him grappling with giving this performance each time as if it were the first time—my God! Glorious! No word should be uttered unless it is important enough to be uttered beautifully. So the pace at which Sean Connery speaks stems from a decision he's made. And every single vowel delivered is with respect for the language. But he delivers it so naturally and with so much humanity that you don't realize that, technically, he is giving a master class in how to deliver a line. And because I watched him do this thing over and over and over again, I would never have seen it otherwise. This is something I've taken with me for the rest of my time as an actor: Don't say a word unless that word is worth saying, and if that word is worth saying, say it beautifully. I learned that from Sean Connery. And I've never delivered a line the same way since.

A lot of people say, "Well, he was 007. He's no big thing as an actor." Fuck that shit. He is a fucking master. He is good as anybody I'd ever seen. In fact, it's always the ones who look so incredibly natural who are constantly being accused of not acting; those are the ones who are the most sublime of professionals. He is somebody who truly loves what he does and does it as if it is the most important thing on Earth. Completely on top of the fact that he is a complete OG—son of a coal-miner, dirt poor childhood, would never take himself seriously, loves to play golf, loves to party, loves to eat well, loves to have a great drink, and loves, loves, loves to laugh. What a combination. But what an incredible example for a young actor to take away from someone who put in that much time, spent that much time with greats like John Houston, Alfred Hitchcock—you name it. He worked with the greatest of the great, and all of them regarded him highly. His legacy has proven itself out.

My favorite interaction with him occurred in a night scene we shot together. It was about three-fourths of the way through the film and took place in the cemetery adjacent to the monastery, where we bury our own. In the scene Sean's character is in the process of narrowing down who the killer is, who's responsible for all these deaths taking place throughout the storyline. He's at a frenzied point of the film, for he knows that unless he unearths the killer, responsibility will fall on him, thus destroying him.

So he comes upon me in the cemetery in the middle of the night, and I'm chasing rats and killing them for a midnight snack. He's supposed to interrogate me for clues because he knows this is where I hang out and from this vantage point, chances are I saw the murderer. So it's this thing in which he's dealing with this guy who's mentally challenged and doesn't quite understand rational thought, and he's having to speak to me as if I'm some sort of child, but he is desperate for vital information, which, at its very core, is life or death. And I am trying to hide the fact that I'm only there on a rat-hunting mission. He said to me during our first rehearsal, "My God, that's really funny, that thing you're doing with the rats. How about I do this when you do that so it's even funnier?" And suddenly I felt this guy was going full vaudeville on me. He's a bigger scene stealer than I ever thought he was—he was trying to turn this into an Abbot and Costello moment. I fuckin' love this guy!

We started off playing the scene one way, and by the time we were finished with it we were out-hamming each other to the point where it's completely different from how I imagined it was going to be. It was like these two fucking teenagers having the time of their life, stealing each other's thunder.

Something else happened on the set of *Name of the Rose* that was one of those solidifiers, completely epiphanous in nature, sublime. It was about five o'clock one afternoon, and we were on the exterior set perched on a hillside about twenty kilometers outside of Roma. And the crew was dashing around, trying to get a shot right at magic hour, that tiny little window between dusk and nightfall when the light is different from any other part of the day, light that is just magical on film. Hence, *magic hour*. But the window to get the shot is tiny, thus preventing us from having too many takes at it. So the pressure was on to get it right and quickly.

Now, I didn't happen to be in this shot, so I was up there, having a smoke and enjoying the respite. And observing! And the energy that was going into the making of this magic moment to be forever captured on celluloid is insane: there were about 150 adults running around egolessly as if they were kindergartners preparing for the school pageant. Except they probably had around forty-five Oscar nominations between them. There was Dante Ferretti, the production designer; Tonino Delli Colli, director of photography, after having done six Fellini movies; Jean-Jacques Annaud, director; Manlio Rochetti, makeup artist; Gabriella Pescucci, costume designer; Jake Eberts and Bernd Eichinger, producers; Sean Connery and Oscar-winning F. Murray Abraham, who was just coming off of *Amadeus*, and on and on and on—all running around like kids, like their lives depended on it to get one tiny moment in this huge moving mosaic. All of which had sprung out of the imagination of a man with a Nobel Prize. And it hit me: if this ain't *the* coolest art form ever invented, it'll do till the real thing comes along. And if I ain't the luckiest white Jew to ever make his way to just outside Roma, then I'd like to meet the schmuck who beat me!

> Every time I've seen Sean since that film he's been just like family. He's just incredibly loved, giving his signature big bearhugs. It was clearly one of the most pleasurable collaborations I've ever had with anyone. And the fact that it just happened to be Sean Connery makes it all the more magical.

When the film was done I went back to LA to our Hollywood quasi hotel/apartment. The experience of having shot this movie infused me with just enough resolve to feel Hollywood might in fact truly be the place I needed to be. But if I was gonna stay the course, some career adjustments should probably get made. So to balance out the past and pave the way for the future, I called my then current manager with an edict: no more roles in which I am obscured by heavy makeup. That's when he decided to send me a script for a new TV pilot that was beginning to cast. Curiously it was called *Beauty and the Beast*. I called my manager, saying, "This is for the role of the Beauty, right?"

(CHAPTER 13)

Birth of the Beast

"Close! The role does start with a B; it's just not Beauty," my agent
said.

"Don't send it!"

"Hear me out. The writing is great, the team is great, and CBS
has ordered a go pilot. And you are on a very short list for one of the
leads."

"The Beast, right? Don't send it." The two films I was most known
for up until that point had me completely and unrecognizably covered
in makeup. And I kinda had this gut feeling that maybe my time spent
behind bars like that had served its purpose. I'm thinking that if I had
been in *Quest* and *Rose* in roles in which people knew it was me, then
maybe I'd be getting better offers. I didn't know whether I wanted to
be the Lon Chaney of my generation. But the next morning, when I
open up the front door to get the newspaper, instead there's an envelope from my agent with a copy of the pilot script for *Beauty and the
Beast*. I called him up, saying, "Did you not fucking hear me? I told
you. I told you not to send me this script. Why'd you do that?"

"Hey! You want to work? You're not the boss. I sent it. Deal with
it."

I said, "All right, fuck you, I'll show *you* who's boss! I'm not gonna
read it." So anyway, the newspaper finally arrives, and after I read it

from cover to cover and then was reading the back of cereal boxes and the label on a can of Lysol, I ran out of things to read and couldn't avoid it. So I picked up that envelope, thinking, *Lemme just read page one.* By the time I got to page twenty I called my agent and said, "Okay, who do I gotta kill to play this fuckin' role?"

"I knew you were gonna say that, ya little prick! So you read it anyways, right, you little lying fucking little prick?"

"Yeah, I couldn't help myself. Fuck you." My manager and I were very fond of each other!

So Erwin, my new agent/manager at the time, set up a very high-level meeting with Tony Thomas (Danny Thomas's son) and Paul Witt of Witt/Thomas Television, who at the time were incredibly prolific at half-hour comedies. They'd done a show called *SOAP*, and they were doing *Golden Girls*. They were also known for an amazing track record of getting pilots to series. In this industry, considering the amount of scripts floating around at any given time, the chances of getting a green light for a pilot are at about one in a million. Then after a pilot, there's maybe a one in a hundred million shot of having it being picked up for even a few more episodes.

From reading the script of *Beauty and the Beast*, I could see it was going to be the very first ever for these producers and a one-hour, one-camera drama. Everything else they had done were half-hour sit-coms, filmed in front of a live audience. So I went and had the meeting with Paul and Tony, and that led to an audition at the network. It was the first time I had ever gone to a network to audition for a show. The way it works is that they negotiate your contract prior to you going in for the audition, 'cuz if they fall in love with you, they don't want you to rape and pillage them after the fact; they want you to negotiate when you have no leverage whatsoever. So we negotiated a deal, and then I went in there. I was in a waiting room with three other guys who were also auditioning for the Beast. We were looking at each other and thinking, "I wanna fuckin' kill you right now, you cocksucker . . ." But we exchange the "Hey, how you doing? Nice to see you! How's the wife, how's the kids, you've never looked better"—ya know, all the shit that is sometimes unfortunately required for living in a civilized world.

I did my reading at CBS with Paul Witt and Tony Thomas in the back of the room. Tony is a very funny and witty guy, son of one of the greatest of all time, Danny Thomas (and brother of Marlo) and an example of the apple not falling far from the tree. He was actually yelling out catcalls while I was auditioning, and this was the biggest audition of my life. But he was trying to keep it really light and loose. And I guess I realized at that point that he was in my corner, that he was trying to say, "This is no contest. You know, the other three guys are basically the beard, but this is our choice." Anyway, I walked out of the audition and felt like, on a scale of one to ten, my audition was probably a strong nine. You know, I was nervous, but not too nervous that I completely sabotaged myself, which happens a lot in big-time auditions, especially to me.

An hour and a half after I got home and changed my clothes, my manager called, using a phony voice: "You got the gig."

"Fuck you, you prick. Who is this really?!" Erwin laughed, which gave him away, and he hung up.

There's a lot of pomp and ceremony when you're going to a network. There were only ABC, CBS, and NBC back in the day. A lot of actors go to the network three, four, five times a year. They're just TV material. Because I never was TV material, it took a show that was as obscure, obtuse, and off the beaten track, requiring this kind of special effects and transformational makeup acting, to get me this offer. I soon found out the reason I was on the short list. It seemed that the first person who got hired when they were crewing up, when they decided to actually pursue doing a pilot for *Beauty and the Beast*, was Rick Baker. It was his design for the Beast that captivated everybody, but especially the network. At the time Baker had already won an Oscar for makeup design and special effects, and he would go on to win seven more times! He was the number-one guy in the industry in terms of creating the transformational makeup the Beast would need.

Rick was instrumental in providing my name to these guys. He didn't do *Name of the Rose* or *Quest for Fire*, but he was very, very good friends with the people who had done them, and he had already heard stories about how I was one of those guys who was kinda comfortable in the chair, kinda comfortable with the rubber on. I didn't let anything bother me. There are a lot of actors who just can't stand hanging out in the chair for more than fifteen minutes, whereas jobs like this take four hours to execute. You don't want to hire a guy who can't do that time in a chair without revolting, which could definitely fuck up the rapid shooting schedule of a series and cost the producer headaches and money. I was flattered that there were apparently glowing reports about me in the makeup world as someone one who could handle the process. It's always nice to get good feedback, 'cuz it's not a given, but for someone of Rick Baker's genius to be advocating for you—that was big.

The makeup for the characters I played in *Quest for Fire* and *Name of the Rose* both took about four or five hours to apply, depending on the weather. The Beast took the same. You got to be still, keep your face unflinching all that time. You can't just fall asleep; rather, you have to engage in the transformation. I guess that's the mindset I have when I get into the chair. It was easier for those long hours for *Quest for Fire* and *Name of the Rose* 'cuz I was so grateful to be in those movies. They could've hammered nails into my palms and feet, because this was my shot. This was the only way I would be invited to that particular party—if they wanted to completely disappear fuckin' Ron and reappear something else, then I was all for it. And the exercise, as I mentioned, of creating a character under those conditions, which were very abstract, because nothing like it existed in the real world, to solve the riddle of where the humanity is, that is what made it all the more fascinating to me, engaging me multidimensionally. Because how to bring your intellectual recognition of who that character might be as well as your own self and the behavior that lies within you and then marry the two, therein lies the riddle. A lot of that happens in the chair as you see yourself physically transformed by the prosthetics seamlessly joined with exquisitely and artistically applied makeup.

Now the notion of doing these long makeup sessions for a TV show, which was open ended, was another story. If the show actually got picked up, I would be working on it for nine months out of the year, which would be a different exercise from what I had experienced to date. With movies, no matter how much you're suffering, you know you're going to be going home in a few months when shooting ends. Whereas with a TV series, this is gonna be a real test because, potentially, there was to be no relief in sight. And sure enough, the pilot got picked up—they order thirteen episodes. But the networks generally wait to see how the public receives the first four or five before they decide to order the back nine, thus giving the show a full first season.

But whether this show would ever get past the pilot was anyone's guess. I would have been betting against it. The first time I sat in Rick Baker's chair he already had something in mind, but of course, my face was the canvas, so I was interacting with him to a degree. By the time I got hired, his designs had already been approved, so they already knew what the Beast was going to look like. This all happened without me knowing it, happening off to the side, before I even knew there was a project called *Beauty and the Beast*. But he was so sure he wanted me for the role that he actually sculpted the makeup onto my face prior to ever meeting me, making a bust of me from an eight-by-ten headshot. And so by the time the network saw me at the audition they were already slightly pregnant with the idea that I was gonna be the guy. All I had to do was fucking not trip over the furniture and be able to read the lines in English, and I think I would have had it.

Of course, I didn't find this out until well after the fact. But the makeup he designed for the Beast needed to be sexy as well as otherworldly, 'cuz, after all, it was to be a highly stylized gothic romance with two main figurative lovers, the Beast being one of them. So when he showed me the sketch of the makeup he was going to build and, ultimately, apply to my face, it looked like I was fucking Rod Stewart—

just total rock star! I mean, he had this kind of, like, blond mane and an exotic look around his eyes. He had this leonine royalty to him, and if you just wanted to put a couple of piercings and a few tattoos on him, you know, you're talking about "hot" bro. Like fantasy hot. I said, "Holy shit, man. I *wish* I could look this fuckin' good!"

And Rick said, "Gimme four hours!"

So sure enough, now that he had me, now that the network had approved me and I'm the guy, I'm hired for the pilot, now I'm going to be in Rick Baker's studio day after day, getting a life cast done on my face so he could actually sculpt the makeup and apply it to me, custom made. The process is rather arduous, very exacting, and trippy. For the Beast I was in the makeup chair every single morning at four to be ready to shoot at eight. And even though Rick was working off a master plan, the makeup kind of evolved once he had the real human to apply it to. Rick was taking what his forebears had given him, mainly Dick Smith and a few others, and was raising the bar in special effects makeup to places former generations only dreamed of: inventing compounds that were incredibly supple, magnificently lifelike, and really user-friendly to make it through the arduous demands of a fourteen-hour shoot day. That was all Rick Baker just elevating the state-of-the-art to something of pure artistry and elegance. It wasn't a mistake or a coincidence, his winning eight Oscars.

He made pieces of foam rubber for facial features. I'm not sure what animal they got the hair from, but it was real hair. With regard to the Beast there were probably three pieces that went on separately and had to blend into one another so you couldn't see the seams or where they joined to my face. There were parts of me that were uncovered, so there had to be a seamless transition between my own features and these features that were glued on.

I happen to have allergies to most of the glue, so they had to invent special glue that was hypoallergenic for me. And to this day it's the only glue that can be used on my face. Originally called 355, it was taken off the market because of its deleterious effects on the environment and replaced with something called Telesis. Back in the day the only glue they had was spirit gum. Weirdly enough, if you even open up a bottle of spirit gum around me and I smell it, my face breaks out. Truly ironic that I entered a world that was exclusively about makeup, but I possessed skin that refused to tolerate it. Rick kept saying we gotta find a way to make this work and not kill the guy, not destroy his face. I was the guinea pig for a lot of products that ultimately ended up becoming state of the art.

Even before I sat in Rick's chair and watched his physicalization of this most exotic creation, I had a profound notion of the magnificence of this character called Vincent. He was an incredible distillation of all the characters who moved and touched me throughout my own life. And his poignancy lay in the fact that due to an accident of birth that places him in his outcast state, he is prevented from participating fully in the world he so loves in the most uncommon of ways, thus forcing him to exist in the shadows, where his interactions with the world are disturbingly minimized. The sadness that befalls his situation, juxtaposed against the magnificent force of nature he turns himself into, made for as tragic a character as I'd ever seen in popular culture. He was the outsider I felt myself to be during so many of my early years. But I chose to counteract whatever might compromise him with grace, elegance, kindness, and a self-given education to all things sublime that made him extraordinary.

Ron Koslow lovingly conceived the character. Ron had to be *the* most romantic of screenplay writers in all of Hollywood. I know of no other writer who could have created this particular creation. As Koslow conceived it, Vincent's world was a counterpart, a juxtaposition to the gritty world of New York City, underneath which existed this almost Swiftian subculture that made up the Beast's lair. Vincent chose for himself an Elizabethan style of dress and even worldview, possessing a rich ease with the works of Shakespeare, Milton, Byron, and Shelley, totally educated in the arts and all things classical, all the way up to current cultural forces.

When I was first starting to absorb the fact that I was to create this character, I recalled the first time I saw Charles Laughton, in *The*

Hunchback of Notre Dame, on that rotating torture wheel where he's being whipped, shunned, laughed at, and having things thrown at him, and suddenly, through the crowd, moves this stunning waif in the guise of the beautiful Maureen O'Hara, approaching him, caressing him, feeding him the sips of water he so desperately craves. That was the seminal moment for me, when I decided what an actor could do, given the right set of circumstances. And here it was, that self-same dynamic, without me seeking it, somehow magically falling right into my fucking lap in the form of the Beast. In prime time. On CBS, the Tiffany network. And not only did it go to the pilot—which to me, was miraculous—but it also got picked up for the first half of the season, then it got picked up for the second half of the season. And then suddenly people were getting nominations for things and winning awards for things, and suddenly I'm on the cover of *Us Weekly* as one of the twenty sexiest men in the world. And then suddenly . . . and then suddenly . . . and then suddenly . . . and this shit was starting to rain down on me as a result of what can only be described as the greatest free psychotherapy of all time, which was me getting a shot to play this thing that lived inside of me, something innocent and precious and dying to be heard. I was getting to finally live out, act out, and exorcise that very bestial thing that had been such a harbinger of pain throughout my formative years. But I'm getting ahead of myself.

It took about four days into the filming of the pilot for the Beast to be called in to work. But when I finally did walk onto the set in full beast regalia, man, it was like, "Whoa, dat is some crazy shit right dere! Dat shit is off the chain!" I mean people were looking at me with total shock, wonder, and fascination, like I was Buddy Love in *The Nutty Professor* and just sauntered into the room. There was an excitement to it that was palpable. So one of the first ones to see me walk on was Linda Hamilton, because my first scene up was with the Beauty. So Linda saw me walking through the doors to the set. She ran over, gave me a big hug and a kiss, and there we were. It was like Gable and Lombard, Hope and Crosby, Tracy and Hepburn, Ginger and Fred! There was an iconocism to this union that was immediate and palpable and classical from the start.

I didn't know her beforehand and only met her when we both got cast for the show. And we had done a little bit of having some dinners together, having a few drinks together in the run-up to doing the pilot. But my knowledge of her was very superficial prior to this first day of filming. So we were walking arm-in-arm together, as if already a couple, even though we just met. And you could tell that there was gonna be this chemistry. I could tell immediately, just by the way she was just kinda looking at me in awe. And of course, if you remember what Linda Hamilton looked like on the show . . . not too shabby either—she was clearly among the most beautiful things I had ever set eyes on. I mean, not in Opal's category, but then, who is?! (Don't want to be sleeping on the fuckin' couch for the rest of my fuckin' life!) But Linda's beauty was quite unconventional, and although she was drop-dead gorgeous, a lot of it had to do with what was shining through from within. It was an accessible kind of beauty, which made our coming together even more within the realm of believability. Quite brilliant casting, if ya ask me.

However, I might've known the experience would be, well, unique, for lack of a better word, when, on that very first stroll, as Linda and I greeted each other on the set for the very first time, she leaned real close and whispered into my ear, "I don't know about you, but for me, it's two years and out!" And as I violently fought the impulse to blurt out loud how weird a thing that was to say even before we've even rehearsed our first scene together, instead my response was, "My, what a nice-looking crew!" Of course my inner monologue was a little different: *Two fuckin' years? Whuddya, nuts? We ain't gonna finish the pilot before they realize they made a horrible mistake!* I mean, television hadn't been known back in the day for doing much other than what it did best—sitcoms, cop shows, doctor shows, shows about private dicks, and variety shows. There simply was no precedent for something as ethereal as *Beauty and the Beast*. And I couldn't see any reason for them to start now.

Anyway, once we got through with the peppy banter, we got on with the business of the moment. The first scene Linda and I were to do together happened to be the last scene of the pilot: everything has transpired, and I am now walking her to underneath the building where she lives, which is as far as I can take her. We have a beautiful exchange and part ways, an iconic moment that became a lasting image throughout the run of the series. Our good-byes include her saying, "I owe you everything," and me responding, "You owe me nothing." We do take one; she says, in a normal voice, "I owe you everything," and then I say in a whisper even I couldn't hear, "You owe me nothing." That would be the first line I ever uttered as Vincent. Out of the corner of my eye I see the sound guy in full panic, turning dials and levers, breaking out in a sweat. We finish the take, and this same fellow, Pat, a veteran sound guy with longstanding credentials, awkwardly approaches me, not knowing how he is going to ask the question, one that I knew was coming: "Uh, sorry Ron, I hate to ask this, but, uh, boy, this is really difficult to ask, but, uh, do you think you could possibly give me a little more?"—volume, that is!

I thought for what must have seemed like an hour to poor Pat, beads of sweat forming on his brow, and said, "Jeez, sorry, Pat, but I don't think I can!" Pat hurried away, mumbling to himself, like I just gave him a terminal diagnosis. We finished with the scene. And the one after that. And three years later, when we finally got canceled, Pat was the only original crew member who was still on the show. I guess he figured it out. I have no idea how, 'cuz the Beast, even to *my* surprise, spoke so quietly, even I couldn't hear the sound of my own voice.

Finally, the pilot was finished. We packed up our gear, went home, and waited around for a few months. In May of that year CBS, as well as all the networks, went to New York for the Upfronts, where they announce their slate of shows that will appear in the fall. I have no idea why, I have no idea how, but *Beauty and the Beast* made the cut. We were, indeed, on the fall schedule. All because a guy named Erwin More ignored me when I ordered him not to send me the script.

(CHAPTER 14)

Beauty in the Beast

It was huge. *Beauty and the Beast* was gonna be on CBS, 8 p.m., Friday nights—prime time, baby. And being one of the title characters for the first time, I was in a position that, if I go, so goes the show. Because prior to that, I never thought of myself as anything other than a character actor, somebody who provided a bit of color in the overall piece, but carrying the show was never in my pay grade—that is, until *Beauty and the Beast*. So it was a real sea change. It was a tremendous transition and affirmation in so many ways. I had to pinch myself to see if it was all real. Prime time network television—highly coveted. How long the gig would last, nobody knew, but what I did know was that this was different from anything that had ever happened to me before. I was thirty-seven years old. And after twenty years of being on stage, finally, not only would I be seen by all of America, but I would also get paid for the privilege!

Our debut brought with it surprisingly good notices. Critics were taken by the show's exotic nature and originality. It was not comparable to anything that had ever existed on television before. Not only did the critics single us out; we also got a lot of love from the artistic community at large and, more importantly, from the viewers themselves. We were never in the top ten; it wasn't getting that kind of love because we were never that kind of a mainstream show. But there was a seriously devoted fan base, which exists to this day. Too esoteric to be a top-ten show, we always managed to dwell respectably in the twenties or thirties. And as more episodes aired, more phenomenal notices from all the right kinds of publications started to come in: the *New York Times* wrote love letters to it, as did *Newsweek* and *Time*. All the things you would hope to get, we were getting. So when the show got that order for the back nine episodes, it wasn't as much of a surprise as everything else had been.

TV works like this: After the pilot is picked up, the network only commits cautiously, and if it's getting sufficient ratings, they give you what's called the back nine, so thirteen becomes twenty-two, which is a full season. When they green-lit our back nine, we had probably already aired five or six episodes. Because you're so far ahead when you're in production than the airing, you're always five or six episodes ahead, so they make the decision to give us enough lead time to write the last few shows. The first weeks of airing is a very dramatic time period, because the reviews come out, the ratings come out, and you start to see whether people are maybe going to start getting big press, maybe a couple of mentions for awards. You have the Golden Globes coming out in January, the show airs in September. The Golden Globe chatter starts around November, December. If you start getting mentions of things like that, you know the deck starts getting stacked one way or the other: you're either looking like a hit or a goat.

Who would've thought a show about a woman who works for the district attorney's office in New York City, who gets mistakenly beaten and left for dead and is mysteriously carried off to some bizarre lair underneath the city and nursed back to health by a creature whose very existence is an impossibility, would work? It was just way too exotic for television, but the chemistry between the two forbidden lovers, beautifully rendered by Ron Koslow and his magnificent staff of writers, really drove it. A writing staff, I might add, that included George R. R. Martin (*Game of Thrones*), Howard Gordon, and Alex Gansa (*24*, *Homeland*). There was an array of elements regarding the success of the show that were really foreign to me. For although I had experienced short-lived momentary visits into and out of the limelight, this was on a scale I was totally unfamiliar with. This was mainstream success, and when it came, what struck me most dramatically was how unprepared for it I was, how it was something I would never have allowed to enter into my consciousness, so I would have remained completely unentertained. What this strange wonder stirring inside of me was is something I will discuss, but one thing is for sure: success felt way different from failure, but it was also way more complicated to navigate, especially when one is hardwired to always stay a part of the pack.

When one, as a graduate of the school of aiming low, is educated to always be waiting for the other shoe to drop, it's not surprising when he starts questioning the degree to which all this newfound success is truly earned or how much is just a mistake, how much is just dumb luck—they got the wrong guy, and this will come crashing to an ugly end. *Beauty and the Beast* was probably the quintessential example of that because I was given a character who represented my very own mission statement concerning my incredible longing and yearning to heal a very open wound that I secretly lived with. So to win the opportunity to play a character who was a distillation of all that discomfort, who would almost allow for an exorcism of it, who would provide my very own catharsis to take place in front of 20 million people, this all seemed way too good to be true.

Then there are all the other things that change. You go from being a guy who never had two dimes to rub together to, all of a sudden, having to think about who's gonna advise you on how to deal with that rather robust steady income that suddenly appears. Now you can afford a *nice* car, can maybe even wanna start thinking about buying a house. You ask around about who's the right lawyer, start thinking about getting a publicist, about a whole lot of shit you never thought about before. So I jumped in rather small: I bought my first car. I see this gray Jaguar XJ6 for sale on the side of the road and say, "Fuck it, I'll buy it." Now, don't get me wrong—it wasn't a *new* Jaguar. I still had that Depression-era sort of mindset my folks passed down to me. No, this baby was two years old and had twenty-five thousand miles on it.

But it was like, holy shit, I never met anyone personally who drove a Jaguar. That shit was for other fuckin' guys.

During the first season, even though I hadn't been nominated, the Hollywood foreign critics asked me to be a presenter at the Golden Globes. That was kinda like the first time the world would get to see the guy behind the Beast makeup, what he really looked like as his mild-mannered self. So when my time came, they plucked me out of the audience, escorted me backstage, threw some makeup on me, and, while they were instructing me on how to enter the stage and read off the teleprompter, I felt a tugging on my jacket. I turned around, and it was Sammy Davis Jr., who went out of his way to introduce himself and tell me how he was a big fan of the show. Eventually this turned into an amazing friendship that I'll get into detail later. That meeting, though—like, the man himself—was too good to be true. Whoa . . . this new gig of mine was getting me more and incredible fringe benefits. Sammy fucking Davis! Just before I walked out onto the Golden Globe stage I looked heavenward, and there was my old man smiling ear to ear.

This whole deal made for a serious fuckin' high 'cuz, although I always hoped to one day get a chair at the big table, I never had any real plan of seeing it through. But here I was, feelin' like I was in this very select club that not a lotta guys get to join. And even though I finally got a coupla bucks, people wanna give me shit for free. They wanna know what I think and have me at their restaurant or club. And on top of all of it all, I'm plying my craft on the regular, playing a character I was so honored to play that I'da done it for free. Well, maybe not that last part, but you know what I mean.

And then, holy shit, we got picked up for a second season, and *boom*, I got nominated for a Golden fucking Globe. And the night comes and, *boom, boom*, I fucking won. And I got nominated for a People's Choice Award, and, goddammit, I won. And I got nominated for my second Viewers for Quality Television Best Actor award, and I won. And I got nominated for an Emmy, and . . . well, I didn't win. But hey, things are just flying at me. And little by little, fantasy is beginning to overtake reality. But let's back up a minute, 'cuz, well, it's worth it, goddammit!

The Golden Globe Awards are hosted by the Hollywood Foreign Press Association, now in its seventy-first year, and it remains a well-attended celebrity ceremony each January. It's a huge Hollywood event and the first of the trifecta of the three most major and respected showbiz awards. And unlike the Oscars and the Emmys, the Globes award excellence in both movies and television. So in a way it's larger in scope than the others. Either way, they all have one thing in common: hype. 'Cuz the nomination for these statues and, even more, the winning of these statues represent big bucks for the entire food chain. Publicists get busier, agents and managers start positioning their clients for bigger pieces of the pie, and lawyers are sharpening their fangs in anticipation of greater leverage. And then there's Dior, Hugo Boss, Armani, Van Cleef and Arpels, and so on and so forth. And the networks are lookin' at big event–type ratings and the prestige that comes with airing these shows. This stuff is *way* more than just a big party. Although, don't get me wrong—it's that too. And all three safeguard their nominee selections with fanfare and secrecy, as if they were guarding the code to launch a nuclear missile attack. There's buzz of who might be nominated, with bookies making odds and critics offering their likelihood of shoo-ins.

For the decades before, when I watched the program from my tenement apartment couch, I always wondered how the inner workings of such ceremonies operated: How did nominees feel when the camera panned on their face as their names were read? What was whispered in the ear of the presenter when the winner was called to the stage? From the moment I was nominated I was certain my chances of winning lay somewhere between none and most assuredly none. And sure enough, when Opal and I were ushered to our seats, it was clear that the guys planning the event were in total agreement. 'Cuz the only thing behind us was a wall. And just behind that wall were the restrooms. It brought me back to the nosebleed bleacher seats my

old man and I used to get at Yankee Stadium. But hey, I ain't com-
plainin'—at least I made it into the program. Most people, when they
watch these awards programs, want to know whether the nominees
prepare speeches or do they feel it might be a jinx if they do so. I was
on the fence about that, but many actors are superstitious and have
certain rituals, as I'll get into in a later chapter. As for myself, I wrote
down nothing.

It was only while in the shower getting ready to attend did I think
to make a mental list of all the people I would need to thank in the
unlikely event I was chosen. 'Cuz, like Sonny said, probably not a good
idea to come out with just my dick in my hands. I didn't want to leave
out any names because, as I believed and said as much when I was
amazingly called to the podium, this type of recognition and spotlight
shines on a person only when a whole bunch of people around him
or her do stellar work. In this most collective of endeavors it takes a
village to shine. But once again, I get ahead of myself.

Before that day arrived, there was about a month of being an official nominee, which instantly bestows upon you an entirely new set of
credentials. When I returned to the set of *Beast* the next day, of course,
everyone was aware of my nomination. I always had to show up four
hours earlier than most of the crew to get my makeup applied, but I
soon sensed that a lot of things had changed, literally overnight.

For someone who had not only been overly concerned with what
people thought of me but in fact felt downright measured by it, this
was one of those moments that went a long, long way. This was the
very first time I got real acknowledgment and encouragement not
only from a major portion of the country but also, and even more in-
toxicating, my peers in the industry. There was a validation that gives
way to many other things, but if one is not supercareful and does not
fundamentally recognize that this winning/losing thing is pure fantasy, signifying absolutely nothing of real consequence, one could be
walking into the trap of all traps. Was my opinion suddenly more
weighty than before, or did I just think it was? Of this, though, I am
certain: people were clearly acting differently toward me. Oh, not all

of them, but enough so as to make one raise one's eyebrows. Because the people who truly wish you well are not as great in number as you might have assumed. Someone's good fortune might simply be a reminder of what others haven't yet achieved, that they were far more comfortable in the relationship when obscurity was a shared virtue.

However, I straightaway gained a new bunch of "friends," all of whom wanted to grab onto the coattails of someone on the rise. Even though at the time I thought it was cool, those friendships turned out to be fleeting, and very few remained for long. Now don't get me wrong, the nomination brought with it a new confidence that perhaps bordered on a self-assurance, which may have been taken as something more deleterious, maybe even a perception of arrogance, and that's maybe why I lost friends. I doubt it, though. I hadn't really changed. I had always held the character of Vincent in high regard, possessing an intensity as to how he should be played, but I always strove to leave that on the field and not carry it around with me.

In any event, it's such a strange experience to be in that moment in time when others suddenly start treating you as if you're a "somebody." Reporters suddenly wanted to know who I thought would win an election, for example, or who was my favorite painter or songwriter. It's easy to get swept into this weird vortex that very well might be over the minute the show gets canceled. Anyway, lemme finally get to the point regarding my night at the Globes.

In the front rows all of the biggest movie stars, directors, and powerful money men and their perfectly manicured wives or dates are placed. The staffs of such stars negotiate with the Award planners with threats of not attending if they're not given the seating placement they deem they deserve. Nevertheless, the seating arrangements each year are actually a game of musical chairs of popularity, although it really boils down to a person's earning potential or how much money they already made or have.

If there would've been a camera on my face when my name was called as the winner, it would've been a profile displaying one of pure and authentic shock. When my name was announced, I was so far in the back of the ballroom that, even though I nearly sprinted to the stage, the applause had ended two minutes before I got to the podium. The woman who opened the envelope and gave the award was Valeria Golino, who played Tom Cruise's girlfriend in *Rain Man*. It looked like I was giving her a kiss, but I actually leaned in close and asked her to show me the envelope with my name on it because I seriously, even then, thought they'd make a mistake.

Immediately after making a brief speech, the winner is led from the stage, and someone guides them to a pressroom to have this mini-news conference. Flashbulbs are going off from all angles like a fireworks display, and, for me, still in shock, I had to look my best and come up with intelligent responses to reporters who were throwing the really tough questions at me, stuff like, "How do you feel, Ron?" And "Who are you wearing?"—ya know, real existential stuff! Then the winner eventually goes back to their table with the statue.

I couldn't take my eyes off it, sitting there in all its beauty among napkins and lipstick-rimmed wineglasses. After the show and the Governor's Ball, winners, losers, and most of the attendees go out partying somewhere. My manager wanted me, as a winner, to do a hopscotch of stops to different iconic after-parties. All the time I was carrying this heavy Golden Globe Award, with its marble pedestal and the gold world on top. The thing weighed eight and a half pounds.

I remember being asked, at one restaurant, by the hat-check girl, "Excuse me, sir, would you like to check that in?"

"Are you fucking kidding me?" I said. "It took me two decades to get this. I ain't letting nobody hold it." She shook her head and laughed as if to say, "You can put a kid from the Heights in a tuxedo, but he's still a hick." The actual trophy is eventually returned to the Globe's committee so they can engrave your name on it, a tradition that is shared with the Oscars and the Emmys. You hope they get your address right.

I falsely believed that with me on magazine covers and everything like this, it was a sure bet that this was what life would continue to look like. I was pretty sure that the money was for sure gonna keep rollin' in, so I started thinking about how I better start being smart with it, maybe hire one of them *financial advisers*. Ya know, 'cuz they care so much. This is something I never had to have a concern about, nor did anyone in the Perlman family for that matter, in all the generations leading up to mine. And then I started going around looking for a house. Because it seemed like a sure bet at the time that we were gonna be around for a while. But then, at the end of the second year, Linda got pregnant and told the producers she wanted be written out of the show by the end of that season. I don't know exactly what happened behind the scenes, but the discussions culminated with them giving Linda her way. They said, "Okay, we don't wanna keep anybody if they don't wanna be here. You want off of the show bad enough, you got it."

I really enjoyed working with Linda Hamilton, but with Linda back then, there was just a slight inconsistency. On the days when Linda was doing well, and I say this without trying to be hyperbolic, she was amazingly good. She was the sweetest, most charming, most generous woman I had ever met in my life. Then there were these other days when this kind of darkness overcame her, and I really wanted to keep my distance so as not to add to her uneasiness. It was clear that she was capable of saying things that were less than politic.

The unpredictability of those two different swings made people curious. Nothing more than that—nothing alarming, nothing serious, but just curious. And it turns out—and this was long after *Beauty and the Beast*, long after the second *Terminator* movie, when it made more sense—that after her marriage with Cameron ended I guess something about her own life patterns inspired her to go check herself out. After much consultation she got diagnosed as bipolar, and then shortly after that she decided to become a spokesperson for it, and I mean in a very big way. She went on *Oprah*; she went on *Larry King*. The way she described this and unflinchingly used herself as an example of the potential tragic effects this particular mental illness could have on a person's life was, to me, among the greatest pieces of work she'd ever done. I will always remain a huge admirer of her as an actress. But her willingness to sacrifice herself no matter what anyone was going to think or say about her—that was class. That was brave. That had character. And knowing her as I did, I wasn't so much surprised, just real damn proud. She was saying things like, this is what I had, these are all the years I didn't even know I had it, and this is how it fucked up my life, my career. And she went on to encourage anyone who felt a lack of control in their lives to not sweep it under the rug, to grab hold of it, because once you do, there are things you can do to help it. Linda—what a beauty!

She was magnificent to work with, even on her bad days. Even on her down days she always looked into my eyes and could see this undying admiration from me to her and know that she was safe, she was okay, and she didn't need to feel threatened. So no matter what, she and I got along phenomenally well. With regard to wanting off the show, I decided that this was her business. I thought that for me to try to convince her of something that she was determined to do would have run counter to our friendship. So I stayed out of it. I never had a conversation with her about it. In retrospect Linda leaving didn't directly cause the show to end; after all, there are plenty of shows that transitioned smooth enough when one of the main leads exited.

But anyway, six months later we closed on our house. And Opal was pregnant with our second kid. And the regime had just changed at CBS. And the first order of business for the new head of programming was to cancel *Beauty and the Beast*.

(CHAPTER 15)

How You Doin'?

Season two was essentially the set up for Beauty's demise. She and Vincent consummate their love, and she gets pregnant. Meanwhile a mysterious, diabolical industrialist is watching us, and he becomes obsessed with owning the offspring of such a union. Beauty is kidnapped and held till she delivers the child, thus leaving Vincent on a frenzied search to rescue both mother and child. By the time he catches up with her, it is too late. The bad guy takes the newborn, leaving Beauty poisoned. He escapes in a helicopter one moment before Vincent arrives, leaving Beauty to die in the Beast's arms. Fade out. End of season two. Nobody wants to write out the main character, but if you gotta go, surely this turn of events made the most of it.

Where to go from there was anybody's guess, so the run-up to season three was a scramble, to say the least. One thing was certain: there was no *Beauty and the Beast* without a Beauty. So the search went on. We ended up with a sweet girl named Jo Anderson. She was to play a New York detective investigating the disappearance and eventual death of Beauty. Throughout the investigation, as she is gathering clues, Vincent is observing her from the shadows. He comes to feel there is something about this girl he can trust, so he reveals himself to her. That's right, sports fans, for those of you who guessed, she was to be the *new* beauty . . . well, you actually don't win anything, but hey, good fucking guess! Anyway, we played out this little charade for another twelve episodes, with me telling the whole crew to take the money and stuff it in a mattress, 'cuz we didn't have long for this fuckin' ride.

Sure enough, the moment Jeff Saganski took the reins, before they even showed him to his fucking desk, his first official act as the president of CBS Television was to cancel *Beauty and the Beast*. He fuckin' hated us—well, he hated how emblematic the show was of the guy he replaced, Kim Lemasters. Lemasters was personally involved in developing *Beauty and the Beast* when he was just an executive at the network, so when he became president our show was his pride and joy. As long as he was around, he was going to give the show every opportunity to thrive and flourish. Which he indeed did. In trying to keep it going during that third season, he really went out of his way to give us the benefit of the doubt when a lot of other guys would have seen the writing on the wall. But Saganski's attitude was, "Nah, let's not throw good money after bad."

So just at the point at which Vincent finds the boy and is getting ready to become the kid's father, they canceled us. And because we were in the middle of transitioning to a new storyline and had broke for Christmas holidays, when the edict came down, there was no real closure—no good-byes, no group hugs, and no time to mourn. Nobody was really prepared for it, but everybody was prepared for it. We just went home one day, and while we were chilling we got the call telling us there was no need to return. Everything changed again. I remember how the last day of shooting of the second season was so incredibly different, so joyous; it was almost too painful to recall, knowing that instead of having this state of grace to return to, the era had ended. But what memories! Milestones! New friends!

As I mentioned before, nothing to date had ever topped meeting Sammy Davis Jr. But if I wasn't totally blown away by just the fact of that, what truly took me by surprise was the regularity with which I would hear from him. He would check in on me every couple of months either to arrange a dinner, a boy's night out, or just to shoot the shit. Hard to believe, but as I will get into later in more depth, I never took advantage of these gestures. I truly felt outclassed, not worthy, even. And it wasn't because of Sammy—he couldn't have been nicer, warmer, more welcoming. It was me. Because even though I was a grown man and had withstood some pretty tripped out episodes and begun to make a small splash, there were still personal ghosts lurking within me that hadn't truly been addressed. But more of that anon . . .

Somewhere around April during season two Sammy called and said, "Hey man, I don't know if you've read about it yet, but me and the fellas are going back out on the road together one mo time. It's gonna be called, 'Frank, Dean, and Sammy Together Again.' And we're hittin' about thirty states." *Wow! That is gonna rock*, I was thinking. Then he said, "The weird news is, you're never gonna guess where we're rehearsing." He proceeded to tell me that of the two sound stages that were at Desilu where we shot our show, the one we were not using to shoot the *Beast* was gonna be turned into a rehearsal stage for the tour and that their two rehearsal days were gonna be my last shooting day of season two, followed by my first day of freedom. "Ya gotta come by, man. It's gonna be very groovy!"

So I got to work really early to shoot what was to be the last day of season two. And the amazingly brilliant Margaret Beserra, the makeup artist responsible for transforming me for three years, and I were in my trailer, into about hour three of the four-hour dealio. Someone knocked at the door, and before we had a chance to say come in, we heard, "Hey man, is the Perl about?" Margaret hit the fuckin' floor. That's right: she looked up, saw Sam, and her legs literally went out from under her. We managed to get Margaret back on her feet. Sam gave us both hugs and kisses like only Sam could and told me to come see him and the boys when I got a break.

We worked like slaves that last day. We hadta get a lot of filming in, and we hadta finish that day, no matter how many hours it took. It turned out we worked twenty-three hours that day before they wrapped us. They didn't wrap us till around 7:30 the following morning. And because my shoot day was so work intensive, all I had a chance to do was sneak over to the other stage for five minutes, hang out in the shadows in back so as not to be seen, check out this stage they had built to accommodate the three greatest entertainers *of all time*, see the seventy-five-piece orchestra that had been assembled and surrounded the stage, see hundreds of people scurrying around doing whatever to make this into a giant event, and then close my slacked jaw and go back to work.

Anyway, I then ran home, took a shower, changed clothes, and came straight back to the studio because I was gonna spend the whole day hanging out, watching these guys rehearse. Sure enough, I came in and George Schlatter, the guy who produced *Laugh-In*, was there with a TV crew. He was filming the rehearsal because they were gonna do a big behind-the-scenes documentary on the making of *Frank, Dean, and Sammy Together Again*, so there were probably forty people from that alone. Then Sammy had an entourage. He had his own orchestra leader named George Rhodes. He had his own costume people and his own makeup people. And he had this guy who was his personal assistant named Jolly Brown. And then Frank had an entourage of probably about forty or fifty people, not including the orchestra. The leader of Frank's whole clan was a guy named Jilly Rizzo, who was famous for his restaurant in New York called Jilly's. He and Frank had been partners in the joint, but then Frank made him sell out so Jilly could spend all his time just running Frank's life for him. He was Frank's best pal; they came up together. Coupla goombahs from the ol' days. So there was Jilly for Frank, and there was Jolly for Sammy. And I'm with one of my best buds, David Schwartz, who to this day I lovingly call Jelly.

Dean Martin showed up in just a Cadillac. All he had was a driver. He had no fucking band leader, no makeup artist, no entourage—just Dean and a guy sitting in his Cadillac, waiting for him to fucking say, "Okay, we're out of here." He didn't talk to anybody or engage with anybody, but for reasons one might not expect. Dino was *the* most beloved guy in all of showbiz. He was the coolest, the funniest, the kindest, and the smoothest, just purely loved by one and all. But by this time he had already lost his son to a plane crash—his favorite son, the kid who hung the moon for him—and from the time he lost that kid and forever onward, Dean's fire went out. He was basically sleep-walking through life; it was a well-known fact. So he was not part of the falderal; he was just like, "Okay, let me come in here, spend a couple of hours rehearsing with the boys, and get the fuck out of here." He stopped playing golf and stopped hanging out. He stopped partying. He was a shell of a man by that time. The loss crippled him, just stopped him in his tracks, which spoke volumes about the facade of Dean Martin and the real Dean Martin. You know, the guy who seemed to not care, who seemed to have a laissez-faire attitude about everything, who seemed to always be drunk was actually the most loving, caring, wonderful, beautiful, generous man to come down the pike in showbiz.

> Strangely enough, to this day I'm more fascinated by Dean than any of them because the older I got, the more I realized the qualities that he was able to maintain through all those periods in his career were truly what separates the men from the boys. And it is said he died richer than any of them because nobody ever let him pay for anything 'cuz he was so fucking loved. Unfortunately, I never got a chance to even get a glimpse of a window into where Dean was at that point. Just as well. All he wanted was to be left alone.

But for the rest of the day I was watching these armies that sur-rounded Sammy and Frank as well as this army that was shooting, with George Schlatter involved, all running around. So I walked over to the buffet table, got a little bite to eat, and tried like hell to be unob-trusive. I was standing off to the side, and all of a sudden, out of the corner of my eye, I saw Sammy Davis Jr. with a hanger over his shoul-der, and he was kind of dancing up to me. Like he was doing a little dance number up to me, and he was singing some little ditty. "This is for you, my friend, the Perl!" He handed me a crew jacket that said on the back, "Frank, Dean, and Sammy Together Again," and on the front of it, on the left-hand lapel breast of the jacket, it said, "The Perl"—

P-E-R-L. He even found out how I spell my nickname. I have that jacket, presented to me by Sammy Davis Jr., to this very day.

So I was hanging out, watching this thing like a kid in a candy store. Dino only stuck around for a couple of hours. They did a few. of the numbers that they were all gonna do together in the medley, and then he got in his car and split. Sammy ultimately split too, so it was then three to four o'clock in the afternoon, and Frank started rehearsing by himself, just him and the seventy-five-piece orchestra. He wanted it that way. He wanted all the shit to die down; he wanted all of the hangers-on to split. And he waited for there to be as much peace and quiet as there possibly could be, considering the surroundings.

He sat on that stage, on a stool, and worked with the orchestra. He sang as quietly as I've ever seen him sing. He was just basically marking time, but he was working on every single note of every single song he was going to sing. And these are songs that he had been singing for forty, fifty years, arrangements that I'd heard from the days of my pop's Victrola. But any time anybody in the orchestra played a note he didn't like or he thought was too loud, too soft, or came in a half beat too soon or a half beat too late, he would stop. He'd say, "Okay, let's go back sixteen bars," and he ran this fucking thing, this rehearsal like Michelangelo would run a sculpting session on the Pietà. It was the most eye-opening of things to see.

I was standing there—pretty much by that time the crowd had died way down—and I guess my mouth was down to my knees. Out of the corner of my eye I saw some guy standing next to me, starting to look at me, but I didn't pay him any attention because I was just mesmerized by Frank. I could not take my eyes off of him. I could not believe his work ethic, his aesthetic, how much control he had of every nuance, every moment, every song. I just couldn't believe it. It was like an acting lesson. It was like watching the guy who made everything look easy be the guy who never took anything for granted, never finesse anything, never kind of just halfway do anything. He was involved with every minute of every single song. I was standing in a pool of my own God-only-knows-what. But I continued to see this guy out of the corner of my eye, and I was hoping, *Shit, whoever the fuck this guy is, I hope he goes away, because I'm in my own private Idaho over here. I'm mesmerized. I'm having a religious moment.*

Sure enough, I heard this guy say, "Holy fuck," and I turn to look at him. It's Jilly Rizzo.

He was looking at me, and I looked at him and said, "Hey?"

He said, "Holy fuck!"

"What happened?" I asked.

He said, "You're that fucking guy."

"What do you mean?"

"You're that fucking guy, right? You're that fucking Beast guy. You're that fucking Beast guy on fucking television—Hey Frank!" And he started yelling at Frank, who was in the middle of singing "In the Wee Small Hours of the Morning." He did not want to be disturbed, and Jilly was yelling, "Hey Frank, look who this is! It's that fuckin' guy! That fuckin' Beast guy!"

I was telling him, "I don't think he wants to be disturbed right now."

And of course, Frank was so used to this shit that he completely ignored it, but Jilly started saying, "Holy shit, it's that fuckin' Beast guy from television. You know how much we love you?" He took his arm and wrapped it around my head like the Italians do when they go, "This kid is beautiful. I love this kid!" He was pinching my cheek like I'm some fucking guy from Hoboken he grew up with. He said, "Ah, I love this guy. Does Frank know you're here?"

"I don't think so," I said, "but I really don't think we should disturb him right now."

"Fuck that," Jilly said, "Frank! C'mere! You gotta meet this fucking guy. It's the fucking Beast."

Eventually I got Jilly to calm down. He and I were kinda standing there, chit-chatting, getting to know each other, and at the end of that song Frank came down off the stage and went through three or four people, passing words with his orchestra leader, his driver, and then he finally got over to me and Jilly. Jilly said to him, "You know who this is, right?"

Frank asked, "How you doin'?"

"This is that fuckin' Beast guy." Jilly said. "What's your name again?"

"Ron."

He said, "This is that Beast guy—Ron."

"Hey, how you doin'?" Frank asked again.

"I'm doing really great, Mr. Sinatra," I said. "Really great."

Jilly then asked, "Have you guys met?"

"No, not yet," I said. "This is a huge honor for me."

And then Frank asked, "Hey, how ya doin'?"

So I said, "I'm doing really fine. How are you doing?"

"I'm doin' okay," he said. "How are you doin'?" This conversation went on like this for about three more minutes, and all he says to me about eighty times is, "Hey, how you doin'?"

I told him, "You have any idea what my dad would do if he knew I was standing here right now with you!"

"So how you doin'?" he said.

I told him, "You know, 'In the Wee Small Hours' is the greatest album ever recorded in any genre, by any artist in the history of music."

He said, "So, how you doin'?"

After about sixty, seventy times of this, I realized I'm not gonna get anywhere. I'm not good at conversations to begin with, and then standing in front of me and my dad's number-one icon. I finally said, "Well, it's just a thrill to meet you. I'm here because of Sammy. I became kind of friends with Sammy. I don't want to take up any of your time—I know you guys are putting together this thing. You must have a million different things to do. So I just wanted to tell you, man, thanks for letting me hang. You're fucking beautiful. What an honor."

"So, how you doin'?" he asked.

"I gotta go, Mr. Sinatra," I told him. "I gotta go."

But that wasn't gonna be the last time I saw Frank. Every year the family and I went back to our apartment in New York City during Christmas and summer breaks. The next year we just packed everybody up and got on a plane. My wife preferred about twelve suitcases, and that's if you're gonna stay less than two weeks. There's fourteen if it's longer. So I get to my pad in New York. Got the kids, the wife, and a moving van full of suitcases finally up to the door of the apartment, with sweat coming down my forehead, when I hear the phone inside ringing and ringing. So I finally put down my suitcases and say, "Hello!"

I heard, "Perl, Sam." Now, I never told Sammy I had a place in New York, much less gave him the phone number to it.

I said, "Sam! You okay?"

"I'm a little beat, man," he said. "I'm gonna take a little nap 'cuz we got a show tonight. By the way, what are you and your bride doing at eight o'clock this evening?"

"We're free," I told him. "Why?"

"You're gonna have two tickets waiting for you. Hot seats on the aisle, eight o'clock, Radio City. I'm taking a nap now, so I gotta go."

I turned to Opal and said, "Unpack quick and put something nice on. We just got invited to Frank, Dean, and Sam Together Again at Radio City Music Hall by fucking Sammy fuckin' Davis fuckin' Jr." She unpacked and got herself all dolled up. By this time, by the way, Dean had left the tour, so it was Frank, Sammy, and Liza Minnelli. We showed up at Radio City Music Hall and told them my name. We got escorted to the tenth row, right on the aisle, center. The whole first act was Sammy, then the beginning of the second act was Liza, and then the second half of the second act was Frank. And then there was a medley with all three of them. Anyway, Sammy did over an hour. I had already seen him live now, four, five, six times, so I was used to being dazzled. But on this particular night, in New York City, in Radio City Music Hall, in what he probably knew was gonna be the last time the Rat Pack roared, he was magic, and he did like an hour and ten minutes. He was mesmerizing.

The minute he sang his last note, as the house lights were getting ready to come up and the stage lights were getting ready to go down, this guy put his hand on my shoulder and he said, "Mr. and Mrs. Perlman."

"Yes?" I asked.

He said, "Would you please follow me?" They took us around the back of Radio City, of the theater, and then down the first aisle, all the way down to the stage. We got to the stage, and there's Jilly Rizzo directing traffic. He said, "Hey, Ronnie! How the fuck *are* ya? Is this your beautiful wife?"

"Yeah."

"Frank's waitin' for ya. Go ahead. Straight to the back of the stage."

They escorted us to the back of the stage of Radio City and took us in this tiny little elevator up to the fourth floor, which is where the dressing rooms are, way up in the rafters above the stage. I was in this packed elevator, 'cuz there are all these people, all these special guests who have been invited to go backstage during the intermission. The elevator doors opened, and there was Sinatra in his tuxedo, warming up his voice, pacing like a sixteen-year-old kid giving his first recital. I said, "Hey, Mr. S. How you doin'?"

"Hey, how you doin'?" he asked.

I said, "You know, I knew you were gonna say that."

Anyway, we got escorted into this room off to the side. It's obviously where you entertain guests; this is not an actual dressing room. This is an antechamber where guests wait for the stars. There was a table that ran the length of the room on which was about a hundred bottles of Cristal champagne, about thirty bowls of Beluga caviar, and smoked salmon. You name it, every delicacy in the world was on this table. It was gorgeous. In the room, waiting to be greeted by the Rat Pack boys, was Bobby Short, Gloria Vanderbilt, Jackie O.—the whole fuckin' New York glitterati. It just so happened that this was opening night, and the crème de la crème of New York society was in this room. Opal and I found a spot and sat down kind of just waiting around. Five minutes in, Sammy came out in a robe. He had got a towel around him and was pouring with sweat. He just gave the most incredible performance. His adrenaline was still pumping.

He started saying hello to everybody, giving hugs and kisses like only Sammy could give. Then he got up to me, and, now, he had never met my Jamaican wife, Opal. He said, "Perl," and I stand up.

I gave him a hug and said, "Sam, I don't think you ever met my wife."

He looked at my wife and then said to me, "Hey man, this is your wife? No bullshit?"

And I said, "This is my wife, man. Mother of my children."

He said, "You never told me you had a secret weapon, man." And then he went off and spent some time with Jackie O. I basically was thinking, *I'm definitely not worthy. I'm getting the fuck out.* I had a little salmon, a little caviar, some champagne. I hung around a little bit, but I did not want to get in Sammy's way. Then we went back downstairs and saw Sinatra and Liza, and then the three of them got on stage, and it was just one of the most magical nights ever. And I believe that was the last time I actually saw Sammy, because right after that he got diagnosed with throat cancer. And when news started to spread that it was inoperable, all of Hollywood Royalty came out to put on a beautiful tribute show. By then his voice was gone. And then a few months later he was gone. I went to his funeral and hung out with his wife a bunch of times after that. But before I had a chance to actually know him, he was taken.

I did, in fact, see Frank Sinatra a bunch of times after that because I got invited to the Frank Sinatra Golf Tournament in Palm Springs for a number of years. Yes, I actually started playing golf. I guess once you start making money, it's obligatory that you learn to play golf, right? Go figure! But anyway, Frank was already married to Barbara at that point, and she was very philanthropic. So she talked him into having this Frank Sinatra Charity Golf Tournament in Palm Springs. I was at the very first one. Frank was very much alive. It was two days' worth of golf, and then Saturday night, the night of the second day of golf, they had a huge banquet and show. Opening act: Tom Dreesen. Second opening act: either Tony Bennett or Steve and Eydie, or Liza Minnelli or Natalie Cole, or somebody, and then Frank. And it was all black tie. I went to all of the Frank Sinatra Golf Tournaments I could while he was alive, all the way up until when he died, in 1998. I saw him perform at all of those things. But I used to run into him at the banquet. He always recognized me, actually stopped whatever he was

EASY STREET (THE HARD WAY)

doing, shook my hand, gave me a little pinch on the cheek like from the neighborhood, and always, always, always said, "How you doin'?" But the thing was, he meant it. He really wanted to know. He wasn't just saying, "How you doin'?"—he really wanted to know. I said, "I'm really good. How you doing?"

He would say, "You know, I'm the luckiest guy alive. What could be better?" That's the most I ever got out of Frank.

Years later, long after he was gone, I saw Frank Jr. at a delicatessen. After he left, the waiter brought a note over to my table that Frank Jr. had written. It was for me, and he told me about every single movie I'd ever been in from the first one all the way to the most current, and what a fan he was of mine. I was a regular at this particular deli, so the next time I was in there and saw Frank I went up to him and said, "By the way, I never got a chance to thank you for that beautiful letter you wrote." He invited me to sit with him, and we became friends. We exchanged phone numbers and everything like that. And a few years after that, I had a notion to do a movie that was gonna be a homage to Sinatra. But it was going to be a very small, funky kind of quirky tribute to Sinatra, like a road movie about a guy who was bipolar and who had these fantasies that involved Sinatra, and all this shit. I needed the music in order to make the movie all that it needed to be. So I gave Frank Jr. a call. Now, when Frank passed, his estate was divided up between Barbara, Nancy, Tina, and Frank Jr. And he thoughtfully left each of them exactly what he thought would be most useful so they could carry on without him. What Frank Jr. got was the rights to all the arrangements of all the songs Frank ever sang, knowing that Jr. could carry on the legacy by touring the world with the Frank Sinatra Orchestra. And have a good life. To this day, that is what Frank Jr. does: playing the songs his dad sung, note for note, exactly how they were on the records. So he was the perfect guy to call for what I needed, 'cuz I needed to have, note for note, these iconic arrangements. So I took him to dinner and said to him, "I'm gonna tell you a little story. And when I get finished telling you this story, you're either going to give me a hug, or you're going to punch me right in the fucking mouth."

"All right, that sounds fair."

I said, "Let's order first, because when I get punched, I like it to be on a full stomach." So we ordered some food and wine. And before I described the movie to him, I said, "I gotta do this movie because I have to thank the two men who made me everything I am right now. That's my old man and your old man."

He asked, "Well, how does my old man figure into it?"

So I told him. I told him what his old man meant to me and how he saved my life countless times when I was suicidal in fucking Moscow making a shitty movie. I put Sinatra on, and all of a sudden I was whole again, home again. My old man handed all of that down to me, and although Frank had a lot of devoted fans, none more so than my dad. So I told him my idea for the story. He got up and said, "Stand up. Take it like a man." Okay, I guess I got this comin', right? He gave me a hug and said, "I'm in. Whatever you need, you got it. You want every arrangement, you got it. I'm in. I love this."

So we sat down and finished our dinner, and he said to me, "Do you know my dad never missed *Beauty and the Beast*?"

"What?!" I said.

"We had strict orders to tape that show wherever he was. And the minute he was free and got home, he watched every single episode. And one day he and I had a long talk about you. I said, 'You don't know this guy, he's not just from the show.' Then I showed him *Quest for Fire*, and *Name of the Rose*, and you became one of his favorite actors." As he was telling me this, I'm going over this tape in my head: every time Sinatra saw me, when he said, "How you doin'?" he kinda knew who I was, but he never said anything except "How you doin'?" And I didn't realize it until it was way too late to do anything about it. But if Frank was here now, now that I've resolved all of my "I'm not worthy" issues . . . well, coulda, woulda, shoulda. All I'm sayin' is I wish I had those moments with Frank again so we could really talk! Really hang out together. But hey, I shook the hands of a man who shook the world!

You would think that I should've been booming with confidence when *Beast* ended after rubbing elbows with such icons and heroes.

You'd think all of the circumstances, like the Sinatra thing, would have cured me of whatever it was that ailed me. But I'm here to tell you that it doesn't come from how you're doin' on the outside; it comes when you're determined to work on yourself, exorcise demons, and *really, really* get rid of shit. Not just give it lip service, not just read a book and say, "Okay, I'm good now," not just buy your way into happiness. Money will only take you so far—and it'll take you pretty fucking far, trust me. It's pretty important, and I fucking love it. I love making money. But it will only take you so far. And there are certain things you need to do the hard way, from inside out. I mean, you take yourself with you, whatever your circumstance, wherever you go. You can be in a palace or in a shack; you can be handed an award or waitin' in the cold for an open audition call. But you've still got to take yourself with you. It would take some time to figure this out—two and a half years or more of nothing before I even began to see things this way.

So the show got canceled in January 1990, and my son, Brandon, came in March of 1990. The timing was a little weird, but there was nothing we could really do about sending back the kid. And then there was this big, beautiful expensive house I had just closed on. Hey, I chucked a few Hail Marys into the wind and said if there's a God in heaven and he means for me to keep all this, then fuck, I'm good! But I'm certainly not pulling out now. This time I'm battle-tested and brimming with self-confidence. I mean, for sure, the fact of being on a prime time show for two and a half years and getting these fuckin' awards, accolades, magazine covers, and all this incredible love that's come my way—something hadda give. Am I right?

I was never more wrong in my fucking life.

(CHAPTER 16)

Not So Good . . . Until

If Frankie woulda asked anytime during the next two years, "How you doin'?" I would've said, "Don't ask." I mean, yeah, now that I have the luxury of perspective, looking at what represented one of the most painful, confusing times I can remember from thirty thousand feet, when I'm no longer in the middle of it, I see the shape of it. And the rhyme and reason of it. I came to the conclusion that for those who are dreamers and are animated by first having a dream and then putting together a road map to go about achieving at least some version of it to the best degree that they can, there is merit in that, in and of itself. Even though most of the time you fall short of it, every once in a while you exceed it. But very rarely does it come in the form you imagined it. When *Beast* was canned I did not know that and only hoped more roles would come, and fast.

But then reality came a-callin', and once again the phone flat-out didn't ring, just as it had been at the end of all the other great gigs I had completed. After a couple of months I saw that the Beast was yet another one-off, so unique in his very nature that the role turned out to be a road map to nothing. No new prime time series that featured a beast was in the works anytime soon. It's like almost starting out at the beginning again, just like every other time. That's what it felt like.

Even though that was probably an overstatement in the big scheme of things, that's what it felt like for me.

Eventually the quietude evolved into a malaise; the energy that had surged through me for the three years of *Beast* was slowly seeping out of me. All directions seemed to melt together into no direction at all. I didn't know it at the time, but the symptoms I was feeling were classical in nature, clearly precipitated by events of dramatic proportion. Because at forty years of age the cancellation of *Beauty and the Beast* coincidentally coincided with the ending of the first half of my life. This was a midlife crisis of a supersized, soul-searching order, made more pronounced by how close I had flown to the sun, because clearly the higher you go, the further you fall.

So what had been a period of intense displays of highly energized events quickly turned into one of complete inertia, in which stagnation replaced energy. And it wasn't as if the world around me stopped; this was a self-inflicted self-removal. For even when the phone *was* ringing, I had no interest in answering it. The fire had gone out. Days on end were spent in pajamas on the couch, listlessly half-watching bad television. My normal range of emotion and mood swing just flat-lined.

There was a part of me that suspected, even then, that when the wheels come off, it isn't a random event; it wasn't a mistake that the axle broke. They were always eventually gonna come off, because what you're driving is, fundamentally, a lemon. But the unease emanated out of me, way more than it was circumstantial. All this time I had fooled myself into thinking that if I just got successful enough, wealthy enough, respected enough, it would mean that I finally *was* worthy. I finally *was* the man I always longed to be. I finally could coast along on Easy Street, where troubles are bubbles and everything ends happily. The hoopla that accompanies the brief moment of career success made me forget what I had already learned: that I never learned a fucking thing while I was succeeding. All of my learning, and I mean *all*, had come when I was struggling, failing. All of my growth came when things were at their worst. All of the character that I had, if, indeed, I had any at all, came from the really, really challenging times when I was anonymous, when I couldn't get arrested, when nothing was going right, when it seemed God had abandoned me. This is a conversation I will get back to later on, but suffice it to say, there was no abandonment on God's part; in fact, it was just the opposite. He was surrounding me, lovingly seasoning me, showing me that the house that needed to be put in order was my own, that there were to be no easy answers from the outside to make everything inside right with me.

Despite all of this, there was an unequivocal shining star around which to rally: the birth of my son, Brandon, in March of 1990. I suspected he was the Golden Child the moment I laid eyes on him. Turns out I was right. I have to believe that the circumstances surrounding the birth of both my children were, as difficult as it seemed at the time, surely the result of a greater plan than I could ever have devised. For in both cases, and not because I planned it that way, I was out of work for the first two years of their lives, meaning there was nothing to prevent me from being with them from the first bottle in the morning to their last bedtime story at night, and pretty much everything in between. If you asked me back then would I rather have been working, the answer probably would have been a resounding yes. But as I look back, what a blessing this dad got to have what so many others miss out on—the profound presence in their kids' lives in their first and most important years. That is palpable and forever. And I would like to believe the uncommon closeness we enjoy to this day has something to do with that. So from where I am currently perched, if that doesn't seem like part of God's plan . . . well, I'm just sayin'.

So I immersed myself in spending time with my newborn son. Not only was it a pleasure; it was the only thing that seemed worthwhile to me. All things showbiz had completely lost their allure. Everything that came across my desk seemed pallid, ordinary. After coming off not only being the straw that stirs the drink but also being on a project with the dignity and integrity of *Beauty and the Beast*, nothing even came close to living up to that. So I hid out. I stopped answering the phone, just listened to my messages, and nothing was going on that titillated me in any way, shape, or form. So what started out as cool detachment slowly started morphing into complete disinterest, which in turn led to the malaise that gives way to total inertia. In other words, at a certain point I couldn't do anything to jumpstart myself even if I'd wanted to.

And it wasn't as if I had the luxury of resting on my laurels. Aside from my firstborn, who at this point was six years old and already enrolled in private school, and a beautiful adoring wife who I wanted the best for, there was this new fucking house. Lemme paint you a picture.

Opal and I started lookin' for our first house in '87, just as the series started to kick in for real. We had a budget and a few neighborhoods we dug. Now, I have no idea what was up, but in the year we were house hunting it appears that all 13 million of the other muthafuckas who lived in LA got the same notion. 'Cuz it was frenzy time. In the year it took to finally close on a place, real estate prices in the 'hoods we were looking in pretty much doubled. It got to the point at which you went to an open house, and there would be about seven other couples there, and the joint was decent—not great but decent—and by the time you turned to your wife to ask what she wanted to do, two other couples just bid fifty thousand bucks above asking.

So now the heat was on. The longer this took, the more expensive shit got. We finally found a place we both liked—really liked. And we saw it before anybody else, so we were gonna be the first bidders. The problem was that it was exactly twice what we originally wanted to spend. *Twice*! So I invited my spanking-new financial fucking adviser to come have a look and give me his educated opinion. He told me, "Nice house, very nice. Looks like it would make for a solid investment. I like it."

And I asked him, "What would make it a stupid investment?"

"Well, in order for it to be a really stupid move," he replied, "virtually three things would have to happen: they cancel your show, you don't find another job to replace it, and . . ."

"And what?"

"And the bottom would have to fall out of the real estate market. But it's so hot right now, that's a virtual impossibility!"

Funny how life works. The month after we took possession of this "solid" investment, the show got canceled. Then right after that, suddenly people are shying away from real estate, so a major correction is under way, eventually leading to my house becoming worth half of what I paid for it. And then . . . well you know about this new phase of my career I lovingly call profiles in-ertia! So aside from the two kids and the wife, I got other issues.

Then I find out that, in all the confusion with the network ultimately deciding to cancel the show, the producers drop the ball and forget to formally submit me for an Emmy. The way it works is nominations are not automatic; one's name has to be put up for consideration as well as an episode you would like the committee to watch before they vote. And considering I was twice a bridesmaid, I figured I had a decent chance of maybe winning now that the show was history. So I found out I'm not gonna get the nomination 'cuz of a technical snafu, and I went nuts. Ends up I fire my manager, which was really stupid, 'cuz he was also one of my best friends at the time. But I was seeing red so I was hardly thinking straight and needed to lash out. Dumb fuckin' move. And one of the only moves I ever made that I have never stopped regretting. Erwin "Levon" More. The guy who sent me the script for *Beauty and the Beast* even though I ordered him not to. If ya haven't figured it out by now . . . sorry, pal.

So with all this on my plate and pressure building, tension rising, there was this one unrelenting reality that was overwhelmingly trumping everything else: the fire had gone out. Which confused me. That had never happened before. Regardless of the slog that these first forty years were, I can say I was never disengaged. There was always a hunger that saw me through, charted my direction. But not now. And as concerned as I was about doing what was right for the family and myself, the will to do it was nowhere in sight. Makes a muthafucka wanna go *hmmmm* . . . !

I hate using clichés! I hate terms like *midlife crisis*. But you know why a cliché becomes a cliché? 'Cuz it's fuckin' true, that's why! And

I didn't know it then, but as sure as I'm sittin' here, I sure do know it now—that's what the fuck was goin' down! I was in the midst of a classic, full-bore midlife crisis. Because having gone through it, here's my definition: whatever it is that drives you for the first half of your life to right around forty, you have either by now achieved or you realize the dreams you dreamed are no longer pertinent, no longer seductive enough to energize you. So the fire goes out. The crisis part is that sticky period it takes till you get a new dream to replace the old one, one that is powerful and compelling enough to propel you forward into the second half of your life. And why I insist mine was classical in nature is because I was exactly forty when it came on; the beginning of it was clearly and powerfully precipitated by coming to the end of an incredibly defining episode in my life and was ended by an even more defining episode, one that has had the juice to propel me to this very day.

The call came in 1992, two-plus years after the Beast was laid to rest, and, interestingly enough, it came from my old dear friend Bobby Littman, from whom I had been estranged for quite some time. Seems he was helping find Hollywood actors for this movie that was to be shot in Mexico for a first-time filmmaker by the name of Guillermo del Toro. He said they were prepared to make a firm offer pending my reaction to the material, and would I consider reading the script? Now, by this point, I wasn't quite finished with my malaise, so my first reaction was no, thank you. But before I could say that, I thought about the fact that it was Bobby, for whom I always had a soft spot, as well as the notion of Mexico, which bore an exoticism to make it potentially interesting . . . and oh, by the way, I hadn't had any income in two years. "Send it over!"

The script arrived accompanied by a beautifully handwritten note from this young unknown would-be filmmaker. The letter, which I still have, was the most moving I had ever received. He talked about him having to turn himself into a special effects makeup artist because there was no one in Mexico he could find to execute his designs. He talked about studying my work, virtually all of it, in his personal journey to learn what he needed to know from the masters. And he said what a privilege, on the auspicious occasion of his foray into filmmaking, it would be if I would take the leap of faith and join forces with him in this adventure. I was charmed.

I read the script on the stationary bike at the Hollywood YMCA. There was another young filmmaker on the bike next to mine whom I had never met but would eventually direct me in a movie called *The Last Supper*. She was reading the script over my shoulder and complaining that I was reading too slowly—remember the dyslexia from Chapter 2? Eventually we engaged in a real conversation. She asked me what the fuck I was reading, and I told her it was this unique and sophisticated vampire movie to be shot in Mexico. She asked whether I was going to do it, and I said, "This script is way too original to ever be done in Hollywood, so, for that reason alone, I guess I should say yes."

Before I could respond to the offer, Bobby called to say that Guillermo is coming to town, and would I like to join him for dinner? Well, join I did at an Indian joint he picked out on Wilshire Boulevard. Within a minute of meeting him there was an ease that was uncommon among people who are just feeling each other out. By thirty minutes into the dinner it was as if we had known each other for twenty years. He had boyish joy and enthusiasm just pouring out of him and an adolescent sense of humor identical to mine. But mostly what he had was vision. Whenever the discussion veered back to what this film he was about to make was going to look like, he was overcome by a slightly different persona; he stopped being this funny, self-deprecating kid and started looking like a Renaissance master. This was my very first glimpse into the glorious, twisted, classical, rebellious, unique, and original mind of Guillermo del Toro. The malaise was over! I was finally in the presence of greatness, but this time of a scope I never conceived could exist. Start the clock, 'cuz the second half just got under way . . .

It turns out that Guillermo came to know me by a plaster cast bust of my face. He had been writing, directing, and producing anthology pieces in Mexico, sort of like *Twilight Zone* or *Zane Grey Theater* shorts, which focused on paranormal and horror characterizations and plotlines. His only problem was that there were no special effects and makeup studios in Mexico that could do the work to match his vision, so he started his own company, which he named Necropia. First, he managed to get an invite to the United States to learn from the masters of the craft: Dick Smith, of *Exorcist* fame, and Rick Baker, who not only pointed to Dick Smith as the Jedi master but who also eventually created Vincent and, later, the masks for *Hellboy*. My plaster face, with all its transformations as Rick turned me into Vincent, were all around Baker's studio. Guillermo fell in love with my anatomy before I ever met him.

Cronos, or *The Cronos Device*, as it was originally called, was to be the first look into what has become the magical and singular world of Guillermo del Toro. Essentially a vampire movie, it was like none other you had ever seen. The backdrop for this extraordinary look at the obsession for eternal life was quite ordinary: an old antique dealer and his granddaughter upon whom he dotes are at the center of the story. So for the first time, but not the last, in Guillermo's world pure innocence and the protection thereof are juxtaposed against a crept-out world of corruption, cynicism, and a lust for the unattainable. There was elegance to the storytelling, a sophistication and purity; one almost envisioned Cary Grant as our lead character. (Instead Guillermo got Federico Lupi, the South American version of Cary Grant and a beautiful actor in his own right.)

The grandfather is a sophisticated man of letters with a poetic soul, a beautiful human being, devoted family man, who, in his world of collecting and selling rare antiquities, happens upon this thing that's in great demand from this underworld.

He tries to figure out what this thing is and why these guys are killing for it. He comes to find out this beautiful whimsical object grants the user the gift of eternal life. In using it, one becomes undead.

I went down to Mexico and we made *The Cronos Device*. I watched this young fellow, fourteen years my junior, work in the most different way from I'd seen anybody work on a film before. He had a skeleton crew. There was very little money, in fact, even less than very little because one of the investors pulled out moments before the start of principal photography. The crew all seemed like they had known each other their whole lives. And everyone there, including the producers, were lovingly surrounding this young genius so as to enable him all of the creative room to make his movie his way. Nobody was questioning him. Nobody was creating roadblocks that didn't need to exist. Nobody was making his life any harder than it already was. In fact, it was just the opposite. This was as happy a film set as I'd ever witnessed, and it was infectious. And I didn't quite understand this term till later, but what I was involved in was the very first independent film I'd ever signed on to do. And I took to it like a kid who just got the coolest toy in the world. I was suddenly flung back to that original feeling I had when I first discovered the true excitement of being an actor—there was that kind of idealism and enthusiasm. It was boyish, it was naked, it was unbridled. Here it was in full bloom, on a tiny little low-budget movie in one of the funkiest cities on the planet.

Not only was I being asked to come out of my stupor to act again, but the setting of it was also this ideal, beautiful utopian landscape, at least that's how I saw it. For even though it was Mexico City—23 million people, horrific traffic, smog to the point that you can't see your hand in front of your face on certain days—I was deeply in love with all of it. I felt like I had been drugged, and I was becoming addicted to the feeling.

Not only that, but Mexico was completely new to me. I'd never been there before, but it completely and immediately spoke volumes to me, almost as if, in a way I cannot explain, I had come home. I became obsessed with the culture, the mindset, the point of view, the humility, the joy (even in poverty) that I witnessed. They brought humor and goodwill, couched in pure humility, to their every waking moment. They never, ever took themselves seriously. No one in the Mexican culture I ever met seemed like they were entitled, imperious, or dogmatic.

We went out every night, ate, and danced. One night it was Cumbia, one night it was Merengue, one night it was Salsa, one night it was Cha Cha. Every single night they took me to somebody's favorite bar with live music and immersed me in this magical realism that Gabriel Garcia Marquez writes about, which is the Mexican experience. Hell, it was just fraught with magical realism everywhere you looked, 'cuz it's the realest place on Earth, and yet they have this mindset, this way of moving through life, that is very sort of . . . I don't know, two or three feet off the ground. And I got hooked into it in a big way, to the point at which I was looking for a house down there to buy. I was gonna fucking move there. I was gonna chuck everything and become a fucking Mexican. Get myself a sombrero, a poncho, whatever. I bought in, hook, line, and sinker. I was reborn. Praise the Lawd!

So many things have changed, so many things have evolved, so many things have happened as a result of meeting Guillermo. There have been so many new experiences, with so many old ones getting crossed off the list, but the things I learned in those eight weeks on *Cronos* in Mexico I'm still trying to apply to this very day; I'm still trying to duplicate, for this little experience down south of the border was to become my model. And even though my friend Guillermo has become a world treasure, having had bestowed upon him heaps and heaps of resources to make movies, I am still in search of the *next* Guillermo, the *next Cronos.*

When I returned I had the enthusiasm to put this new energy surging through me to work. But, more importantly, I also started to experience some other types of changes in my worldview. Guillermo lit the fuse that would end up defining the second half of my life. The old dream that had burnt out two years earlier was finally rekindled, replaced by a new one, and it was powerful. Like I said, very rarely does change come in the form you imagined it would. When you're in the cocoon you never know what kind of butterfly is gonna come flying out.

(CHAPTER 17)

They Call Them Shrinks for a Reason

We survived those two lean years by burning through whatever savings we had left from *Beauty and the Beast*. And a few little odds and ends that popped up hither and thither. Opal was great. She never put any external pressure on me; in fact, she acted as if nothing was wrong, and another job would come along, just as it always had. However, for me, it was a very worrisome period, tinged with the uneasiness that comes from thinking about the possibility of losing everything. I was obsessed with hanging on. I didn't really have anything very valuable at that point other than the family and the house, but I was still putting so much external pressure on myself because I would have just hated myself if, five minutes after I got it all, I lost it all. So upon my return from Mexico I took whatever gigs came my way.

If you look at my IMDb credits in the nineties, you would say, "What the fuck was this guy belly achin' about? It looks like he was working all the time." And I would say that, with a few rare exceptions like *City of Lost Children*, *The Island of Dr. Moreau*, *Alien: Resurrection*, and then at the very end of the decade, *Enemy at the Gates*, all the other gigs were basically taken out of pure desperate desperation. I wouldn't go so far as to say I was ashamed of them; it's just that I'd rather no one ever sees them. It made me look like a total schlepper. But it was essential I keep stringing together a living: I had kids in private school and a roof over my head that I really wanted to hold onto. So whereas most guys can sweep their embarrassments under the rug, with me, every fuckin' mistake ends up on Cinemax at 11:00 p.m., eight nights a freakin' week.

But on a much more important level the nineties provided just the right amount of turmoil to start me looking inward. I guess I finally got fed up enough with the extreme nature of the highs and lows that I woulda had to be a total schmuck to not start looking for ways to remove some of the drama. I began to grow tired of leavin' so much of my inner peace to outward events—indeed, events I took very little part in creating. Because as much as people want to think I had control over the jobs I ended up taking, that just wasn't so. They just came at me and I took 'em, for the most part. Or they came, and I didn't take them. But nothing that ever happened to me happened as a result of my own efforts; they always came out of the blue. Always.

Nevertheless, I think about the nineties as the toughest decade of my life. But, let me be clear, this decade also had pockets of pure sublimity, pockets of beautiful little things. But for the most part it was a real grind: there were real growing pains, a lot of testing. Our marriage got tested. Opal and I as parents got tested, whether we were good at raising kids got tested, whether I was ever going to be this vision of the man I aspired to be got tested, whether I truly even had any talent was tested. When I think of the nineties I think of it as a time of major assessment, as a period with a lot of sturm und drang. A lot of unease.

Opal and I actually had discussions about how tough it was starting to be to find that couple we started out as. And it didn't take long to admit to ourselves that maybe this was a discussion we weren't fully equipped to have. So she got me to agree and then went out and got the name of this shrink, Phil Stutz, who was supposed to be tops in taps. Don't tell Opal this, but the idea of going to a shrink never really seemed like it was for me. I was never really too sure about this therapy thing. I'd heard about it, of course, because it was all the rage, especially in Hollywood, where, on a per capita basis, it was second only to plastic surgery. And I never did understand how answering the question, "How old were you when you first discovered you hated your mother?" was gonna help me pay the fuckin' rent, 'cuz, let's face it, that was the *real* problem all along. I thought it was kinda like chasing your own tail to talk about psychotherapy. When she told me the shrink's name and I told her that our friends went to him and the doctor told them straight out, "You can keep coming to me if you want, but your marriage isn't worth saving," Opal said, "Jesus Christ, how the fuck could my friend recommend me to this guy?" But that's how fucking cool Phil is. He just fucking tells it to you like it is. So after a small degree of deliberation I figured, hey, this could be good just for the entertainment value alone. And thus started my long and beautiful friendship with what I endearingly refer to as the fourth leg of the stool, the other three being Ralph, Jean-Jacques, and Guillermo.

We went and saw this guy for six to eight months before we came to the conclusion that we were paying this doctor so we could fight in front of him. We could have done that for free in our house. We both said, "This fucking therapy is not working. Nothing is improving in our relationship at all. And if our relationship is gonna improve, it's gonna have to be 'cuz we want it to."

So once I realized we would not be coming back to him anymore, at the end of that last session I said, "By the way, would you consider treating me on my own?" 'Cuz by that point I really dug the guy. He looked at Opal, and he said, "Well, since you came as a team, I would have to get permission from your bride."

Opal said, "Jesus Christ, just fucking take the fucker, man. This dude is fucking nuts. Maybe you can do something with him."

Looking back on it now, I can honestly say that going to him in the first place had less to do with the dynamic of me and Opal and more to do with the dynamic of me, myself, and i (and yes, it's supposed to be lowercase). Because my main problem with Opal was that she was simply the closest one there to take all my own frustrations out on, the closest one to blame for everything not being perfect, the closest one to pin all the shit that was really about *my* shortcomings on. Even though there was no blame to begin with, it was just the way shit was. And if you're somebody who hasn't ever really worked on yourself and then tried to understand who you are on a core level, then you don't really have very much to fall back on.

I'm fortunate to be able to say that I was obsessed just enough with not wanting to go back to certain painful things that I was willing to do the work. But the work that needed doing never, ever, ever had anything to do with when I was on a lucky streak or when things were going well. It all happened when the wheels just completely came off, because that's when you realize how fucked up your thinking is, how completely short-circuited you are. He taught me to look at things I had never taken a good long, hard, objective look at before so that, with any luck, I would drill down to a sort of core that I could depend on that wasn't based on what I was doing, how I was doing, whether I was doing.

I didn't know to what degree I needed that kind of help except for the fact that there were so many ups and downs and so many highs and lows in that ten-year period that I was forced to turn inward and deal with the misery and the vast mood swings. I didn't know how to begin to figure out what was wrong until I started to see Dr. Phil Stutz on my own. And although all I could see was the haze of what seemed at the time as an excruciating journey with dubious results, finally I had taken the first real step to confronting the issues that had my fingerprints all over them. This amazing shrink changed—or shrunk— the notion that I always had, that all of my wiring was intertwined with fame, success, the accumulation of wealth, how many friends I had, and so on and so forth—how often I worked, what my TV queue was, how I was regarded. All this shit completely means fuck all unless there's a *you* there that it all can reflect off of.

Once the real *you* emerges and appears unfettered, naked, and completely in touch with the good, the bad, and the ugly, then you really meet yourself. Then all those things take on a different perspective as well. Certain things fall away. Certain things are not quite what they were cracked up to be, but you begin to understand that yes, there are certain things that would make your life a lot easier. But they're not panaceas. They're not the answer. It's no longer dependent upon if this or that happens to me all of a sudden, then I'm good from here on out. Then I have no problems, I have no issues, it's all smooth sailing. That's just an illusion. That's just a lie.

So a lot of this stuff was revealed to me when I began working with Dr. Stutz. It couldn't have been couched in a better period because the nineties were so challenging on every level, thus allowing me to bring into the conversation Ron at his most fucked up, most terrified, most negative about his own self-image. The decade touched on all the little cracks that still existed and that, if left unchecked, could have flooded into irreparable damage, so it provided me with all the ammo I needed for full self-examination: there were career problems, money problems, parenting problems—you name it, I had it.

In short, I couldn't have been a better subject to test out the theories and efficacies of the renowned Dr. Phil Stutz. His beliefs sprung forth most specifically from the teachings of the great Carl Jung and the amazing Rudolf Steiner. Of course he threw in dashes of Freud and sprinkles of Nietzsche and Schopenhauer. But by the time Phil got through distilling them down, they were pure Stutz. And tailor-made for the sick, twisted wannabes who get off the bus every single day looking for fame and fortune in Hollywood. He is a truly, truly brilliant man, and what is beautiful about Phil is that whenever I was on the skids I could see him; there was never any of the bullshit formality of making and keeping sacrosanct weekly or biweekly appointments, with all the self-important crap most therapists throw down to confuse real help with rigid dogma.

Phil didn't give a fuck whether I saw him once a week, once a day, or once a millennium. I could call him when I needed him, and he would figure out a way to make time for me, just like ya'd do with any other doctor. If I needed him really bad, he'd make time for me quickly. If it was not such a big thing, he would fit me in. But he was in a lot of demand, so I was one of many people who depended on him for balance and equilibrium. That was the pattern in the nineties, when I went to see him a lot. The problem was that he was the most expensive shrink there was. No one in the world charges more than Phil does. So sometimes my real problem was, "Phil, I don't have any money. And that's fucking me up. I gotta come see you. But you're really expensive and I really can't afford you." That whole thing was a catch-22. So I had to be very careful about how I administered his therapy and made sure I never took anything away from the other needs in my life that sometimes a dearth of resources were needed to cover.

He worked things out so even when there were certain months when I couldn't pay him, he'd wait. When I got a gig, I would make it all up to him. There was no issue that was coming up for me at that time that I wasn't able to call him up and address. And the way it worked with Phil was, whereas most of the people I knew who were in therapy would lie there on a couch or sit there in a chair and talk for forty-five, fifty minutes and every once in a while the shrink would say, "And how do you feel about that?" and you'd be fucking talking and that's what therapy was, Phil would listen to your version of what was fucking you up for about fifteen minutes, twenty if it was *really* serious, and then he'd talk for the whole rest of the time.

Phil taught me that there are things that don't square up inside of most people, but these are just distortions—they're really not real. They're just things you think are real because that's what you've been wired to think. And low self-esteem is just another example of a bunch of bad assumptions, assumptions you are making that are reality to you, but they don't have anything to do with real reality. It's based on a bunch of assumptions that are the result of misfires or bad judgment. And those things don't get removed if you make a lot of money, get lucky on a TV show, start driving a fucking XJ6 Jaguar, or are getting head seventeen times a day from hot supermodels. You know, all that shit is just a distraction. Well, maybe not all of it . . . but you know what I'm sayin'. The real work you do on your life is a question of how well you can recognize that you need to work on your life and how determined you are to look it straight in eye and figure out how to remove it and replace it with something that's closer to real reality instead of the bullshit that got foisted upon you either by bad parenting or whatever other fucked up stimuli you experienced in your first five to ten years of life.

Most people have the biggest trouble seeing life through their own eyes. They don't have as much problem seeing someone else's life objectively, but they have no way to see themselves with the same clarity. This is particularly the case for people who haven't worked on their core, don't have a whole lot of self-awareness, when the real you is a ghost.

Essentially any search for inner truth begins with replacing all of the illusory things you think you perceive with the things that are really there. In other words, you must begin to train yourself to make all your judgments on the reality of a thing rather than the distortion that occurs when you look at the world through a distorted lens. This is the power of cognitive thinking: there is an objective truth to it that is undebatable. Hopefully you learn to get to the point at which you could now look at something in a way so that it becomes an offshoot of logic and, thus, a problem infinitely more solvable. And very often Stutz would give me a diagram that encapsulated the universe. He taught me the tool called *The Grateful Flow*. I think Carl Jung talks about that, in which you just begin by saying, "I'm breathing right now. I'm not in pain right now. I'm sitting down right now. I'm in a warm comfortable room right now." You begin to list all the positive things you're experiencing in the right here and now. And then the list is usually so vast that you completely obliterate and expunge any of the negative forces trying to invade you. So these tools were instantaneous—if you just took the time and accessed enough self-discipline to use them.

And 100 percent of the time I would walk out of Phil's office with such a cleaned-out vision of the world and myself in it that I had no recollection of ever even being in trouble in the first place. I could always leave Phil's office with a complete spring in my step, completely unfettered, when nothing was bothering me, nothing. And he would do that in not a week or a month or three to six years, like I hear about from my friends with their own shrinks; he would do this in fifty minutes. Every time. No matter what shit I dragged in with me, he would get right to the matter. He would identify what the disconnect was, not ever giving a shit where it emanated from, that, "So when did you first discover you hated your mother"–type of shit. Instead he gave me specific ways of not only rethinking a situation but also provided a tool to help me get back to this place where I was able to remove it from allowing whatever it was that never existed in the first place to become a part of my perspective. And these tools were incredibly user-friendly, unbelievably accessible, guaranteed to be effective! As long as you were willing to call upon them regularly.

I traveled great distances with Phil. Between my abbreviated description of the conditions that I was bringing him and his fine-tuned intuitive ability to not only identify it by name but also surmise the characteristics in me that made those conditions possible, Phil developed a mastery of me that is equal to none. Which allowed him, as we traveled along together, to zero in on my mishigas and cut right to its quick, by first identifying it, then obliterating it, so rapidly, so effectively that it seemed almost like magic. But there was no mumbo-jumbo, no psychobabble. Everything was in layman's terms. And there was not one moment in all our years together of analysis when we drudged up past bruisings in pursuit of current events, because at the end of the day who gave a fuck what it all meant, these conditions of yours. Instead, here's how you kick its fuckin' ass. Here's how you identify the high ground and then get yourself there.

After years of working with Phil—'cuz that's what it was: work, not treatment—we started to develop a deep fondness for one another, one that obviously sprung from mutual respect but nevertheless transcended normal doctor-patient protocol. "You lost a brother," he said, "and you almost lost yourself. If you had gone to a hundred shrinks, ninety-nine of them would have had you on meds. What we did was work diligently and single-mindedly to teach you how to manage yourself out of harm's way whenever it appeared. Because make no mistake, it will keep reappearing till they close the lid on you. But if you can get good enough to call upon a tool to redirect the flood of shit that comes to bring you down and you get good enough at it so reaction time is close to immediate, well, that's as close as you can get to harmony and bliss." I was never on a med. Not never, not no-how.

Little by little this shit began to take hold in real time. The goal that Phil had set, which was to take the giant waves that existed between my highs and lows and diminish them to the point at which they were softer, quieter waves, was becoming a part of my everyday experience. And as we got closer to the end of the decade I began to notice a distinctive new level of peace and contentment during my alone times, something I couldn't handle for an hour in my younger years. I became so much more comfortable in my own skin. I became, God forbid, one of my favorite people to hang out with; in fact, being alone started to surpass the need to always be with others, as if I could only feel like me if it manifested itself as a reflection of other people.

Perhaps the hardest tool in Phil's arsenal to master also happened to be the most profound in importance. It sprung from an approach that was central to Jungian philosophy; it had to do with the shadow. The shadow is that little person who lives deep in the bowels of your innermost self and is the part of you that you loathe. You usually perceive it as weak, ugly, twisted, and completely unacceptable. Phil tried to get me in touch with mine for years; I resisted. And each time he took me down the road where my shadow-self lived, I got to slowly and incrementally see what this little fellow looked and felt like, making it clearer and clearer why I wanted nothing to do with him. Well, after much poking and prodding, toward the end of the nineties I saw him, fully formed and in living color. He was very fat, of course. He was very weak, like "You're a pussy" weak, and he was essentially helpless. Phil sensed that I had arrived, that I finally had him in my purview. He said, "Now tell him you love him. Tell him he is precious and beautiful. Tell him you have his back and that you will always take care of him, never let anything bad happen to him, never let him down . . ."

Well, it wasn't hard to see that this was the part of Carl Jung's conclusion around which all others emanated. Just as I had become the parent to my children, I was now the parent of my own child. I was empowered, adult, responsible, and I loved myself for being badass enough to be ready to kick anyone's ass before I would let anything happen to that precious being. Phil said, "That's it. Get the fuck outta my office. You graduated. I got nothing left to teach you!" Well, that'll never happen; I'll always have things I'm gonna wanna hash out with Phil Stutz, my doctor, my guru, my friend.

Phil is now a celebrated author, having written a book with another brilliant psychiatrist, Barry Michels, with whom Phil shares a passion, called *The Tools*. When it got released Phil invited me to do an hour-long interview he and Barry were conducting as part of a series. I, along with a host of others who had spent time with Barry and Phil, shared their experiences and insights. I'm incredibly proud of that interview I did with the lads. (If ya get a chance and can find the link, check it out and lemme know whatcha think.)

I guess there was some other shit that went down in the nineties besides Phil, although all of it pales in comparison. I remember finding voice work in cartoons and falling head over heels for that. The first person who brought me into that world was Andrea Romano, who directed almost all the animation stuff for Warner Brothers that was and still is the biggest in the business. I mean Bugs, Yosemite, Road Runner, Porky, Daffy, and . . . need I say more? Andrea brought me in to do a regular lead role on a show called *Bonkers*. It was really cool, and I had a ball. I found the people who made their living doing nothing but voices to be some of the most raw, flat-out talents I had ever met. And I fell in love with the process: no rehearsal, no discussion—just get in there, give a balls-out performance, and get the fuck out. Couldn't get enough of it, and, indeed, I did a ton of it through the nineties. Kept me busy during the slow times.

And yeah, there were some movies and television thrown in during the nineties, but if you insist on reminiscing, you'll have to take a trip to IMDb, 'cuz I ain't getting into any of it. Suffice it to say, it was pretty much a period to coast, survive, and work on myself—that is, except for one little highlight, a freaky little French flick called *La cité des enfants perdus*, or *The City of Lost Children*.

(CHAPTER 18)

Enfants Perdus

The City of Lost Children required me to effect the most dramatic physical transformation I've ever had to make to my body. I worked my ass off, literally, to look like a street carnival strong man who could break chains with his bare chest. I ain't sayin' I had a six pack, but there was definitely a two-pack, which is twice as much as I normally have. But I was still young enough, hungry enough, and in love with the potential of the project enough to give me the focus to get into some serious shape. Even I couldn't get enough of me!

I got the role because the producers were looking for a foreigner; they were looking for somebody to create a character who was kind of a fish out of water, a country bumpkin, an innocent in a world of decay and decadence. They didn't quite know what his ethnicity would be; they just wanted somebody who wasn't facile with the French language. So after spending a huge amount of time trying to cast the role in France and, indeed, throughout the rest of Europe, they broadened their search even further outward. It just so happened that there was a midnight screening of *Cronos* at a horror festival in Paris that Marc Caro went to. He dug it enough to arrange a screening of it for Jean-Pierre Jeunet the following night. They thought enough of it to reach out to my agents, who shall remain nameless because they never returned the fucking call. Finally, out of pure frustration they called Jean-

Jacques Annaud to ask him how to get in touch with me. He in turn gave them my personal number. I guess the Hollywood types don't feel that dialing long distance to France is an expense worth making. 'Cuz shit, whoever heard of France? Whatever. Anyway, I eventually got word that they wanted to meet me. I was in Los Angeles, they were in France, and so we decided to split the difference.

I flew to New York, where they personally presented me the script, thus planning to give me a day to read and digest it before meeting the next day to make the formal offer. This turned out to be a good move, because it took me eleven hours to get through the fucker. It was so incredibly dense, layered, and textured, and on top of that, I think this English translation was created just so I could read it. I had to keep going back to the beginning. It was almost like trying to read *Titus Andronicus* because there were so many disparate facets to this completely made-up world; it was almost like Dickens on steroids. It was idiosyncratically postapocalyptic, if that's even a thing.

I remember I went to see this French movie called *Delicatessen*, maybe a year earlier, with Guillermo one night when he was in town. We went to this art house theater to see what the highly touted new innovative team of Jeunet and Caro had done. I had never seen anything like it; this was as pure an original form of cinema as anything I'd ever seen. I wouldn't compare it completely to Fellini, but it was certainly as stylized as that. Fellini sometimes made things so visually obtuse that they almost seemed like cinema for cinema's sake. Whether you actually understood them didn't really matter; you were enjoying Fellini's feast for the eye as well as all the other senses. That's kind of what *Delicatessen* was like, in which the world of the film, the logic of it, existed in some parallel universe created exclusively to embody a Rube Goldberg–style universe, where one thing would bump into another thing that would then lead to another that would bump to another. It was fascinating, yes, but also supremely clever and entertaining. And like nothing anyone had ever seen before. So going into this meeting for *City of Lost Children*, I knew I was going to be introduced to iconoclasts of the highest cinematic order.

Getting through the screenplay was akin to getting through *Name of the Rose*—there were many false starts because of the intricate and exotic world of the film. But around the fourth try I began flowing with it and started marveling at the premise of it, the richness of this imagined reality, and the epic scope that underscored its entirety. This was going to be way bigger than *Delicatessen*; this was a masterwork. When I finally got through the screenplay I spent the rest of the evening fretting about what would happen when they realized they got the wrong guy. 'Cuz this shit was way too good to be true. In my mind I had just read a masterpiece, something that, if executed properly, would take its place in the pantheon of film classics, the *Children of Paradise* of its generation. And from what I understood, the next step was to make me a straight offer—no audition, no screen test, nada. It couldn't possibly be me they were culminating their six-month search with.

The next day was to be lunch. At the table were Jeunet, Caro, and their producer, Claudie Ossard, who doubled as a translator because neither Jeunet nor Caro spoke a word of English. And let's face it, the C-minus I got in high school French was not fer nuthin'. No small talk, no foreplay, just right to the gusto: first question, "What do you think of our movie?" as if I were auditioning them! I'm thinking there must be a shoe that's about to drop any second, because no one ever offered me a movie of this sort out of the blue. But then there never was this sort of a movie. And clearly Europeans go about things differently from Hollywoodians. (Hollywoodinistas?) But indeed, these two guys came there to offer me this film on the condition that I liked the script and was willing to go do it—that's the only condition. So I kept saying, "What the fuck is wrong with this picture?" This can't be right. Maybe I *don't* wanna work on this picture 'cuz these guys are too naïve to know how shit's supposta work. And besides, to channel Groucho Marx, why would I wanna join any club that would have me as a member?!

So I started playing it cool and said, "Well, I have to show it to my people, and we have to talk about dates, because, you know . . . I'm very busy . . ." But fuck, if I wasn't dying to do this movie!

So we end up negotiating a deal, and I was off to the races. As soon as I got back to Los Angeles, I hired a trainer, joined Gold's Gym, to which I'm still a member, and proceeded to lose fifty-five pounds and get in as good a shape as I possibly could. I then went over to France for the next seven months and worked on one of the strangest, most intense productions I've ever participated in. It was almost like being on an acid trip, you know; the experience itself was bizarre from the onset. Every exchange between me and the two directors had to take place through a translator because I was the only one on the movie who didn't speak French, and they were the only ones who didn't speak English.

Jeunet had a country house in Normandy on the northern coast of France that he was very proud of and comfortable enough there to almost be a different guy from who he was on set. We used to go up there on weekends while we were in preproduction and have these long discussions about who this character I was playing was going to be, what his background was, and what made him so unique within this strange world of the film—again, every word of it through a translator. Eventually we decided to make the character a Russian sailor, somebody from Belarus, something like that, so he had a very Eastern European, kind of Baltic accent. My task was to learn the role in French and then speak it with a Russian accent. The only people who really understood I was speaking French with a Russian accent were French people because they're the only ones who know the difference between what French is supposed to sound like and what it sounds like when it is being butchered.

Eventually we commenced what was to be a six-month principal photography shoot. The location for the set was an abandoned airplane hangar about thirty kilometers south of Paris. Because everything Jeunet and Caro had ever done involved stylized environments with false perspectives, thus making their various worlds appear a few degrees off from center and slightly surreal, even though they might be shooting an exterior, it was always shot inside so as to manipulate the visuals as their minds imagined them to be. So the set for the movie was the section of a made-up, slightly apocalyptic city, including a harbor complete with ships that moved, neighborhoods, restaurants, butcher shops, patisserie, you name it, all within the confines of this massive space. It was the most magnificent piece of whimsy/harsh reality I'd ever seen. It was like Epcot meets 2036 World's Fair. To light the film they went back to Darius Khondji, who had just gotten finished setting the world on its ear with *Delicatessen* and was on the cusp of being the most sought-after cinematographer on the planet. Darius's plan was to have all of the actors' faces painted almost white so that when he color-corrected the film in postproduction back to natural skin tones, it skewed everything else in the frame, thus giving it a dreamlike-bordering-on-nightmarish quality. Genius, right?

Once we got under way the making of the movie felt like nothing I had ever experienced before—indeed, nor have I seen anything like it since. The tone of the set felt like church: it was the quietest set I'd ever been on, as if we were all involved in some secret experiment and were anxious about how it would come off. The directors' style of shooting was unique: we never shot scenes, we only shot shots. Each shot was a designed and calculated piece of a mosaic they would eventually turn into a seamless painting. But to give you an idea of how this translates, dailies for the first day of filming took twenty minutes to watch, as opposed to the three to five hours it usually takes on a more conventional shoot. Clearly this was no conventional shoot, and these were no conventional filmmakers.

All in all I felt I had been placed in a highly privileged, totally unique dreamscape in which the results were set up to be groundbreaking. Story-wise alone the piece was magnificent: this sick, twisted Dickensian world where just the mere act of survival obliterated love and where children are left completely on their own, to make it or not, and in the center of which is this pristine, gothic romance between the shrewdest, most hardened, gorgeous ten-year-old girl who is awakened to the feeling of love for the first time by this foreign-born country bumpkin who has just lost his little brother and is desperate to find something, anything in this world to care for. Shit, I'm crying while I'm writing this.

I'm pretty sure you're getting tired of hearing this by now, but I believed this project had *game-changer* written all over it. I know, I know, we've been down this road before. But *City of Lost Children*? Come on! EASY STREET. YA DIG?!

This time I *know* it is the real deal, and I'm licking my chops, getting ready to take the muthafuckin' world by storm, baby! By the way, did I mention Jean-Paul Gaultier was doing the costumes? I mean, come on, people! Then, while we're shooting I'm becoming very close friends with Claudie Ossard, who is producing the film. She's produced *Delicatessen*, along with a multitude of classic French films, and she's high-society in France and a real classy dame. Coincidentally, while we're shooting, the Cannes Film Festival was going on. This is Claudie's turf, baby. She is to Cannes what Dorothy Parker was to the round table.

She invited me to go down there with her on a private plane as her personal guest. "I'm showing you Cannes as you've never seen it before. Next year you're going to be here, and you're going to be the opening-night selection, and I want you to be prepared for what you're about to experience." Sounded pretty good to me. She showed me fucking Cannes as an outsider, as a wannabe, because nobody knew who the fuck I was. But by the time she got done with me, I knew that joint like the back of my hand. Because I saw Claudie Ossard's Cannes—champagne wishes and caviar dreams, baby, 'cuz she was French royalty, baby! Oh, and by the way, she turned out to be right: the next year *La cité des enfants perdu* was the opening-night selection at the Cannes Film Festival, or, as Sam Spade would call it, "The stuff that dreams are made of."

The reception at Cannes was tepid, very much like my own reaction to the film. I felt it was nothing like it had played out in my head when I was first absorbing it. And I wasn't all that enthralled by my own performance in it either—it's certainly one of those I'd like to have another crack at. And even though I personally disagree, there are many people, especially in the movie business, who hold that film in high regard. I don't argue. I learned in the aftermath of that film that what I think of me is none of my business. Anyway, Sony Classics distributed the film worldwide, and if the grosses are any indication at all, I'm not the only one who felt that way. *La cité* was the last picture Jean-Pierre and Marc worked on together. I went on to do one more with Jean-Pierre in what turned out to be his foray into big-time Hollywood studio filmmaking. In 1997 we did *Alien: Resurrection* together for 20th Century Fox. He and I remain close friends and are still threatening to find still another project to do together.

Anyway, as game-changers go, that wasn't it. But I am certainly overcome with a feeling of warmth every time I see that on my "shit I have done" list. So there's that—*Enfants perdus*!

(CHAPTER 19)

Como Day Peliculas . . .

So around the mid-nineties word started circulating around and about the environs of Hollywood of a retelling of *The Island of Dr. Moreau*. There were a number of reasons why I would have been compelled to participate in a revival of this tale, not the least of which is the fact that it's a classic title by one of the most brilliant iconoclast authors in the history of writing, H. G. Wells. In this case he wrote something so prescient, so cutting edge, and so, so ahead of its time. It concerned itself with futuristic experiments in vivisection, and he dreamed all this up in 1898, a full one hundred years prior to even a glimpse of a science that would embody these virtues. Wells must've been a frigging time traveler, because he identifies the concept of gene splicing, as the precursor to cloning and all the things that we were experimenting with in the 1990s. Plus, the cinematic versions also had a long history of distinguished people who were involved in it.

Charles Laughton had done a version of it, as did Burt Lancaster, and now there was gonna be a version of it done again nearly one hundred years after Wells wrote the book. New Line Cinema, which was at the time one of the majors, was going to be producing this new version. They were putting out amazing stuff: They were responsible for some of the best, most profitable pictures being churned out at the time, culminating with the *Lord of the Rings* trilogy. Having just come off a little sleeper hit called *Don Juan Demarco,* the nineties was New Line Cinema's strongest decade, and we were right in the midst of that, with the film company flexing its already formidable muscles.

But the number-one reason why one would deign to drop everything and put on four hours worth of makeup again, which, at this point, I was sure I'd sworn off doing, was that this newest retelling had the incomparable Marlon Brando playing Dr. Moreau, or at least that was the rumor. As I mentioned earlier, the chance to even be around this man would have had to be the single-most profound privilege any actor could imagine. From the moment he burst onto the screen he was the most important actor in the history of the medium—indeed, in a class all by himself. His performance in *The Godfather* was the last of three times in his career in which he deigned to turn on this gear that no one else has ever come close to having, and those of us like me, who are real students of the game, can't even begin to analyze how he did what he did, which is another reason for the fascination. Even though generations of us tried to imitate him, tried to find moments, pockets of that kind of clarity, that kind of human behavioral verisimilitude, there was only one Brando. And even he didn't let himself let it all hang out very often, so no one knew when it would come flying out again.

So it was doubtful that I was gonna get the Vito Corleone version of Brando on *Island of Dr. Moreau,* but even if I just got a shadow of the man, I was good to go. What they didn't know was that they didn't even have to pay me. I would have showed up for free just to fuckin' observe the guy, analyze him, breathe the same air as him.

The man whose idea it was to do a new adaptation of *Island of Dr. Moreau* was a filmmaker named Richard Stanley who, according to the last rumor I heard, had gone feral and was living in a tree somewhere in the middle of London. And it all started with *The Island of Dr. Moreau.* The loss of his beloved version of the movie drove him over the edge. But Richard Stanley had a take on why it was a great idea to do another adaptation of this story that was so compelling that he was able to attract even Marlon Brando himself to the idea of being involved with the film.

Brando, as well as Johnny Depp, had just come off *Don Juan De Marco*, so they were responsible for one of the biggest hits the studio had ever enjoyed. It also signaled to the community that maybe the old man was back. So at that point Marlon Brando was green-lighting movies again. If he said he wanted to do a movie, *boom*. Whatever kind of budget they needed, they got. So Brando came on board, Richard Stanley went to New Line and said, "I've got Marlon Brando." They said, "Let's do it." And *boom*, the train starts moving and the search is on to put this bad boy together. The first one on board to play the lead opposite Marlon was Rob Morrow. Next came Val Kilmer and then Fairuza Balk, both of whom were at the peak of their powers. And then there was the rest of the cast set to play the creatures, all hand-picked by Richard Stanley, whose particular expertise lay in the horror genre. It turned out he was a bit of a fan boy of mine, which I didn't know before, and he wanted me to play one of the more featured of the creature parts. It's kind of like he had that same fascination with me that Guillermo had, because he was really into these kinds of transformational performances I was known for. It was clear that I was gonna be in the movie, playing one of the experiments, one of these half-man, half-whatever creatures Dr. Moreau made that lived on this island where he could work on his experiments unfettered, without the watchful eye of society telling him that he was insane and should be in an institution or maybe even a prison cell, which is the premise of the story.

Mine wasn't a gigantic role, but I did have one huge scene and then a couple of little tiny pops. So they hired me for three weeks and paid a decent sum of money for me, which surprised me, as I didn't have a lot of leverage at the time. Once the deal was set, I was due to fly in about ten days, which was already two weeks after filming had begun. The shooting was in the far north part of Queensland, Australia, in a city called Cairns—C-A-I-R-N-S. They pronounce it *Cannes*, but it was a far cry from the French Riviera. It's Cairns, right on the Great Barrier Reef, in the middle of an absolutely pristine rainforest. It was a pretty magnificent location. Perfect for *The Island of Dr. Moreau*.

When filming began I was still in Los Angeles and we started hearing rumors, because this is obviously the movie that we're all getting ready to go do. (The wheels of Hollywood, by the way, are greased with rumors!) So these rumors are filtering down, and I became quite caught up in hearing them but was having trouble discerning which parts of them were true, 'cuz they're all really fuckin' weird! Apparently the first day of filming was a disaster. They got nothing in the can. There was supposed to be all the stuff on the water with Val Kilmer en route to the mainland to pick up a shipment of things Moreau needed for his experiments. Val Kilmer was playing his right-hand man, his facilitator. Then the rumor came down that day two was even worse than day one. Then by day three they had about 6 percent of everything they needed for the first three days in the can, but it was basically a disaster as well. By day four, the rumors said, every time Richard Stanley said "Action!" Val walked out of frame and refused to walk back in. So Val had created a stonewall situation, and it was clear that he did not feel confident with Stanley at the helm.

Now, this was a big movie with a lot of moving parts, not the least of which is that Brando was due to come over around the same time as I was, and the budget . . . well, it ain't small! So they shut down production, and the takeaway is that they relieve Richard Stanley of his duties as the director. For the next week there were just a *shitload* of crazy rumors flying all around town, stuff like questions of whether the movie is going to get completely shelved or whether they're going to figure out a way to salvage it. Then the rumors started coming that there's a parade of filmmakers going up and down Mulholland Drive being interviewed by Brando himself because they're allowing "the man" to decide whether there's somebody else he's even remotely willing to do this picture with, as Richard Stanley was the guy who attracted him to the project to begin with.

I was actually getting calls from filmmakers I knew who were being interviewed, asking me, "What should I expect?"

"Well, I don't know," I told them. "I've not met Marlon yet. All I'm hearing are the same rumors you are. So I don't know what to tell you, but I know for a fact that he signed on for a movie that was a personal vision of a highly invested filmmaker, Stanley." You don't do *The Island of Dr. Moreau* unless you have a really specific vision of why the fuck to do a third retelling of it when there's already been two movies of it already. So it's not the kind of movie where you just get a director-for-hire to come in and pick up the pieces. Richard Stanley was obviously walking around with his concept of *The Island of Dr. Moreau* for a long time and had an interesting enough take on the story to get a whole lotta heavyweights on board. So replacing Stanley was gonna be really tricky.

At the end of the day there was a world-class director who was just reemerging from a twelve-year exile due to problems in the middle of his career with alcohol, which had benched him. But he was one of the greatest filmmakers of the second half of the twentieth century. He created some amazing movies. And then he started making these great MOWs (movies of the week), epic movies for television. His name was John Frankenheimer, and he started winning awards because these huge epic movies for television he was making were phenomenal. So he was clearly sending the signal that he was sober, he was back, and he was ready to play. They were going to give Frankenheimer a shot at a feature film, something he hadn't had in twelve years. And it was gonna be *The Island of Dr. Moreau*.

Apparently Marlon signed off on Frankenheimer and the studio agreed. They weren't sure exactly when I should be getting on a plane, but I was told to stand by because it could be any day. Sure enough, about a week later they said, "Okay, Ron, you go over there now. We need you for preproduction; makeup test, wardrobe, creature orientation, the works. John is reconfiguring the movie; he would like all his cast around him." So I went over there and got on phenomenally well with John. We hit it off immediately. There's a huge amount of warmth and mutual respect between the two of us. So one day, because I'm to play the Sayer of the Law, which is kind of a classic character, I have an epiphany. The role of the Sayer was kind of pivotal because in order for Moreau, in his obsession to civilize the beast, to create a subsociety with the constraint of law and order, there needed to be a figure in that society who represented those conditions—ergo the Sayer of the Law. It was one of H. G. Wells's most compelling creations and had always been given due treatment in all the other adaptations. Bela Lugosi played him in the Charles Laughton version, and Richard Basehart played him in the Burt Lancaster one. When we see the character most heavily featured it is in the mock trial Moreau would preside over for whenever one of his flock crossed back over to primal, animal behavior. The Sayer was almost like the court clerk who, in incantation form, reads off a litany of laws, values, and mores of the community, thus identifying which of the laws had been broken.

Anyway, getting back to me, so I had this epiphany shortly after arriving in Australia: what if I were to play the character blind? Know what I'm sayin'? *Blind*, muthafucka! Ya know, like justice is? Anyways, while you digest that for a moment, lemme say that the moment I let the genie out of the bottle with that one, I couldn't get it back in. I became obsessed with the idea: justice—blind, blind justice. So I went to Frankenheimer with it, who judiciously asked for a day or two to slosh it around his brain. The following day he came to me and asked what it would take to pull it off. I told him I already had a chat with the makeup boys, who said they could supply me with milky, opaque contact lenses that would not only make me *look* blind but would actually *make* me blind. Worst fucking idea I ever had in my whole life. Which, of course, I didn't realize until it was way too late. Obviously, Frankenheimer said, "Ron, I love it. The Sayer is blind!"

Meanwhile every night we have a welcoming party for Brando 'cuz every day he was expected to arrive. The only problem is, with each passing day, no Brando. We say *fuck it* and keep the parties going just in case; we knew we were gonna get lucky eventually. Rumors are abounding as to when and also from where the man will be flying in. First we think he's coming from his house in LA, so a PA is stationed at the local airport greeting every flight from there. Then we hear, no, actually Marlon went to Japan, so then this poor girl is meeting every flight from LA and from Tokyo. Next thing we know the big B decided to stop off at his island near Tahiti. So now this poor girl is meeting every flight from LA, Tokyo, and Tahiti. Finally the producers pull her from her airport detail and, whuddya know, fuckin' Brando shows up on the next fuckin' plane from LA and there's nobody at the airport to greet him. So he charms his way through customs as only Marlon could do and ends up takin' a fuckin' cab to a hotel. I still have the *Cairns Tribune* newspaper from the next day that said, NO ONE TO MEET MARLON!

Meanwhile, Frankenheimer had been falling all over himself trying to figure out what the fuck to shoot 'cuz Marlon wasn't there. So he was making shit up; he was vamping. He was shooting this and shooting that. While the cast and crew were starting to bond, all of us tickled with excitement—we all knew we were about to meet a living legend, a god, somebody who occupies a space that's never been occupied before on the highest mountain in all of filmmaking. That's what was sustaining us.

Marlon's entire entourage consisted of three people: a woman by the name of Caroline, who does everything for him (yeah, everything!), a makeup artist named Fred, and Fred's wife, who does his hair. But she doesn't really do his hair; she's just Fred's wife, so she's on the payroll. Oh, and by the way, Fred doesn't really do his makeup; he's just a dude who used to be an actor. They met on the set of *On the Waterfront* and had been buds ever since. Fred's acting career never got into gear, so Marlon found a way to keep him in his life. What Fred really did was hold up a mirror while Marlon did his own makeup. Damn good at it too. And that was the entirety of Marlon's entourage.

And I've seen entourages. One ex–movie star, who shall remain anonymous, traveled with a dozen people, three trailers—a gym, a kitchen to make him designer food, and a mini–country club to hang out in. The entourage had twelve actual people, including bodyguards, accountants, stand-ins and doubles, chefs, and the PCBJ, otherwise known as the Person who Coordinates . . . you can figure out the rest. But Marlon's got this chick whose main gig is to sit there on the sidelines saying his lines into a microphone so Marlon can hear them in his earpiece. That was his new way of working. He used to have cue cards; now he has an earpiece. And this makeup artist who doesn't do makeup and his wife who's a hairdresser who doesn't do hair.

By the time Marlon got there, the budget for the "Welcoming Marlon" parties had already dried up, so the night he arrived there was no party—indeed, no fanfare whatsoever. I, however, having done my homework and knowing all things Brando, knew what a freak he was for Afro-Cuban music, and I happen to own quite a good and obscure collection of it myself. So I put together my five favorite CDs and sent them to Marlon's room as a welcoming present. Anyway, the next morning, the morning when he was supposed to come to work, I had a three o'clock call because I have a four-hour makeup session, and they wanted me ready by seven. All of us, all the creatures are in the makeup chair. Marlon was supposed to be arriving at eight. We all kind of have our ear to the window, waiting to hear his motorcade pull onto the set because we were all dying for our first glimpse of the man, the myth, the legend. Everyone was kind of on the edge of their seats because we knew he was on his way to base camp. This was like you're an eight-year-old kid and Santa is about to come down the chimney for real and you're going to finally find out whether he is indeed a myth or there's actually blood flowing through his veins. And whatever the fuck else you can get.

We all got finished with our makeup as we were ordered to be, by 7:30 to 8 o'clock in the morning. But we really can't shoot anything without the man himself 'cuz we ran outta shit days ago, so the whole schedule for that day is based around his scenes. Eight o'clock, no Brando. They tell us, "Have breakfast." We finished breakfast by 8:30, and then we sat around: 9:30, 10:30, 11 o'clock—nuthin'. You could hear your own hair growing. Then suddenly, around 11:30, we saw this energy field kinda materialize, like a twister is coming through town, and a whole bunch of people were mobilizing. Sure enough, this retinue of vehicles came bursting up the road, and the word is that the man was in one of those cars. So everybody suddenly wanted to look casual. But they couldn't help themselves. They got as close to the road as possible to get a glimpse of him getting out of the car. But all we got was a cloud of dust and gas fumes as his car blew right through base camp and kept going for another mile down the road. What the fuck just happened? Everybody was like, "Isn't this base camp? This is where his trailer is, no?"

We came to find out that he had his trailer stationed half a mile away from everybody else's, so he was gunning it right through base camp on his way to his little Marlon village. From that moment on, everything was communicated via rumor, with little tidbits of information funneling on down through the grapevine.

So by now, a half-hour, hour went by, and it was around 12:30. We weren't hearing very much. We did hear that, yes, in fact, that was Marlon's car. And yes, in fact, he was in his trailer, but nobody was ready to shoot anything and it was going to be a while before anybody would be. So they break us for lunch. Lunch was really the first thing that happened since breakfast. So at least we'd all be well fed on this particular day. Lunch came and went, people started breaking out in chit-chat clubs, and folks were running into town for decks of cards. Some of the Chinese people were playing Mahjong. It was just like, let's kill the fucking afternoon. At around four o'clock we were all kind of in our bathrobes and underwear and shit. We still had our makeup on. All of these exotic makeups needed to be touched up every few minutes, certainly once an hour because they tend to move and evolve, and compromise, and so forth. And it was fucking hot 'cuz we're in Australia and there's no fuckin' ozone layer. It's now nine hours since we got finished getting made up when all of a sudden the word came down: "Everybody get dressed and get in a vehicle immediately. We're going for a shot!"

So there was panic in River City. And sure enough, everybody was runnin' around like idiots and was just grabbing whatever vehicle, whatever van they could get into, going where, no one the fuck knows. The location they were going to shoot the shot in is half a mile down the road, right near where Marlonville's little trailer park is, the irony of which didn't escape me. I piled in a van with a bunch of other creatures, but nobody knew any more than anybody else. One thing was for sure, though: there was a lot of high-pitched yelling and screaming. We saw way off in the distance that there was an entourage of vehicles, one of which was like a Popemobile. It was a jeep that had a platform on top of a vehicle, upon which sat a throne-like chair. Off in the distance we saw a large figure, all in white, being helped onto the top of this Popemobile, and then we heard a lot of ADs over the radio saying, "Everybody get ready for the take."

Meanwhile nobody knew what the fuck we were shooting. No one had told us anything. We were all just assembled and gathered, and we knew that this thing is about seven hundred feet away, this vehicle with what we can only assume is Marlon atop. And it's going to be coming toward us, and they're going to be shooting something. Sure enough, we heard, "Action!" We saw this caravan of vehicles beginning to move forward. By the time the shot got done, it was about five minutes to five. You lose the light in far north Queensland that time of year at around 4:45, so it was almost dark when we got done with the shot. Then the first AD yelled, "Great day, everybody. That's a wrap." Everybody knew the shot was completely unusable, but they were shooting something because, if they didn't shoot something, they would have had to put another wasted day on the production report. That would mean that somebody else's head was going to roll along with the dozen or so that had preceded it. We had already lost a director, two or three production managers, and three of the stars, and we hadn't even really started yet.

Everybody just stood there, waiting around to see what happened next. Marlon was up on his perched platformy throne-like thingy, atop this moving vehicle. People were whispering things at him, and he was saying things to them, and we were really too far away to know what was going down. But apparently he said, "I would like to meet the rest of the cast," because he spent the entire day in a private rehearsal with David Thewlis, Val Kilmer, Fairuza Balk, and then the makeup emissary from Stan Winston. Oh, and the director, John Frankenheimer.

That's what was happening all day; that's what brought us to four o'clock in the afternoon.

So they paraded us out to meet Marlon, and the first person Frankenheimer thought to introduce to him was me. He said, "Ron Perlman, come over here and meet Mr. Brando."

I saw Brando saying, like for the eightieth time, "John, I told you. I'm not Mr. Brando. I'm Marlon." So he started this mini-argument with Frankenheimer, and he was looking around as I was walking up to him, and he was saying, "Jesus Christ, these makeups are amazing. Who did the makeup?"

Just as he asked that question, Frankenheimer said, "Marlon Brando, meet Ron Perlman."

Now, I was dressed as a goat with ram horns in a Dashiki, and he said to me, "Oh, you did the makeup. Wow, that's fantastic. Can you tell me what your process is?"

"Sorry to disappoint you, sir," I said, "but no, I didn't do the makeup."

"Well, who the hell are you?" he asked.

"I'm just playing a character in the movie, sir," I said, "named the Sayer of the Law."

"Oh, okay," he said. "So you didn't do the makeup."

"No sir," I said. "Stan Winston did the makeup, sir." And suddenly Marlon was looking really sad that I had the balls to not be the makeup man. And that was my first exchange with Marlon Brando . . . not exactly like I drew it up.

So anyway, once he got over the disappointment that I was not who I said I was, they kept introducing him to the rest of the cast one at a time, and there continue to be these rather awkward exchanges while he was taking in the marvels of the world that Stan Winston had created. Finally the last person who got introduced to him was a little guy named Nelson de la Rosa from the Dominican Republic. I say little guy: Nelson de la Rosa was the smallest mobile human being on record, standing tall at twenty-seven inches. (There's another guy who was twenty-six inches, but he couldn't move, so we couldn't use him.)

Now, Nelson, who was in the Guinness Book of Records, had a bit of a following in the Dominican Republic. He was sort of a celebrity down there because he was a regular on one of the more watched variety shows. When they were about to introduce him, Marlon leaned forward and seemed to be in shock.

Yes, Nelson was able to move about, but with some difficulty, so, as much as possible, one of his handlers carried him around. He had these two very young, very sexy girls who he'd brought with him from the Dominican Republic to take care of his every need. They were kind of cute and personable, and Nelson spent all of his time just tweaking their nipples because Nelson was a sexaholic. Like totally out of control. So as they were carrying him over to meet Marlon, Nelson was actually trying to remove this girl's breast from her blouse and her bra. He didn't have a clue who the fuck Marlon Brando was; he was just looking for someplace to stick his little boner. When Marlon finally focused in on this thing that he was about to meet, his eyes got so big they nearly fell out of his fuckin' head, just like one of those cartoons in which the eyeballs are on springs. He looked like a kid who was watching Santa opening his favorite toy. Originally Nelson was basically just hired to be a background player: I mean here we are doing this exposé on this uniquely freakish subsociety, and . . . you get the picture. But as soon as Brando got a gander at this little dude, *BOOM*, a star was born. Brando said to him, "How many movies have you been in?"

There's nuthin' from the little guy. Somebody yelled out, "He only speaks Spanish Mr. B."

Brando segued, "Oh. Uh . . . como day peliculas a tu uh, been in?"

"Oh, dos," shot back the little guy, proudly holding up two tiny little fingers.

And before I could restrain myself I blurted out, "Yeah, and both of 'em were this one!" Another sad look from Brando. This was not going well for the Perl.

From that moment on Marlon became so fascinated with this character that he elevated him to being a kind of mini-me. He became Dr.

Moreau's alter ego. And every time you saw Dr. Moreau on the screen, Nelson was there, dressed in the exact same outfit as him, only tinier. There's even a scene that Marlon created in which Moreau is playing a baby grand piano, and he had the art department build a tiny baby grand to sit on top of the real one while they ferociously played duets.

At any rate, from the moment Marlon laid eyes on little Nelson, Marlon saw an opportunity to build his entire world using this device as a lynchpin to unearth the experimental nature of Moreau's obsession with creating the ultimate subculture. And we all saw it happening right in front of our eyes. Marlon Brando! Like him or not, he was flat-fucking fascinating.

CHAPTER 20

The Doctor Will See You Now

The only real scene I originally had in the film was a big trial scene. In it, one of the members of Moreau's merry band of freaks crosses the line of civility and must be dealt with summarily. The Sayer of the Law had the task of reciting the litany of laws in a ritualistic form to remind everyone of the limits of their little society. The speech was lifted straight out of the H. G. Wells novel, thus maintaining purity to the storytelling that was sacrosanct. "Do not slurp but sip. Do not go on all fours"—weird shit like that. The Sayer's job is to remind the villagers of unyielding absolutism of these laws, that there is a corporeal implication for any behavior that falls short of human. The scene I was essentially there to do involved one of our members' brutal taking down of prey. By slipping back into the feral, he had broken one of Moreau's most sacred trusts. The individual is put on a trial conducted by the Sayer. Moreau is the judge of the trial, and the entire community is present. It was a huge, complicated scene, with a lot of moving parts.

It was during those days I was acting with the great one, because he's sitting there on his makeshift bench like you see in courtrooms, but in an outdoor amphitheater of sorts. I was standing by his side with a rod, as if I'm some sort of symbol of justice. I was saying these incantations, and when I get to the incantation, "Thou shalt not kill," Moreau stops me and says, "That law has been broken." And the trial ensues. So this scene was scheduled to take a day and a half to shoot; it ended up taking five and a half because it was a hot mess. There were 250 extras and a lot of disorganization. There was a lot of reinterpretation taking place when Frankenheimer saw what Marlon wanted to do and how he wanted to fold little Nelson into the scenario. There was a lot of planning and replanning and then throwing everything away and replanning anew.

But luckily for me, that meant I was enabled to do multiple takes with Marlon, shooting from a number of different angles and in a number of different ways. Five days is five days—you really get a chance to spend quality time with a guy when he's two feet away from you on a stage and you are depending upon each other to conduct the shape of what transpires.

Because this was a day scene and we needed to catch as much light as the winter months would yield, each day we were in the makeup chair at three in the morning in order to be shoot-ready at seven. Whoever had picked this location thought that because we were in the South Pacific, the days would be really long, when in fact we only had daylight from around 6:30 in the morning till 4:30 in the afternoon, which was a major snafu for a film company that's depending on fourteen hours of sunlight a day to keep anywhere near budget. For the first couple of days Marlon arrived at 8:30 or 9, and it took him a while to get up to speed as to what was going down. Once he got up to speed, he was terrific. He was fantastic. And he was very much like a kid in a carnival, especially in this scene. He was surrounded by these incredibly exotic, truly imaginative creations that Stan Winston had spent so much of his time and artistry to develop. You could sense Marlon really appreciated this creativity and was wide-eyed and enthusiastic about being a part of this incredibly well imagined world. He would turn around and say, "Look at that guy! That's some weird shit right there."

He was this beautiful, innocent, very fun, very loving guy who really, really just wanted to fit in. Just wanted to entertain himself. He just wanted to entertain others. He was very curious about who you were, how you got here, what you were doing later: Where do you eat around here? Where does a guy get a drink? Blah blah blah. Don't get me wrong—Marlon had developed a series of little tests he put people through, but I came to understand that it was just his way of separating the people he could trust from the sycophants. But once you passed through his little ritual and were given the seal of approval, the man let down his guard and became as accessible and wonderfully human as anybody I'd ever met. And so after a bit of test specially designed by Marlon himself, suddenly the mystique of him melted away, and what replaced it was sweetness, kindness, and a childlike obsession to spend as much of the day as possible just laughing and cutting up. He hated pretense and despised anyone who treated him like anything other than just one of the boys.

This was the first movie he had done since the incident when his son Christian shot his son-in-law Dag Drollet, a wretched affair that had unfortunately played out in front of the eyes of the world. The family had been through a horrific trial in Los Angeles, in which Christian ultimately ended up being found guilty of manslaughter and sentenced to five years in prison. As a result, the people of Terraria turned on Brando, making it clear that he was unwelcome back in the community. What made this even more tragic than it already was, was that the island of Terraria, which he had bought while filming *Mutiny on the Bounty*, was the one place on this Earth where he could go to find true peace and contentment. It was a place where he could just be Marlon, or Pops, as he liked to be called, without the ugly glare of the public eye invading his precious desire to just be normal. He lost his safe haven, and his son was in jail. And on top of that, in the aftermath of this incident and as a result of this emotional sorrow, his daughter Cheyenne, who was the apple of his eye, killed herself. So we were getting Marlon in a state in which he was trying to put on as good a face as possible, trying to be as professional as possible, but you could tell he was profoundly wounded emotionally and had suffered a really horrific blow. At the end of the day, even though he wasn't a traditional parent—he had probably eight kids who he actually took care of—he truly loved his family and truly took care of anybody in his orbit, so this was a blow to him.

So for Marlon to be in the South Pacific, on the one hand, the rain-forest was soothing him somehow by reminding him of his beloved Tahiti, and yet, on the other hand, it was causing him to feel a longing and sorrow. In my obsession to observe him, I was really seeing a man who was actually holding on for dear life, trying to find some sense to it all and some equilibrium. He did his very best to remain positive. I learned that if you had a joke to tell him or a funny story to tell him, he would completely just drop everything he was doing to hear it. And then he would return with two or three other funny stories of his own. So he was a guy who was very, very happy to be entertained and to be around entertaining people. There was this kind of adolescent, wide-eyed innocence to him that was infectious, and that was quite beautiful. He had the capacity to be very generous and very kind.

One of the first things that happened on day two of the filming of this trial scene was that Frankenheimer decided to do Marlon's close-ups. He wanted to do a medium shot and a close-up of Marlon so that the crowd that we're playing to, the community for this trial, is behind him. So Marlon said, "Okay, so if you're setting up to do coverage on me, I want you to take these two hundred people and put them in the shade—we don't need them now."

But Frankenheimer said, "Well, Marlon, I'm going to keep them here. I need them here for reaction."

"John," Marlon said, "I don't think you heard me. We're in Northern Australia. There's no fucking ozone layer. The sun is beating down on these people in masks and heavy clothing, and you're asking them to stand out there in this field, uncovered and unprotected, while you're shooting through them onto me. So I want you to put them in a shady place. I want you to get every one of them a Coca-Cola, and if I gotta pay for it, just put it on my bill. I want you to take care of that right now, 'cuz I'm not going to do anything until you do. And by the way, get rid of this guy, because he's bothering me." The "this guy" he was referring to was me. Then he said, "And then I'll be ready to do my close-up."

"Marlon," Frankenheimer said, "you don't understand. The crowd must stay because I need to feel free to move the camera and maybe get a glimpse of them."

And, shrewdly, Marlon said, "You mean you think you might see a reflection of the crowd through my sunglasses?"

John answered, "I'm actually going to try to get that."

To which Marlon said, "You're never gonna be able to get that."

"What do you mean I'm never going to be able to get that?"

"Because I'm gonna play the whole fuckin' scene like this," and Marlon put his head up so he was facing the sky, so the only thing you could see reflected in his glasses was clouds. Marlon said, "So fuck you, you're not getting the crowd. Put them in the shade and give them a soda because you're a fucking Nazi, John."

"I am not a Nazi, Marlon," Frankenheimer said. I'm standing there looking at this thing. These guys might actually be getting ready to start throwin' fists!

"You're a fucking Nazi, John," Marlon said. "A fucking Nazi wouldn't want to put these people in the shade. You're a Nazi."

"How could you call me that? That's a horrible thing to call a person."

Then Marlon said—and this was my favorite part—"Have you ever seen a movie called *Young Lions*?"

"Of course I did," Frankenheimer said. "It was directed by Edward Dmytryk. It was you, it was Montgomery Clift, it was Maximilian Schell, it was Dean Martin. You played a German officer. You were great in that movie!"

"That's right I did," Marlon said. "I know Nazis. And you're a fucking Nazi, John!"

So Frankenheimer said, "Okay, I'll tell you what. I'll make a deal with you. We'll put the crowd in the shade. They don't have to be here, but Ron Perlman stays."

"Why, John?" Brando asked. "Why does he gotta stay?"

"What is it about him that's bothering you?"

"He's saying these fucking words that are so fucking weird that I don't think I can concentrate. Every time he speaks, he throws me off."

"Well, those are the words, the incantations that are in the script," Frankenheimer said.

"Well I don't give a shit, it's bothering me," Marlon said. "We gotta cut 'em or something."

Finally I chimed in: "H. G. Wells himself wrote those words. I'll do anything ya want, but it'd sure be nice if we could figure out a way to keep 'em."

So Marlon said, "Okay, okay, you can stay, but fer Chistsakes, can you say 'em a little quieter, like almost so I can't hear you?"

"Yeah," I said. "Whatever you need, Pops. Whatever you need." So that was my really true first working exchange with Marlon. What started out as awkward is goin' downhill fast!

I realized, okay, I'm in some sort of game here that I'm not quite sure how to play. But he just kind of singled me out. He doesn't really know me. He's kind of thrown down some sort of gauntlet, and I actually feel like I'm being challenged in some sort of way. I've got these goat horns on, and I look like a fucking idiot. I got to say these stupid words that were written in 1896 that are really tough to say without sounding like a putz, but hey, that's how H. G. wanted 'em. So as much as I don't like being here anymore, clearly Marlon likes it even less. The whole thing is fucked up, but we're going to have to do this, like it or not, for the next however many hours—shit, days—'cuz we gotta get this muthafucka in the can.

So, sure enough, they broke for lunch to light the scene so that they could start shooting Marlon's coverage. I walked away from set, but I didn't go to lunch. I went straight to my trailer to throw up. Thank God for the makeup, so no one could really see my face, but I was an inch away from ballin' my eyes out. Here I've come 16 gazillion hundred fuckin' miles, put fuckin' horns on my head, studied my ass off so I could finally, finally be in the glow of the greatest of all time, and as soon as it's showtime, he decides to obliterate me.

It took me the whole lunch hour to pull my shit together, but as work time was approaching, I started saying to myself, *I'm a professional actor. I've been hired to do a job. I have not only a right but also an obligation to be here. I sure wish my hero hadn't broken my heart, but he did, so that's that. Fuck what he thinks of me. Let's do this!*

We took our places on set; Billy Fraker, one of the greatest cinematographers of all time, finished tweaking the lights; and the first AD rolled camera. Frankenheimer yelled, "Action!" and it was fucking on. I said a line, and he said a line back, and then I said another line, and he said another line back. And suddenly it was startin' to cook. And I'm feeling so proud of myself that I start celebrating in my head. And then there was this long, awkward silence. I was looking around, thinking, *Hmmm, somebody done fucked up here.* I heard Marlon say, "It's your line."

Now you have to understand, I had these lenses in so I was completely blind. I couldn't see my hand in front of my face. I could only hear Marlon. I didn't even know that he was physically there because I couldn't see anything. I was wondering who he was talking to. He was saying, "Hey! You with the horns! It's your line." It was the first time in my entire career that I had gone up on my lines because I was so caught up in the coolness of this. For all I know, they'll be comparing this to the taxi scene between him and Rod Steiger.

So when I finally realized that it's just him and me in the scene and that I'm the only one wearing horns, it hit me: *Oh shit, he's talking to me!* And I said, "Oh, I'm sorry, that's my line, isn't it?"

And Marlon said, "That's okay, let's go back. Let's start again. Let me know when you're ready." Little by little I could see he was beginning to become sympathetic toward me because he was seeing that I was really standing my ground, driving the scene, proving myself to him, just like he designed it when he was giving me shit earlier. Then he said, "Let me know when you're ready." I had him. He was on my wavelength. We were gonna fucking act this scene—together!

He let me kind of run that scene from that point on, and we ended up doing about two or three takes from each angle. With each take I could feel him coming with me deeper into dialogue. Without saying a word to each other, he figured out exactly what I needed to drive the scene, and I got more and more specific the more he gave me. And it didn't take too long before he said, "I like that one. How did you feel?"

"I'm good too," I said.

"Yeah, I think we got it," he said. "Let's move on."

By the end of all the coverage, despite a little bit of a rocky start, we were two guys that had been on the same wavelength for a little while. That's a feeling I just can't describe. But it's beautiful. It's why I love this thing that I do, that I've done for forty years. Except this time I got to do it with Zeus! So for the next three and a half days, till we finished this thing, it was clear sailing with me and Pops. In fact, I'm *so* loose that the jokes start flowin'. That's when I realized for myself what I had heard from people for years: that if you could make Marlon laugh, you owned him.

Anyway, for the next four days we were shooting this same scene. And for four days, after we finished a shot, Pops would split back to his trailer and wait for the team to change set-ups. But because I kinda got nauseated every time they popped my lenses in or out, I decided to just keep them in. So instead of leaving the set, I just sat there and waited. Which meant that every time Marlon got called back to set, he'd have to move his 320-pound frame around me on the tiny platform to get back to his throne. And I'd hear him mumble shit, stuff like, "Jesus, you're not a small guy, and I'm not a small guy. You could at least gimme a little room to maneuver here." And I'd throw out some little barbs that got him to chuckle, and we'd go back to work.

Finally, on the fifth day of shooting this scene I was sitting on my little stool, waiting, when I felt these two hands violently grab my shoulders. I mean, I jumped out of my fucking skin! I jumped up and turned to figure out who the fuck just did that, even though I couldn't see shit. After a few seconds I heard Marlon say, "Holy shit, what's that in your eyes?"

"What do you mean?" I asked.

"Wait a minute," he said. "Holy shit, are you . . . are you playing this character blind?"

"Marlon, yer fuckin' with me, right?" I said.

"No man," he said. "I'm asking you if you're playing him blind?!"

"Marlon," I said, "we've been doing this fucking scene for five and a half days, and you're asking me now if I'm playin' the fuckin' guy blind? You're kidding, right?"

Then Marlon said, "Hey John! He's playing the guy blind! Oh man, we've gotta start again."

"What are you talking about, Marlon?" Frankenheimer said.

"If I knew that he was playing the guy blind," Marlon said, "I would have played it completely differently. We gotta go back and start again!"

"Fuck you, Marlon," Frankenheimer said. "We're not starting again."

"I was just kidding, John." And then Marlon turned back to me and said, "And by the way, are you the guy that sent me all that Afro-Cuban music when I first got here?"

"Yeah," I said. "I was wondering if you got it, 'cuz I never heard from ya!"

"Oh man, Caroline just told me it was you. That shit is great! You shoulda come to my trailer. I been dancing my ass off the whole time!"

"Wow," I said. "That would have been fun. Maybe when we do *The Island of Dr Moreau II!*" And he gave me a hug and a kiss on the face.

Then he said, "You're playing blind. You're playing the guy who's responsible for justice, blind. That's fucking genius." He was whispering this shit to me. That was the first time he realized I was not this fucking lump who had just been sitting there in his way every time he had to get in and out of his chair, that I had actually given this thing some thought. Shit, I'da never thought of something like that had I not been a voracious student of the Marlon Brando School of Acting! It was kinda nice to see that he approved.

Meanwhile, Marlon, without the sanctuary of Tahiti, was robbed of that last place on Earth where he could truly find the solace he so desperately craved. By the time I met him, he was somewhat of a tragic figure. Somebody who, in spite of whatever he tried to do to create a peaceful world for himself, was just destined to have it elude him. I got all of that from watching him in his quiet moments, from watching him fight back the tears when he knew nobody was looking because of what he was going through at the time. I could see the heaviness visit itself on him and would watch him wrestle to distract himself from it. I saw all that. And I felt for him, for how deeply I could see him caring about things he couldn't control, but only when nobody was watching. I adored the guy . . .

I never pursued a relationship, even though I probably could've. I'm sure that if I had knocked on his door and said, "Hey Marlon, let's have a drink," he would have welcomed me in. A few weeks after we had shot that scene I started wondering what else there was for me to do on the movie. Frankenheimer answered me before I even got a chance to ask the question: "Do you know why you've been here this long?"

"No," I said. "I don't know, John. I've been wondering about that."

"Because every time we talk about our approach to a scene, Marlon says, 'Have the guy from *Name of the Rose* do it. Give this stuff to the guy from *Name of the Rose*.'" Apparently Marlon had loved *Quest for Fire* and *Name of the Rose* and watched them multiple times. He never said this to me, of course, but he did say it to Frankenheimer, who related it to me. He said, "You mean Ron Perlman?" He said, "Yeah, the guy who played the hunchback in *Name of the Rose*. Take it away from Val Kilmer and give it to fucking Perlman. There's a guy who could actually handle it."

As I said, Marlon was a guy you could talk to about anything in the world. He was an information junkie—anything except of course the one thing everybody wanted to talk about with him: acting. And those who either didn't know this rule or did and decided to ask anyway would see him grow cold, distant. Now little Fairuza Balk was playing his daughter in the film. She was Moreau's pride and joy but also his most flawless creation with, unlike all his other creations, almost no evidence of having anything other than purely human features. Well,

Marlon had a weakness for beautiful women and was not shy about making his predilection known. So little Fairuza got nothing but affection and warmth from him. So she decided, "Well, if anyone can cross the line, it's me." As they're getting ready to shoot their most important scene together, in which the true dynamic of this deeply emotional bond is really on display, Fairuza said, "Marlon, can I ask you something?"

"Sure, baby, anything you want," he said.

Now because Marlon was doing a performance that he was making up as he went along, anyone who acted with him had no way of knowing what to expect. So Fairuza said, "It's really important for me to know more about our relationship as you see it so I can play our scene together more effectively. How do you see our relationship in this film?"

Sure enough, the sweet old man's sweetness drained out of him. "Relationship? Did you just ask about our relationship? Okay, imagine a basket the size of Wyoming. And imagine that basket filled all the way to the top with dollar bills. Got it? Well, that's how much they're paying me to do this fucking turkey. And *that's* our relationship, baby!"

I guess if you search far and wide enough you could find exceptions to this rule. Maybe when he was younger, when he was still enthusiastically playing the game, I don't know. I do know one story, though, in regard to this that's worth telling. Ever since Eddie Albert Jr. did an arc on *Beauty and the Beast* he and I turned into fast pals. Eddie virtually grew up at Uncle Marlon's knee, 'cuz Eddie's dad, the great Eddie Albert Sr., did a few flicks with Marlon when Eddie Jr. was a tiny kid. So they had a really close bond.

Anyway, Eddie Jr. had just finished doing a piece-of-shit action flick in the Philippines that was destined to go straight to DVD. The movie kicked Eddie's ass. So he decided to stop off on the way home at the neighboring island of Terraria to see if Uncle Marlon was around, maybe stay a couple of nights, kick back on the beach, charge the battery. He showed up at Uncle Marlon's door unannounced, and Marlon came to the door in a sarong, his preferred mode of dress, particularly in his later years, and was just delighted to see him. "Eddie! What are you doing here?!"

"Uncle Marlon, I just had the snot beat outta me in the Philippines. Mind if I hang out here for a coupla nights?"

"Of course not. C'mon in. I was just makin' dinner."

Dinner was a pot of boiling water with a can of Campbell's soup heating up in it. Meanwhile, Uncle Marlon opened up a rare bottle of gorgeous Bordeaux, and they got off to what turned out to be a scintillating evening. One bottle of Bordeaux led to two or three more, and they were having a beautiful night and the conversation was flying, and that's when Eddie figured, okay, it's now or never. "Uncle Marlon, you've known me my whole life, right? And I know what the rules are. I know you as good as anybody on the planet, but Uncle Marlon, I'm an actor and I care about acting."

Marlon said to him, "Eddie, don't fucking do this. I just spent two thousand dollars worth of wine on you. Don't ruin the evening."

But Eddie said, "Marlon, you can excommunicate me, you can disinherit me, you can kick me the fuck out and send me packing to the airport. I'm going to ask you one question because if I don't ask you this one question, I'll never be able to live with myself because you're the only guy I would ever be interested in the answer to this from."

"Eddie, you're fucking me up here. You're ruining a perfect night, and if you keep goin' down this road, I *am* gonna throw you the fuck out."

"Uncle Marlon, throw me out, whatever you gotta do, but I'm going to ask you the question. You don't have to answer if you don't want to, but I got to ask on behalf of every actor I ever worked with."

"All right, Eddie. Because you are your dad's son, because I love your dad so much, I'm gonna let you ask one question. But just one. And if you ever tell anybody what my answer is, you *will* be excommunicated." Then he said, "What's the question?"

"Here's the question, Uncle Marlon: how do you know when it's working?"

So Marlon said to him, "You had to ask me that one, didn't you?"

"Yup," Eddie said. "That's the only one I want the answer to. How do you know when it's working?"

"All right," Marlon said, "I'm gonna give you the answer, but if I ever find out you've told another actor this, you're toast, ya hear me? You'll never hear from me again! Deal?"

"Of course, Uncle Marlon, deal!"

Marlon said, "I check my asshole."

"Come on, be serious."

"I am being serious, motherfucker. I check my fucking asshole."

"You check your asshole?! That's the answer you're going to give me?"

"Yeah, that's the answer I gave you and I'm giving you."

"What kind of fucking answer is that?"

And Marlon said, "Think about it, Eddie. I check my asshole, and if it's tight, I know it's not working."

So the first thing Eddie did when he came back to the States the next day? He found out I'm shooting some piece a crap some place in downtown LA and paid me a visit. And the very first thing he did when he saw me is tell me the story—word for word! He said to me, "I knew you would fucking love that story, so I hadda tell it to you." So then I proceeded to tell every single actor I've ever worked with, from that moment forward, the asshole story. And so now, between Eddie and me there are, I swear to God—and you can ask around—there are generations of actors all over the world right now who, when the AD says, "Roll camera," they put all their attention on their assholes. And if you're on the set with somebody else who knows the story, you say, "Checking?" and they say back, "Checking!" To this day, even though it doesn't work at all, I check my asshole whenever anybody says, "Roll camera." And that was Marlon's big fucking joke on actors everywhere. Like, "You fucking idiots, how am I supposed to know when it's fuckin' working?!"

CHAPTER 21

Piled Higher and Deeper

Funny how life works. Actually, lemme rephrase that: funny how my life works! In fact, now that I'm well onto the wrong side of the hill, among the many wonderful things I have obtained is perspective. I would imagine that it was the prime driver that led to my even entertaining the idea of ultimately sitting down and putting thoughts to paper. Writing enables so much perspective. It brings with it the beginnings of objectivity, which, as I tried to identify through all the years I've described here, was what I craved most, even though there was no way of knowing that until I actually began to have it. Because, clearly, what I was in the midst of living was an incredibly blessed life. It was as easy to see it as the nose on one's face. I'm sure it was obvious enough so that everyone around me could see it. Everyone except me. And why I've identified the nineties as the most tumultuous of periods for me is because of how close I was growing to—with apologies to Jim Morrison—breaking on through to the other side. Looking back, the closer I got to finally reaching some semblance of happiness, balance, and self-worth, the more anxiety that possibility triggered. I don't know, maybe no matter how fucked up a thing in your life is, the notion of changing it, of letting it go, is obviously way scarier than living with it. I mean, Christ, you see it everywhere you look: people stay in bad marriages, bad jobs, cities they don't belong in—why? Because any alternative to what is familiar, that "undiscovered country from whose bourn, no traveler returns," is terrifying!

So if you look at my life in the nineties with any objectivity at all, it looks fucking beautiful, carefree, and dreamy most of all. So why could every muthafucka see it but this muthafucka?! I mean, you just look at the series of events, the body of work, and the people I got to be around, it musta looked like I was set for life. And yet . . . and yet! But hey, good news! I had already opened the box wherein lie the genie. And I was close, way closer than I even knew. The thing, the one thing that could put me over the top was determination. A determination to square up finally these absurd incongruities. 'Cuz let's look at it: *A Few Good Men* on Broadway, *Cronos*, *City of Lost Children*, *Bus Stop* on Broadway, *Alien: Resurrection*, *Enemy at the Gates*—that's not a good decade; it's a GREAT one!!! So how in God's beautiful world could I still be calling Phil to essentially discuss the merits and lack thereof of being a loser?

Phil never looked at it like that, never put it in those terms; in fact, he never put it into any terms at all. Why would he need to when I was so good at it? No, he would just spend those first fifteen minutes of the session doing what I chose, that time totally fashioned according to my needs, my urgency, my call to make the appointment, and he would listen, unprejudiced. I say fifteen minutes 'cuz that's how long it generally took to describe the malaise du jour, and certainly he never needed more time than that to identify the disconnect. Because that's what it was: a disconnect. A viewing of a set of circumstances that I was immersed in that in fact had nothing to do with what was truly happening and only to do with how I interpreted what was happening. It was baggage, and it was old baggage at that. How it got there, why it got there was none of Phil's concern—only that it *was* there. And in being there, it was in the way. And the process Phil was able to bestow on me to get me to rearrange the wiring and, in turn, reinterpret the perception, objectify it, show me how little if any I even had a part in what I was describing was simple and effective. It was usually accompanied by a diagram that was passed down to him from one of his gurus, either Jung or Steiner, and the very fact that there was a diagram for exactly what I was describing was indicative of the fact that, shit, I must not have been the first one to feel this way, a fact that in and of itself granted comfort. But the tool that accompanied the condition illustrated in the diagram was really simple, really user-friendly, and really easy to do, and, once I did it, it completely granted relief. One hundred percent of the time.

So the late nineties were like grad school. I began to sense that if I devoted myself voraciously to allowing Phil to one by one address each of these distortions I carried around with me like old friends and I used these completely effective tools like I used the barbells in the gym, in which with each rep I got faster and stronger, I would create for myself more and more moments of real peace through clarity. It was good! Good . . . it was genius! It was the best I could hope for. Because, as I said earlier and as Phil intoned religiously, there is no life free of pain, loss, despair, confusion, violence, and, yes, even death. To make it a goal to think you could ever live a life that avoided all these things is pure folly, and you can only fall short. What there is, however, is the ability to manage one's way through these things so that, in addressing them, you remain as whole as possible, as present as possible, as undaunted as possible. For that is the closest you are ever gonna get to real, real contentment. And if that ain't the name o' the game, well, I just don't fucking know!

So, yeah, I got back from Australia, and, sure enough, a whole shitload of time went by before something happened to replace the feeling that that gig gave me. That gig or any gig, in fact. Because no matter how fucked up the circumstances are on the gig, they're a lark compared to the downtime, the not knowing, the wondering how to manage the money 'cuz you're not sure when the next batch is coming, the *between* gigs. There are loads of reasons ya don't wanna be outta work, but when the work is the direct link to your self-worth, then what would normally be an annoyance looms into something way larger, with overtones ya don't, once you've had a bellyful, ever wanna revisit again. Plus, I'm just happier when I'm working. I love the stimulation of it, the amount of me that it engages. I love the mind part of it, in which fitting myself into a picture is tantamount to solving a riddle. And I love just being on a movie set, 'cuz like the song says, "There's no people like show people, they smile when they are blue." And because I'm a bit of a clod in real life, I love how well I know my way around when I'm on a movie.

But never did this dilemma come into such stark relief as it did in the late nineties. It had been too long getting fixed. And the determination I was putting into it demanded a follow-through that I hadn't heretofore applied. So I used those years to double-down with Phil Stutz. I became obsessed with closing the gap between the reality of how good my life really was going and this nagging feeling that it wasn't going well at all. Nothing could have provided me as great an opportunity to bring all the elements to Phil that ultimately needed addressing than the lead up to the actual shoot and then the aftermath that was *Alien: Resurrection*.

I heard about the project when I got a really strange call from one of the higher-up production executives at 20th Century Fox. They were preparing to launch what would be the fourth installment of one of the most successful franchises ever. They were putting together a list of possible directors for the movie, and very high up on the list was my old friend Jean-Pierre Jeunet, with whom I had done *City of Lost Children*. Having done only independently produced movies in France, no one in Hollywood had a handle on JP's ability to wield a big-budget important studio franchise flick. So, knowing I was the only American who had ever worked with him, they gave me a jingle to ask about my experience with him. Of course, my report was glowing: not only was Jean-Pierre a brilliant, innovative filmmaker, but he was also a devoted movie buff who had a real feel for international cinema and adored the great early American movies. Plus—and this was the surprising thing— he had confessed to me a real desire to make a big studio movie one day in Hollywood. I thought he would be a perfect fit and said as much.

He ended up getting the film and returned the favor by helping me win the role of Johner in the movie. The character was an over-the-top loudmouth who fashioned himself a badass and had the attitude to prove it. As a guy whose work on big Hollywood studio movies is limited, needless to say, I was thrilled. The film also boasted Winona Ryder, who was at the peak of her powers then, and a coupla guys who remain friends to this day, Leland Orser and Raymond Cruz, great dudes, both!

Unlike most of the studio movies I'd made, this one shot right on the Fox lot in Century City, so I had the extra added luxury of sleeping in my own bed every night for a change. So I was able to take advantage of this good fortune by folding regular visits to Dr. Stutz into my schedule. And trust me, there was plenty to talk about. For instance, there I was, a forty-seven-year-old father of two, with a long successful marriage and a pretty decent résumé under my belt, and yet I can't tell ya how much time I spent thinking about how I really didn't deserve to be there. I mean, don't get me wrong: I got through the movie just fine and for sure no one except me and Phil knew of these feelings, but they were there. So Phil and I handled those. Then there were the instances in which whenever anything went the slightest bit wrong—and trust me, the pressure on a big-budget studio movie is palpable—I always knew it was because of me. Unfounded? Of course. But I never referred to myself as rational.

Then there was the aftermath, ya know, that period right afterward, when the news is bad. And then right after that, when it gets worse. And finally two years go by, and there's no news at all—*that* period! So Dr. Stutz and I had mucho, mucho, mucho to discuss. And discuss we did. And I started noticing signs of improvement—little things, like my highs and lows diminished by around 88 percent. And my demeanor at home got calmer, more dependable, and less unpredictable. And I became way more cognizant of the world around me and finally started to have an awareness and an empathy for what "the other guy's" life might be like. And so I started looking for ways to put all of my attention on the outside world, on ways I could use my blessings to lighten people's loads, even if it was just with a fucking smile. And discoveries and epiphanies started exploding inside of me.

And things Phil had warned me about, if applied assiduously, started to become just another part of my day. Things like the more I took the attention off of me and put it on the things around me, the bigger and more powerful I felt, and not powerful in the yucky way people in high places lord over the world, but rather a true power, one that lived deep inside me that no one could feel but me. This was the beginning of something big.

Another thing happened in my sessions with Phil, and this time it wasn't something that came from him; it was the other way around. I started talking about a relationship that had formed and was evolving in my life that added a dimension that finally addressed the collision of the real with the mysterious that I had danced around my whole life, the things that seemed coincidental but years later were things I clearly knew had happened for a reason, and I had nothing to do with them happening, even though they were the most definitive forces guiding me. And with these realizations came a relinquishing of needing to be in control of every little thing every minute of the day, for there was a force way outside of me that was doing more to chart my path than a gazillion plans I could've made myself. So I gave this force that lovingly surrounded me a name, and because I couldn't think of anything original to call it, I simply referred to it as God. And I—this son of an agnostic, this individual who, like my father before me, had nothing but disdain for organized religion—was filled up. This force for me was humbling in the purest form of the idea. And I loved him. And talked to him, sometimes eight or ten times a day. And I knelt before him because, even through turmoil, with him present I could feel only love.

I mentioned this relationship of mine that came from no one but me, that meant nothing to anyone but me and to Phil. He got a look on his face I'd never seen before, like a tinge of disbelief. As I was waiting for the explanation of what might have caused him, after all this time, to finally be caught flat-footed, he took over the conversation. Now, having not studied under the geniuses he did so as to make him equipped to be who he turned out to be, I wasn't aware that apparently all these guys, no matter what viewpoint they started from, all eventually had the same epiphany—the God epiphany. And once they did, their teachings transformed themselves to include a mystical force one is able to give over to that makes everything else profoundly enhanced. All Phil's heroes, many of whom had been sworn atheists, not only came around to God but also became realigned. So our discussions going forward always included this all-encompassing force that, because of which, one's relation to self is never the same. It's interesting to think that maybe that's how the whole ball got rolling in the first place.

Anyway, *Alien: Resurrection* had a decent opening, grossing around $38 million on the Thanksgiving weekend it got released. And then, in week two it disappeared. No legs, as they all too often say in Hollywood. So, rather rapidly, excitement gave way to disappointment, which gave way to embarrassment, which gave way to another two-year stretch during which the phone *literally* didn't ring. I don't mean literally, I mean *LITERALLY!* Like not even for any Saturday-morning cartoons, which had sustained me through so many of the lean times. But this one felt different from the others. This radio silence was such that, with every passing day, there was less and less reason to believe it would turn around and more and more reason to think, *Well, maybe my luck finally ran out.* There appeared to be no prospects in movies, even less in television, and the voiceover thing seemed like even that had had its day. So as good as things were going in my personal life due to the real connections I was making with Phil, there was an alarm building as to how long I could hold on to it all.

One of Phil's tools that had always proved really effective for me was the "Contingency Plan," whereby you focus your mind on the worst-case scenario . . . I mean short of a devastating health diagnosis—that's different. But rather, worst case, what happens if . . . and then once you put yourself there in that hopeless place, what are your options? Say you lose everything—the house, the school for the kids, the ability to interface with what had been your lifelines—what do you do? And whuddya know, I came up with something! I saw myself as a teacher at NYU or some noble institution for the arts, back in New York City, living in a two-bedroom in what-the-fuck-ever neighborhood we could afford on a teacher's pay. And it was good, it was fine. Life went on. And it was a good life. And suddenly calm washed over me, almost as if to make me fearless. Because I just dealt with the worst-case scenario and came out the other side unscathed, with everything intact. And I even had some amazing memories of all the glory days I had in showbiz. I was smiling. Fuck, I was happy. And the energy changed. All of a sudden I was giving off a different brand of pheromones. Calmness replaced anxiety. My worst fears had been addressed, and I still had everything that matters, and then some. And sure enough, a funny thing happened . . .

Out of the muthafuckin' blue! Out of the blue, for no reason at all, as I hadn't spoke to the dude in, like, twelve years, Jean-Jacques called: "I'm in LA for a few days—why don't we get some dinner?" We made a plan, I met him, and he looked every bit as good as this handsome elegant Frenchman with movie-star looks ever had. We had some small talk—how's the kids, how's the wife, bullshit, bullshit, bullshit—and as the salad arrived at the table J. J. said, "So I have a movie, and it's not quite green-lit yet because we're waiting for a movie star to say yes, but if he does, the movie goes. And I just want to prepare you because I wrote a part for you, and it's juicy. It's not big, but it has all the quirky character and charm of Amoukar and Salvatore. Knowing you, you'll steal the picture!" And all I could do was stare into his face. This normally overly expressive smooth-talker was suddenly speechless. And goddammit if, after about a half a minute, I didn't start crying. Jean-Jacques, not knowing what the fuck was happening, started looking around the restaurant, making sure nobody was seeing this less-than-manly display. He asked, "You alright?"

"Fine," I said. "It's allergies!" I didn't share with him what he had just done for me. I chose not to tell him how, just the day before, I was on the brink of selling everything and leaving the business. I never mentioned how I thought the world had forgotten me and that the scope of not only being remembered by someone but also being handed a little tailor-made jewel to boot, that had my name on it, meant so much to me. I knew that Jean-Jacques along with Guillermo and Ralph and Phil were my four angels of the apocalypse, but this was huge. This was life altering. This *was* a game-changer. J. J. saved me from a God-knows-what kind of life. Because Jude Law did indeed say yes, and the movie did get green-lit, and when Jean-Jacques found out how much money they had offered me, he stepped in and made them double the offer, saying, "This is Ron Perlman. He is my friend. Treat him right!"

On a personal note, and I think by now we can get personal, don't you? I've always been obsessed with doing whatever I had to do to begin to approach the man my dad was, the men my dad worshipped as heroes were. So there was a drive to close gaps, to address the synapses, to ameliorate the conditions preventing me from reaching that goal. Because to me that was Big Casino, which was the one element that would inform all the others: being a good husband, a good dad, a good citizen, someone who, when I said I got your back, I wasn't giving lip service. I'd seen plenty of that, especially in Hollywood, and personally, it turned my stomach. So I couldn't live with myself if that was ever gonna be the dealio.

'Cuz what good is it to have a hero if you didn't emulate the values that made them such in the first place? What good is it to complain about cowardice or the lack of resolve or the lack of backbone in people when you're gonna end up just like them? That would have been the ultimate hypocrisy, and that just wasn't okay with me. Those heroes I talk about, they were not just heroes; they stood for elements of the human condition that were noble and worth aspiring to, even when standing up for them cost them personally. And unless you're prepared to emulate these heroes, to learn from them to the degree to which you're willing to have that same swagger as they have and maybe even be willing to put yourself in a little bit of danger for the greater good, what good is having those heroes?

Frankly, I'm not entirely sure what my rep is around the movie business. But I'm pretty sure it ain't wishy-washy. I'm pretty sure if ya ask a cross-section of people I've either met or haven't in my travels, they would say, "Oh him . . . what a dick!" I'm also pretty sure if you asked 100 percent of all the crew guys I worked with over the years—the below-the-line guys, the grips and gaffers, the electrical guys and set painters, the makeup, hair, and set dressers—you'd get a pretty consistently good report. 'Cuz since the beginning, when power was wielded such that the real worker got disrespected, I got in people's faces. When people asserted their authority in ways that divided a company into camps, I let 'em know that that shit was fucked up, even intolerable. I never ever asked for a bigger trailer or better cocaine in that big fat trailer or, indeed, anything that would make the gap any wider between me and the guy who swept the floor. 'Cuz I loved that guy: he got up every day to feed his kids, make a better life for his loved ones, did whatever he hadta do to be in the film business, 'cuz he knew what a privilege it is. And he didn't have an agent, a manager, a lawyer, or anybody the fuck else to fight for him—except me! So if ya wanna know my rep, I guess it depends on who ya ask.

But if you're gonna be that guy, you have an even greater responsibility to find a way to do it so that it is not dismissible. Because it's too important. Yer never gonna get anything done to improve the environment if people think you're shrill, a dickwad, and an asshole. So doing the work I did with Phil Stutz was essential to finally accessing real strength without having it be hindered by the short-circuiting that occurs when wires are crossed.

When you look at some of the greats, they did the same. Hell, James Cagney was the very first president of the Screen Actors Guild. There was no union up to that point to mitigate working conditions for artists. And what people were up against was nothing new and, in fact is a discussion we're still having: big business wants *the* biggest profits possible with *the* smallest investment they can make, and whoever gets in between them and that agenda is to be stopped at all costs. So the notion of unionizing was then, as indeed it still is now, something owners would do anything to avoid. And I *do* mean anything! Can you imagine how miffed they were by the things Cagney stood for? And he was one of the biggest stars of the day, so he had an enormous amount to lose. But the outrage he felt because of the callousness of man to his fellow man was enough for him to throw caution to the wind and piss in their faces. Oh, and by the way, he managed to stay every bit the star he had been, whatever the fuck that means.

One of the by-products of the glare that came with *Beauty and the Beast* was the realization that success is way harder to deal with than is failure. It requires a greater amount of character; the reason why people on top are as self-destructive as they are is because they can't handle the baggage that comes with it. It really is a strange phenomenon. Success puts a bunch of shit into your path that you almost have to be a genius to modulate, to deal with properly in a balanced way. I know a lot of people who, the minute they see their name in print and are talked about in a hyperbolic way they start losing their grip, they start looking for ways to destroy themselves. And but for the grace of God, you just got to hope they're surrounded by really strong friends and family and that there are enough people who are going to say, "Hey, stop the shit. You're blowing it. Chill brutha. Get humble. Grab a hold of yourself. You got the best set of problems in the world!"

And Now a Letter from Dr. Phil

You're probably curious about what it's been like to be Perlman's psychiatrist for such a long period (twenty-three years . . . but who's counting?). People always ask me what it's like to treat stars. It's not a good question. Just like "regular" people, each star differs from the next. But they do have one thing in common: each of them is subject to the whims of public acceptance or rejection, a nasty beast that can effortlessly give them a swelled head and then, just as easily, bite that head off.

Each star deals with this situation in his own way, and you can learn a lot about them by observing how they handle its pressure and temptations. But federal law and simple human decency forbid me from discussing anything about my patients . . . unless I have their permission. Mr. Perlman has given me more than that: he has insisted I write something about our work together.

Time and space are short, so I'll jump right in. The first word that comes to mind in describing my time with Ron is "surprise." Every time I thought I knew him fully I discovered something new about him. In fact, my feelings were hurt when I realized how much of the stuff in the book he had never bothered to tell me at all—not that his job was to entertain me. (He did give me a free book.)

His tendency to reveal hidden talents never seems to end, right up to and including the writing itself. I suspected he could write, but I had no inkling of how funny he could be without at all diminishing the impact of his message. That misperception is fully corrected in the chapters on the making of The Island of Doctor Moreau. In fact, if you're pressed for time, I advise you to skip the rest of my reminiscences and reread Perlman's account of what it was like to meet Marlon Brando on the set of that movie. If you don't find it to be one of the funniest things ever written in the English language, you need a shrink (or a new shrink).

But what surprised me the most about him wasn't his hidden talents, no matter how many of them there were; instead, it was his willingness to face himself honestly at his worst moments. I don't consider that "star-like"; rather, it takes a humble kind of courage, not the first qualities that come to mind when you hear the word "star."

Which brings us back to public acceptance and rejection. Let me be specific: at the beginning of our relationship he would come in depressed and demoralized, trapped in a dark cloud he couldn't see his way out of. The darkness was usually his reaction to professional setbacks. "Setbacks" is putting it mildly: when he says the phone stopped ringing he means that literally. If he got one call all day, it would be from one of those guys who interrupt your dinner to sell you worthless penny stocks, and even that guy would hang up when he realized he'd gotten the coldest actor in Hollywood.

It didn't seem funny at the time. He'd get some kind of an unusual role, play it in a way no one had ever seen before and, for awhile, electrify the public and most of show business. Then nothing . . . and more nothing. This could go on for months.

All the while he'd fall further into his abyss. When all hope was gone he'd call me for a session. (That should be on my business card.)

His sessions always followed the same pattern: he'd spill out his latest tale of woe for fifteen or twenty minutes until he felt I had all the details. Only then would he stop. Okay, sometimes I had to stop him with a judiciously placed, "Shut the fuck up." But at that point he'd look to me to make sense of whatever had just happened to him—near bankruptcy, poor reviews, the cold phone, and so on—in a way that made him feel like it didn't mark the end of the world.

No matter how articulate and persuasive a therapist is, you can't talk someone with a crushed spirit into a positive view of himself or his future. People need tools that give them the power to change their inner state, no matter how bad their outer circumstances are. Without that, your words are just that: words. I call it "loose talk," and I hate it.

As it turned out, so did Ron. Maybe 'cuz we were both from New York, where "money talks and bullshit walks." In this case "money" would translate into "that which has real, permanent value." And spiritually the greatest value is the ability to turn yourself around and climb out of whatever hole you've let yourself fall into. When you can do that, you don't just get through adversity; you grow from it. The real star is the person who has that ability, even if no one has heard of him. Ron turned out to be that kind of star.

But it didn't seem that way at first. In those early sessions, once he'd finish talking, he'd sit quietly while I explained how he could create an identity that didn't require approval or recognition from other people. Then I'd teach him tools to achieve the emotional independence that required. This isn't the place to describe what the tools were, but they work—as long as you use them consistently.

This was where Perlman surprised me the most. In the beginning I had no idea whether he understood what I was saying—or if he was even listening. I certainly had no reason to believe he'd go home and do what I'd asked him to do. Yet that was exactly what he did, time after time. And time after time he'd drag himself back to the realm of *the living. His recovery time—the true test of psychological strength—went from a few days to a few hours.*

A couple of years after I met him I was giving a seminar, and Ron came. There, while helping someone with problems similar to his own, he explained with perfect clarity what they needed to do to heal themselves. He wasn't repeating my words; rather, he was describing his own experiences. At that moment I realized he wasn't just committed to mastering acting; he was also committed to mastering himself. Now you know it too.

—Dr. Phil Stutz

CHAPTER 22

Meanwhile . . .

While all this trivia was playing out, there was something lurking in the nether regions, something that, while starting out millions of miles away from my orb, would eventually wind up not only intersecting with it but also sweeping it up into an energy force responsible for the momentum that led me to this very day.

From the moment Guillermo del Toro and I met, it seemed like there was a really good chance it would lead to one of those rare things not only in showbiz but, indeed, in any endeavor: a real and lasting friendship. And like I said before, having presided over the event that literally set me on the path that was to carry me through the entire second half of my life, which included an enduring love affair with a culture I was to revisit heartily from that point forward, Guillermo had already taken his place among the most important figures to affect my destiny forever and always. All that being said, he was a pal, somebody I couldn't wait to hang with, have meals with, shoot the breeze with.

On one of his growingly more frequent trips to LA now that his career was getting into gear, we went for one of our signature meals of arroz con puerco at one of our most favorite eateries. I was already aware that, among all his boyish obsessions, among his most rabid proclivities was his love of comic books. In fact, even at that young age, he was already on his way to building a collection of comic book art that would eventually rival the most important on Earth. Anyway, as we got closer to paying the check, he hurried me up, claiming that there was something he had to show me. Sure enough, we got back in the car and drove to a very large comic book store on Sunset Boulevard. We walked in the door with great purpose and walked up to a beautiful scale sculpture of this very exotic, very red superhero. "Ron, meet Hellboy! He is my favorite comic book character of all time! In a perfect world, if there were ever to be a movie of Hellboy, you would play him. That is my dream!"

"Wow!" I said. "That's some dream!"

There are just some things that are too good to be true, and this definitely had to be one of them, and I expressed this to Guillermo at that moment and, indeed, many, many times thereafter in the ensuing years. The fact of the matter is that comic book movies are expensive to make, especially those that are heavy on alternate universes. Not only that, but if they resonate to an audience, it can become a franchise, which represents huge profit potentials for studios. So regardless of what you do or do not think about Ron Perlman as a talent, the studio is gonna need, even demand a big-name movie star on which to hedge such a big bet. Nuthin' personal—it's just how it is. But the notion that this movie giant even thought to give me a part that had such a personal meaning for him, well, that made me adore him even more. So anyway, even though the big G insisted on buying me a copy of *Seed of Destruction*, which is the first installment in the *Hellboy* series, and even though I took it home with me, I resolved to never open it, lest I fall in love with the character like Guillermo did and then be invested enough to suffer once I saw the part go to someone else.

It wasn't long before Guillermo did indeed get Universal Studios to purchase a five-year option on his *Hellboy* project. He set up meetings, and everyone was excited to get this thing going, but there was one obstacle upon which the studio heads and Guillermo could not agree. When they asked who would play Hellboy and he told them that Ron Perlman was perfect for the part, well, all he could hear were crickets!

"It's not that we don't like Perlman," Guillermo was told. "It's just that . . . what about Nick Cage?"

"I love Nick Cage," Guillermo said. "Let's set up a meeting." And then for some strange reason, Guillermo didn't show up for the meeting.

A few months would go by, and Guillermo would bring in busts of Hellboy as sculpted onto my likeness just to show them how well this fusion would work, and they would say, "What do you think about the Rock?"

Guillermo would say, "The Rock is great. Let's get a meeting together." And when the meeting time came, no Guillermo. This little charade went on for five long years. Movie stars got mentioned, meetings got set up, and no del Toro. Finally, after five years, with the option running out, Universal decided to wish Guillermo luck and give him his project back because, well, by now, the reasons were obvious.

Meanwhile, the copy of *Seed of Destruction* remained unopened 'cuz I kind of agreed with Universal on that one. In fact, I said as much to my friend: "Guillermo, this movie is too good, too important to not make. I love you for sticking by me, but this is Don Quixote pissing into the wind—it's just never gonna hit the mark! Please go make this movie, and I promise I will cheer you on from the sidelines, be there on opening night to celebrate with you!"

"Yes, my friend, you are right," said the Mexicano. "That is what I will do." The little devil!

Around 2000 Guillermo pitched an idea to do a sequel to the movie *Blade*, starring Wesley Snipes. The studio guys at New Line flipped over it and then proceeded to give him the green light and the funds to direct *Blade II*. So after a long absence between films, the Big G was off to the races again and, not only that, finding a way to bring me along with him. And so off to Prague we went for what was to be our second flick together. Once I was on the set, my small role got bigger and bigger, with Guillermo giving me lines to say and new scenes to play right on the spot. It turned out fantastically and was released in March 2002.

Even more stunning, *Blade II* earned $35 million the first weekend, thus becoming, far and away, the number-one movie of the week. This proved what anybody who knew Guillermo already knew: the hombre knew what he was doing and was more than capable of directing a major-studio, action-packed film. Suddenly everyone in Hollywood wanted to get into the Guillermo del Toro business.

That week Guillermo made a decision to use this moment of being considered a money-making genius to his advantage, knowing that, in Hollywood, windows like this don't stay open very long. He also knew that if, at this time, with all this heat on him, he couldn't get *Hellboy* made his way, on his terms, then he was never going to get it made at all. The town responded in kind. There was no studio that didn't want their next picture to be with him. But they knew enough about Guillermo's penchant for doing original, self-generated projects that most of them were smart enough to ask him what *he* wanted his next project to be. The answer was always the same: "I have a lot of things I have developed that I would be happy to do, but if you ask me what my number-one priority would be, I would tell you unequivocally that it is *Hellboy*."

They would invariably ask who he wanted to star and what the budget would be, and once he told them, for the most part the response was, "We'll get back to ya!" That is, until he got to Joe Roth and Tom Sherak at Revolution Studios. Joe asked, "How do we get in the Guillermo del Toro business?" And he got the same response. Joe said, "I know the *Hellboy* project, and I'm a fan. Are there any caveats?"

G took a deep breath and said, "Yeah, a big one: Ron Perlman plays Hellboy."

"And what's the budget?" Joe asked. And G told him. There was a thirty-second pause, and then Joe said, "Well, I can't do *Hellboy* with Ron—who I like by the way—for that price. But I can do it for . . ." and he said a number that was about $30 million less than Guillermo's. "If you tell me you can make it for that, we have a deal."

Guillermo stuck out his hand and said, "We have a deal." And that, as they say, is that! Seven years, two studios, 875 doors slammed in his face, the prospect of never, *ever* making this beloved project at all, and, as if the whole thing was this well-oiled plan/Apashe dance, *Hellboy*, starring yours truly with an option for two sequels, was a reality. Now I'm no linguistic expert, but I do know that the English translation for Toro is bull. Ya know how to get Guillermo del Toro to really do something? Tell him he can't!

To him, to make a movie any other way than how he envisioned it was a waste of creativity and a betrayal to his art. *Hellboy* was going to be made his way, and he refused to compromise, choosing art over money, and this made him, believe me, a rare type of person in Hollywood. But then again, Guillermo was not from Hollywood. Nor was he *of* Hollywood. No, he was clearly more like the guys my dad couldn't get enough of watching and studying when I was a kid growing up. He was a guy who stood for a principle, even when everyone around him told him he was nuts. I never saw that before in Hollywood. I'm not sure anyone did. And I've certainly never seen it since.

What ensued at this point—and I have to direct hand-to-God and swear to its veracity, because, for the life of me, it has remained to this day something too strange to even process, much less believe possible—is that at the time the offer came in I was looking to move to more exclusive representation: which agency represents an actor plays a large part in the direction that actor's career travels. I felt that by walking into an agency with a firm offer for the title role in a potential huge studio franchise for a world-class director, I could call my own shots, that they'd all be salivating to take 10 percent of a deal they didn't have to work to obtain in the first place. My manager and dear friend Erik Kritzer and I identified the big five we wanted to target, and I asked to put in the calls and set the appointments. It turned out no appointments were forthcoming. One by one, each of these agencies, William Morris, ICM, Endeavor, CAA, and UTA, decided to pass. When all the dust finally settled, I was dumbfounded. I asked Erik how was it possible that none of these players wanted free money? I mean, for Chrissakes, even if they never planned on lifting another finger on my behalf again, WHO THE FUCK WOULDN'T WANT

EASY STREET (THE HARD WAY)

FREE FUCKING MONEY? Wanna know who? Those five, that's who. I noticed that Erik, even as smart as he is, was not able to answer the question. By the way, I'm not ruling out ever having an agent in the future; it's just that I haven't had one since. That was eleven years ago. Fuck me? Nah . . . .

Of course, we ultimately cobbled out a deal, and a few months later, we were all off to Prague, with me getting ready to make the transition to become Hellboy. The great Rick Baker of *Beauty and the Beast* and countless other incredible masterworks was brought on board to create to the best of his ability the elements it would take to transform Ron Perlman's physicality into Mike Mignola's creation. And speaking of Mike, you can bet that before I left for Prague I dug out those comic books Guillermo had given me years before and immersed myself into the visual and poetic world Mike had given way to, finally understanding Guillermo's fascination with it.

As described in the title of Mignola's kickoff introduction to the Hellboy Saga, our hero is summoned to Earth in an epic occult ceremony conducted by the Hitler Regime as the ultimate seed of destruction, with an irrevocable destiny of being the instrument that eventually leads to the end of the world. And, as in the oracle of Greek tragedy, this destiny of his is nonnegotiable. So there is the element of certainty that this Hellspawn will deliver this result—that is, until he is found at the moment of his birth by the benevolent Professor Broome and lovingly raised and nurtured to develop pure goodness with which to utilize his formidable skills and abilities. So now you have a character at odds with himself, and the fascination of watching him is witnessing the struggle playing out as to which of these conflicting proclivities will win out at the end of the day, when the big shit hits the fan.

The road to Prague, though scintillatingly magical and majestic as this insane miracle Guillermo spent seven years in pulling off, was not without its hiccups and speed bumps, many of which exemplified the similarities between me and the distinctly underachieving ways of this most unique of superheroes—underachieving-ness being the quality that charmed me the most.

The first such example came when it was pointed out to me that, although we were still eight or nine months from the start of filming, Rick Baker needed all of that lead time to create the customized pieces that would become the defining physicality of our hero, and that would include his superhuman, muscle-ridden, ripped-to-the-tits torso. I realize that I run the risk of ruining the illusion for all you *Hellboy* fans who were absolutely convinced that those were my actual biceps and eight-packs, but trust me, even a god-like specimen like myself needs a touch of enhancing. So I needed to report to Rick's shop for a series of body castings so as to begin the process of building the pieces. The problem was that, like every other time I find myself "between engagements," I was fifty-five pounds overweight—and happy as a clam!

Well, obviously that first trip to Rick's and all those castings proved to be a colossal waste of time and money, 'cuz no matter how many muscles Rick's design included, they were essentially gonna be applied onto an extremely obese muthafucka. So I got my first call from Guillermo: "Excuse me, Roncito, but Rick can't use any of the stuff from that last session. In fact, Rick is not going to be able to use anything until you are a great deal smaller. How long do you need?"

I said, "Give me a month, and we'll do it again." He agreed.

I go in a month later, and I've lost a whopping four pounds. So while they are applying all the plaster of Paris to create the body cast, I am holding my breath and sucking in my stomach to the point of cramping. But, indeed, nothing I did could make up for the bitch tits that were prominently displayed where there should have been pectoralis majors—*minors* even. Needless to say, the next day the phone rang again: "Ronaldo, you're fucking killing me here. I give you the month, and you lose FOUR FUCKING POUNDS?" We clearly were about to have our first fight.

I said, "What is this bullshit about having to be ready nine fucking months before the fucking camera rolls? When the time comes to play Hellboy, I'll be fucking ready. That's the way it's always been, and, Godammit, that's the way it is now! Godammit!"

"Yes, but Ronaldo, excuse me, but—do you mind if I call you fat boy?—you do realize Rick is trying to turn you into a god, but he needs time."

To which I ran out of defensive answers and said, "If you insist on hitting me with logic, we're not gonna get anywhere. Godammit! Gimme another month."

At this point I just flat-out stopped eating. My breath smelled like the Russian Army at the battle of Stalingrad, but I did manage to lose about 20 pounds, just enough so they could see the effort and feel sorry for me enough to stop bombarding me with what a piece of shit I was. When the cameras finally did roll I was 205 pounds, a full 55 pounds lighter than I was when the process started. But poor Guillermo did get a front-row seat to what degenerative behavior looks like close up. But, gentleman that he is, he only reminds me of that little incident every time I see him. The little devil.

Once in Prague, and as filming was about to get under way, the atmosphere was stupendous. Guillermo had assembled a dream team of artists to surround, support, and utilize in bringing his formidable imagery to life, with a cast that remain among my favorite, both professionally and personally, to this day—Selma Blair, John Hurt, Doug Jones, Jeffrey Tambor, Rupert Evans, Biddy Hodson, Karel Roden, Brian Steele, to name a few. And although the big man poured everything he had into the making of this movie and demanding no less from the rest of us, looking back, I feel that we never really got out of the honeymoon period. That set was as joyous, bright, warm, and fun as any ever and always, and the spirit Guillermo exerted in sticking to his guns to make the movie *he* saw fit to make characterized the entire proceeding in its magical realism.

Hellboy opened to great reviews, with a staggering 93 percent positive, most of which were downright raves. To no one's surprise, Guillermo had made a kick-ass tent-pole action flick, but he fused it with art-house sensitivity, integrity, and intimacy. All the people who mattered to me took notice. The box office was strong; we were number one on opening weekend and hung around the top ten for a few weeks. Internationally we were even stronger, with DVD and VOD through the roof—all in all something to be quite proud of. And although the numbers are incredibly important in terms of measures of success, what I take with me everywhere and for always are the opinions and comments of all those for whom I have deep admiration. On that level *Hellboy* was a blockbuster of uncommon proportion, one that trafficked more in human values than on technological achievements. Because at the end of the day the thing that truly separates my friend Guillermo del Toro from the pack is his heart and what comes seeping out of it as it relates to his view of humanity. There are no numbers to measure that!

There was a validation following *Hellboy I* that was palpable. One could sense I was, although not quite there yet, ever closer to a seat at the grown-up table. It certainly felt like a personal triumph, what with all the elements of the stuff that dreams are made of converging to make it possible. I sure was proud of that movie. And to this day I find that the people who dug it, *really* dug it.

The prospects for a *Hellboy II* were not automatic, not slam-dunk status. For although the first one did just fine at the end of the day, the box office didn't dictate that a sequel was mandated, as they sometimes are with these comic book titles that break box office records. But we had our fair share of angels lurking about that would turn uncertainty into downright enthusiasm. One such angel came with the name Scott Bernstein, an executive who had been in charge of the *Hellboy I* production while he was at Revolution Studios and had moved to a high-level executive gig at Universal, the original scene of the crime, bringing with him a deep and abiding enthusiasm for the title and for Guillermo's prospect of making cinematic history with it. So the discussion gathered steam.

Meanwhile, Guillermo *was* off making *real* cinematic history: when he left Spain two years hence, he carried with him his unabashed masterpiece, *Pan's Labyrinth*, which not only I but also 135 of the top movie critics around the world called the greatest movie of 2006 and among the greatest of all time. It definitely goes in *my* top hundred!

Talk about a game-changer! This was one of those movies—Spielberg has a couple, as does Scorsese, Coppola, Capra, Kurisawa, Ford, Sturgess, Hawkes, Wilder and Wyler, Stevens, Chaplin, and Hitchcock—whereby if it had been the *only* movie they ever made, they would still go down in history as the greatest the art form had ever known. Guillermo returned from Spain a little like Charlton Heston does in *The Ten Commandments*: hair a little whiter, wisdom a million miles bigger. You could see it on him. He had done something earth-shattering, and it was singular, original, and gorgeous. Imagine what the guy who starred in his *next* movie would look like.

Well, as fate would have it, that next guy was me, 'cuz his next movie was *Hellboy II: The Golden Army*. Yes, between the backstairs maneuverings of Scott Bernstein and Larry Gordon, this little miracle took wing, this time for Universal, the studio that had owned the franchise in the first place but just couldn't see their way clear to make it sans movie star.

Although it is always exciting when a real movie comes together, when it is a Guillermo del Toro movie one is making because of popular demand, the excitement is heightened. There was nothing that could top the unimaginable fact of *Hellboy I*. By the second film we were old hands who would lovingly reassemble and once again endeavor to make magic that would cause lasting and memorable cinematic moments for our faithful and stalwart hero. But the newness of the proceedings was replaced by something else. All the same, there are *some* things that *never* change.

Like the call I got the minute the film was green-lit saying that Rick Baker would not be returning to create the makeup but that the amazing Mike Elizalde would take the reins, even including some touches and refinements of his own. An appointment was scheduled for my body cast for the top of the following week. The phone call I got from my dear friend Guillermo following that first body cast this time did not start out with the name "Roncito." Oh no! Roncito was replaced by something like, "You fat tub of shit . . ." Yup; it was nine months before principal photography was to commence, and I was the exact weight I was when *Hellboy I* started. Ya'd think these muthafuckas would learn! Anyway, if ya wanna hear the rest of the story, just turn back a few pages to the *HB I* version and add a lot more cursing.

Suffice it to say, the extended honeymoon that characterized the entire experience of the *HB I* shoot evolved into something much different for the sequel. There was, for my part at least and maybe even Guillermo's, a manic drive to top ourselves, to prove to the world that this fragile second chance of ours was not undeserved. There wasn't as much joy on the set. Don't get me wrong: after Disneyland, a Guillermo del Toro set is the happiest place on earth, so the setting was not devoid of lots and lots of laughter, wonder, and discovery. But there was a grind to it that took a toll on us and, in fact, on everyone concerned. During the seven-month shoot, with six-day weeks and no time to ever charge the battery, Guillermo, the entire crew, and I came away bowed, maybe even a little bit broken. Nothing that couldn't be fixed, but there was a definite price paid. For my money, we *did* surpass the first movie—I mean, not by much, because the first movie was really good. But I gotta give the edge to *Hellboy II*.

The net result was almost identical: reviews that were love letters, big love from the filmmaking community at large, but a box office that, though profitable, was made slightly anemic, mostly because of a set of decisions by some people at the top, most of whom are no longer there, that worked to our detriment, such as the decision to open the movie one week before *Dark Knight*, the second Batman movie and the final Heath Ledger performance. This was a decision that, though we opened with killer numbers, far and away finishing a resounding first, led to being obliterated a week later. All this is what makes the prospects for a third and final film such a heavy lift. Gone is the unabashed passion of any studio to relive these circumstances. In fact, the one thing that keeps the conversation alive, at least in my mind, is the fact that we owe it to the fans to complete this trilogy, to fulfill the promise that was made in the first film and set the stage for at the end of the second. Maybe there weren't as many fans as those who showed up for *Iron Man* or *Thor*, but show up they did, and with at least as identical a passion. They are invested, these fans of ours. They are owed. And so I fight. Stay tuned!

CHAPTER 23

Mudville

By the time you read this, *Hand of God*, a pilot I made for Amazon, will have already aired. The original movement to bring this project to reality began with four players: Ben Watkins, who wrote this as a spec script out of true passion for the subject matter; Marc Forster, the incomparable filmmaker of uncommon brilliance who, prior to this, had never done television before; Brian Wilkins, my brilliant manager, who masterminded the search for the perfect vehicle to follow *Sons of Anarchy*, and myself. We came together out of a mutual devotion to Ben's brave and original screenwriting but also out of a mutual respect for one another. In the process of finding a buyer for this project our regard for one another grew precipitously, to the point at which we were actually finishing each other's sentences. We loved each other's combinations of determination and humility and how quickly each of us was to pay close attention to the others' opinions and ideas. It was, in very short order, a thing of beauty.

By the time the show went into production, what with the filling out of the cast and choosing department heads, all of whom brought with them their own loving family of worker-bees, our little team had grown to some 150-plus. Each and every member of this new and burgeoning family was adored for their passion and their vision. Not only were they welcome, but the opinions and points of view of what would become the world of this show were also essential. And although, as is always the case, the final sets of decisions were the job of Marc Forster, I watched as he lovingly and humanely embraced the input of each and every member of our team. It reminded me of the magic that is the power and the glory of filmmaking. It harkened back to that epiphany I had on that hilltop twenty kilometers outside of Rome on the set of *Name of the Rose* some thirty years earlier—that is, the thing that made the making of movies and great television into the greatest of all art forms, the coming together of the brightest and the best in the world, all with disparate expertise all coalescing with the innocence, naïveté, and energy of kindergartners to paint one glorious picture, all of which is filtered through one amazing artist, the filmmaker. And if you are lucky enough to get a filmmaker who is brilliant, humble, and loves people, loves what they do, and loves what *he* does—one like Marc Forster—you indeed find yourself in a state of grace. That is what it can look like when it happens how it's supposed to happen.

You must know by now my intense devotion to these elements, my unwavering belief as to what a privilege it is to be in this, the most elite group who gets to work in these settings. And how, ultimately, we who get to do this are charged with a set of responsibilities that, when regarded with love and true humility, can elevate us to a state of true nobility. People love movies; they love them because they teach us, they move us, and they remind us of our commonality, of how we are not, not one of us, in this alone. This, to me, is sacred. So when I see it sullied, when I see it misused, it saddens and angers me.

Let me talk for a minute about *Sons of Anarchy*.

There was a whirlwind of press about Guillermo del Toro's next film *Hellboy II* after just coming off *Pan's Labyrinth*, so this whole maelstrom of goodwill and frenzied curiosity was rubbing off on me even before the movie came out. The difference between what the first *Hellboy* did for how I was perceived in the business and what the second one seemed to be yielding was dramatic and decisive. I was part of kinds of conversations different from those I'd ever before been a part of. I was talked about and booked for types of gigs different from those I'd ever done before, many much closer to mainstream than the steady diet of guerilla indie that I'd immersed myself into up to that point. Ultimately all this noise put me on the shortlist for a new FX show called *Sons of Anarchy*. But because the pilot episode for the show was already in the can, the lunch meeting that was set up between me and the show's creator, Kurt Sutter, seemed to me to be about a supporting character who would come in down the road a piece. Much to my surprise, however, Kurt began to explain to me that the network would like to recast the role of the president of the motorcycle club, Clay Morrow, and reshoot the portions of the pilot in which this character appeared. And if they could find the right actor, the network was prepared to green-light an entire first season consisting of thirteen episodes. But because, after making a formidable investment in the original shoot, they needed to be super-sure of the new actor; they were asking whether I would be willing to audition for the studio execs. My response was, as it always is, that upon reading the script, if I felt as though I could be of help to the show with regard to my confidence in my ability to play the character and my enthusiasm for and fascination with the world of the show, then yes, I would be more than happy to audition.

And indeed, the world of the show *was* fascinating. It was a show about a modern-day outlaw motorcycle club, similar to the Hells Angels, operating in Northern California. But the show was ultimately going to be mostly a strong family drama with a superstructure that was borrowed from the bones of Shakespeare's *Hamlet* saga: a prince, whose father, the king, has recently been murdered and who now finds his mother, the queen, married to his father's best friend and confidant, who has himself assumed the title of king, thus usurping all the power. Interesting idea for a television series. Even more interesting was the notion of playing this character, for Clay Morrow was far and away the most serious persona I would ever have to deconstruct. I mean, clearly up until then all the roles I played possessed a duality, an ability to be self-effacing, whereas with Clay, it wasn't as if he had no sense of humor; it was that he had no sense of humor about himself. And even though, in recognizing these traits, I do admit to having second thoughts about whether I could pull this off and balance the idea of trying to do so, of stretching to find this guy's most singular point of view, in the end I felt that the exercise of discovering where this man lived inside of me could very well be a challenge worth diving into. So I agreed to test.

Kurt wanted to work with me prior to going into the read. He said, "They didn't see enough gallows humor in that last actor, that these violent guys have all this dark humor to them that, when added to their explosive natures, provides them with real dimension. I want to bring that out in your reading." So we worked on that. On the day of the test there were at least twenty people in the room watching my performance. Meanwhile, I was scheduled to be on a plane the next day to shoot two movies back to back, one in Detroit and one in Romania, but as I was walking out of the room, all I was thinking about was, "I just nailed this fucker!"

I drove home from 20th Century Fox, which is about an hour drive in rush hour—they always seem to schedule these fucking meetings in rush hour. I know I'm going to get a phone call before I even hit Santa Monica Boulevard, which is two blocks away from the Fox Lot, telling me that I got the show. But the phone didn't ring. I got home. No call. Half-hour went by—nuthin'. Another hour went by. Finally my manager called and said, "I hope you are sitting down."

"Okay, I'm sitting," I said. "Talk to me!"

"They love you," he said. "But they need you to come in again."

"Are you nuts?" I said. "I'm on a plane first thing in the morning. All I got time to do is pack for two time zones and then catch some fuckin' Zs."

He said, "Calm down and listen to me. They thought you were really good, they loved the intelligence and the humor of the guy, but they're a little worried you're not tough enough."

"Oh really? You want to know how fucking tough I am? Tell them to go fuck themselves. If they don't know by now how fuckin' tough I am, they ain't never gonna know. Here's what I know: I'm on a plane tomorrow for two fucking movies. I get the job, I don't get the job—I don't give a fuck." And I hung up.

So my manager, Erik, called them back and told them that. Verbatim. He phoned back in five minutes and said, "I told them exactly what you said. They said, 'Oh yeah, well, fuck him . . . He's got the job!'"

There is no question the impact this show had not only on me but also on the network and, indeed, the entire trajectory of cable television, which was already beginning to trend as the new haven for the most original, cutting-edge storytelling in any medium. We came along just as the show that branded FX, *The Shield*, was coming to the end of its magnificent run. So to say that the timing for us to emerge was felicitous would have been an understatement. Not only that, but at the same time as us, other cable networks boasted the likes of *Mad Men*, *Breaking Bad*, *Dexter*, and *Burn Notice*, to name a few. It was a glorious time. And it gave way to the current crop, which includes *The Newsroom*, *Game of Thrones*, *True Detective*, *Ray Donovan*, and *House of Cards*. So our little motorcycle drama made some noise. As to how much noise, I don't think anyone would have dared to imagine what would ensue.

By the end of season one we were starting to break network records for ratings and viewership that *The Shield* had set. At the beginning of season two we became the highest-rated show in the history of FX. And for the next five years we kept shattering our own records. In fact, every year the *New York Times* business section published an article illuminating what our one show meant to the bottom line of News Corp, Rupert Murdoch's sprawling empire. There was joy in Mudville, you betcha.

For my part, I loved going to work on that show, especially in the early going, when riding the wave was fresh and new. Because there were a lot of veterans on that show, myself included, who knew that that kind of success wasn't a given, that it was rare and that the odds of all the elements that need to align in order to make that kind of success possible were far and away against us. And I loved the guys: Coates and Rossi, Hunnam and Hurst, Flanagan and Boone, Lucking, Siff, Sagal, and Rivera. And then all the ones who came along down the road: the Kenny Johnsons, the Tim Murphys. And I loved sitting around that reaper table, in the chapel, gavel in front of me, stoagy smoking in the ashtray, surrounded by those guys. It was among the greatest ensembles of actors I ever had the honor to be around. And, indeed, yes: there *was* joy in Mudville.

The bond that existed among our group in the early years, how much all us guys liked being in each other's presence, was true, and we had some great times. Later, of course, the story went off in a direction that made everybody very uncomfortable, and a palpable stress crept over the set. Working under those conditions affected all, including me. Eventually I could see that I began to become iced out of the group on a story level. It became clear that as this dynamic of the story changed, people around me started to act differently—not just to me, but also differently. So I sensed among the other players that in the environment being created for us, it might be a little bit dangerous to be Perlman's friend, because obviously Perlman's not going to be around for much longer. My character was going off in a completely separate storyline from the original core ensemble he once epitomized. Clay Morrow was being set up to be a pariah, an outcast, a persona non grata, and it was beginning to look like there was nothing but inevitability that his very existence was nothing short of intolerable. Funny how a manufactured reality can start to blur its way into reality itself, because ultimately it did. And by the end of the show I wasn't very close to anybody.

As for the rest, suffice it to say that our collective time characterized itself with dramatic swings from the highest of highs to . . . well, and as I learned so thoroughly in therapy, highs *that* high don't come free of charge. I mean, clearly, for six years the blessings that were anointed on me for having the luck to land on that show rivaled any I had experienced heretofore. Clearly the show touched off an unbelievable reaction in the public, with people on the six continents I traversed during that time in a frenzied state to share their enthusiasm with me: "Yo, Clay, great fucking show, dude!" Or, "Yo, Clay, not sure whether I hate you or love you, dude!" Either way, it was intense. And clearly, for six beautiful years I got to be around a crew who had enough heart to get ya to the moon and back. And clearly, FX, et al.—the Landgrafs, the Schriers and the Grads, the Sohlbergs and the Pagones, the LaTorres and the Brochsteins and so many others who had become like family to me—were the smartest, warmest, most visionary set of execs I ever had the pleasure to know, to work alongside. And boy, it got to be fun watching us set new bars year in and year out in terms of audience enthusiasm. Good times. Blessed times. A lotta joy in Mudville!

So I guess ya gotta be ready to take the fat with the skinny. I guess ya can't expect life to be all peaches and herb. 'Cuz after all, it was the little things that I missed: the joy that comes with the knowledge that collaboration is not only welcomed but insisted upon; the unencumbered feeling that one could take huge risks in finding the operatic nature of these extremely extreme characters and it would be appreciated, cherished even; the pride of ownership that comes with knowing one's contributions were admired and respected—ya know, the little things. I mean you'd have to be a fuckin' idiot to think you could get all that on top of the glory of making history every day. And I guess just knowing how lucky we all were wasn't enough; we hadta be reminded of it every fuckin' day, like a fuckin' kid whose nose gets rubbed in the chocolate cake he has the balls to not finish. So, yeah, there were *clearly* some little things some of us missed. And clearly that beautiful, ethereal, magical little canvas I tried to paint in the beginning of this chapter, the one that *Hand of God* exemplified with so much elegance and grace, was MIA on the set of *Sons*. 'Cuz in order for that world to be even possible, the guy at the top, the tone-setter, has to be kind, generous, sharing, and secure enough with his own sense of worth that the creativity of others does not make him feel threatened. It's a lot to ask, I know. All that and ratings too. Who the fuck do I think I am?!

You must trust me when I tell you how much I have struggled with myself as to how much of this I should write and how much of it I should simply move on from. But if you've learned anything about me in reading up to this point, then you must know the lengths and depths of my passion for this, the greatest art form ever invented. And what a select club it is. And what a privilege it is to be one of the rare ones who doesn't get left by the side of the road but who gets to participate in something that is this precious, this phenomenal. And when I see someone who is fortunate enough to be welcomed into that most exclusive of clubs but chooses to sully that tradition, someone who never for a moment is humble enough to understand that he or she is a tiny addition who will come and go but instead stands on the shoulders of true greatness, my blood boils.

Let me be clear: the debate as to whether to stay on this show, given the mounting personal price that it exacted from my soul, was among the most dramatic and intense I have ever taken part in. And if ya don't believe me, ask my wife, ask my team of reps and lawyers, ask the rest of the cast, ask my fucking shrink. For me, the joy that had once been a shining light on Mudville was replaced by, well, something short of joy. But at the end of the day I had a show to do, so the decision was to stick with it, for there was a deep and abiding knowledge that I was involved in the biggest juggernaut my career had ever experienced and that situations like this, maybe, if you are really lucky, come around once in a lifetime. And that's only if you're *really* lucky. And for the sake of who I was ultimately responsible to and for what I had worked toward for those many decades, I would try to keep my cool and hold my own, no matter what it exacted from my conscience. And so that is what I did. But it was essential to me to try like hell to do it in a way in which I was as true to myself as was humanly possible.

Regrets? I have a few. But then again, too few to mention. . . .

(CHAPTER 24)

Legacy

It doesn't seem so long ago, looking back as I have had to do in order to write this, that I was the "kid" on the set, the baby, the one everybody worked around because of how little I brought to the table. But when I woke up one day to find these real young 'uns—nineteen, twenty, twenty-one, twenty-two—who had literally just got off the bus that brought them seeking fame and fortune in "tinseltown," walking up to me on movie sets, asking me questions like, "What was it like when *you* started out?" or "You know where I can work on my craft?" or "Can you give me some advice to get me to feel I'm not just spinning my wheels?," I slowly started to get the joke: I'm now the "old guy" on set, the elder statesman, the white-haired, wisdom-bearing, cute old toothless sherpa who has lived *so* long that maybe even I, with my limited abilities, can impart a couple shortcuts for these fresh-faced innocents.

Further, I have kids of my own. And my kids have friends. And they've all gotten infected with the notion that a life in the arts is the coolest thing they could possibly commit their lives to. And when we spend time together I am reminded of how little they have traveled, how much they have yet to see, how confusing it must be clueing into that one moment that gets the momentum flowing. And I put myself in their shoes. And I think back to that very moment in my own life when I had all the questions they did, all the concerns, all the uncertainties. And an obsession grows inside of me, an obsession to say something, something of use, something that can spark that moment from which the rubber and the road finally make contact. And so I am asking you to trust me when I tell you that it is for them and them alone I really write this book. Because Darwin looms! My time is short. My kids and their friends are the new hope, custodians of the new world, charged with making a place that reflects whatever it is they have come to hold dear. And so there is desperation on my part to paint a picture for them, to celebrate good ol' American values that were the foundation that my own journey was a reflection of and to make note of when, where, and why they've evaporated in an anxious hope to light a fire under those charged with rekindling them.

My time here has borne witness to a golden period, when there were real iconoclasts walking the Earth, and I've watched those times evolve into these, when everybody's measure of everything is directly linked to the new phenomenon of social media. Everything has come down to what the next guy's doing—how to either stay with him or get ahead of him in rankings, ratings, hits, and follower counts. That's the mission for many. The solution is not retro so much, because there's nothing wrong with embracing technology for beneficial means; after all, it can reach more people. But the solution is a return to that time when a handshake was a handshake, when you said you were going to do something and then you did it. When, if you had a friend, you helped him and he helped you. When, if you said, "I got your back," it wasn't some hip, empty epithet you heard on Twitter but instead you meant it and didn't run for the hills when the shit started to hit the fan, especially from the very people who professed to be your friends. This is what I was taught by my old man and that "greatest of generations"— the group of people who lived during that time leading up to World War II and right in its aftermath, who were not only capable of putting their own lives aside in the quest for some greater good but were also capable of real, *true* self-sacrifice. Not the momentary kind. Not when it's convenient. Not when it gets you more likes on your Facebook wall.

Not when it makes you more popular. Not when it increases your TVQ. Not when it makes you more attractive as a money earner.

That's not true heroism; that's nothing to truly aspire to. That laundry list of names I made back in Chapter 2, the one that seemed to go on for way too long, that was but a fraction of the real icono-clasts who walked the earth when my values and aesthetics were being formed. Those were the true heroes, truly guys you can envision say-ing, "Fuck this shit, I'm outta here," even when all the lemmings were rushing toward something, no matter how empty and wrong-headed that something was.

You can make excuses till you're hoarse about how those were different times, with different values that are dated, that simply don't apply anymore, but I say, "Really? A hero's not a hero anymore? 'I am my brother's keeper' is not a value anymore? That there are things worth fighting and maybe even dying for is not something to aspire to anymore? Really?" Because if that's the case, if mediocrity finally is the new normal, then maybe we should all just take the fucking pipe. But when I talk about my kids and your kids and that whole genera-tion I am desperate to open a dialogue with, it is alarming. They have no idea of where to begin. Nothing is universal anymore. Nothing is larger than life. There is no unifying cause. Yeah, there are individual little pockets of things we involve ourselves in on a momentary basis, but nothing is being celebrated in our culture that is cathartic, con-structive, moving, and makes the ground underneath our feet tremble to the point that we're shaken to some sort of action or direction.

So yes, if one is looking for and obsessed with finding the elements that exist for our kids today, upon which they can build something of substance, one must first look to the heroes. Who do they have to aspire to? And fuck me, if I can think of a single one! I mean, I don't wanna seem snarky, but who the fuck are they? Are they the people you see in the top forties in music? Are they the sports figures who go from team to team, scandal to scandal? Are they all those amazing philanthropists who populate the seventeen thousand reality shows that clog my fucking arteries, gearing it toward audiences with third-grade educations? Well, are they, punk? Maybe I'm missing something, but no matter where I turn, I can find nothing to point my kids to that even comes close to being an idea big enough to build a set of dreams on. And make no mistake, without a dream, as the song says, you'll never have a dream come true!

So as I approach the rocking chair years of life, I realize that turning our backs on that and looking upon what went before us as hokum, as cornball, is not the best course of action. The things that are celebrated as human decency, true heroism, true self-sacrifice, and with a kind of leadership that was completely iconoclastic during the first half of the twentieth century are nearly forgotten. All of a sudden we started looking inward and becoming obsessed with behavior, idiosyncrasies, human flaws, and all this stuff. Some great accomplishments happened in the second half of the twentieth century, don't get me wrong, but in the process we lost a template of what truly being human looks like. I dare you to look around in this world and show me ten people who I should aspire to behave like, who I should drop everything and study. Oh yes, there are millions of them where they've always been— behind the scenes, making up the backbone of this world, the salt of this earth. But in our leaders? It's not even possible. It's weird, and as somebody who has two kids who are just approaching the prime of their lives, where they should be at the peak of their powers, the world we are leaving to them deeply saddens me. My children have count- less friends between them, and my friends have kids who have friends, so I've seen the ripples of disengagement and uncertainty among a huge segment of our young population. Everywhere I look I'm seeing a generation coming out of school directionless.

I write this book because maybe, just maybe, there are things about my little journey that will make you say, "Sometimes it's not so good to throw out the baby with the bath water." Sometimes it's not so great to evolve to the point at which you lose yourself in the doing, you lose your sense of community, lose your humility, lose sight of the fact that you are part of some sort of collective consciousness, that there is universality of human rights. I don't know what took us here;

I'm not a friggin' philosopher. I'm just a friggin' actor, so I can only just glimpse or guess at what went wrong. But I'm telling you, these are some fucked up times we live in. I've never seen such hypocrisy, such polarity, such hatred, such smallness. I've never seen such bare-faced corruption ruling the day and so many people trying to create so much fear and disdain for so many other people because that's what they think is going to advance their cause. It almost makes you think we're in for some sort of biblical epoch. I mean, shit, every once in a while I say to myself, *Maybe that's what this whole global warming thing is.* I don't know. All I know is that if you turn inward to that degree and your mantra is, "What's in it for me?" then we ain't gonna be around very much longer. And even if we are, who gives a fuck? What the fuck is there to celebrate?

The generation my kids are in seems to have bypassed a sense of perspective when forming their core values. Because their diet has been so steadily informed by the highly technofied, highly corpora-tized world they were born into, when you make references to the bygone days they look at you like you're speaking Namibian, if that's even a language. I am noticing it's hard to miss what you haven't expe-rienced. And so that was the point of this, my letter to the young art-ist, as well: to show me moving through the decades, to gain a sense of perspective of where our country came from and how it has changed. I described what I witnessed around me not only on a cultural level but also on a human level, and I saw how we allowed the corporatization of everything to come to dictate our lives. Everything has become a tiny line item on some vast corporate ledger sheet. Absolutely every-thing. Name the one thing that's not just a line on a corporate ledger sheet. Yeah, I guess you'll still find some old vestiges of the mom-and-pop days upon which the American Dream was founded, but there are only vestiges. Gone are the days of the sole proprietorship. Gone are the days when movie studios were run by movie guys, not lawyers and Harvard business school majors. Gone are the days when competition looked like, "Well, if you're gonna hire Faulkner to write a screenplay, then fuck you, I'm getting Hemingway!"

Where there once were thousands of corporations, now there are hundreds, because they keep swallowing up themselves along with everything else in their paths. I'm starting to be able to envision the day when there will be four fucking corporations, when the real world will actually resemble what some of these cheesy postapocalyptic movies they are making these days look like. I know—I've been in some of them! In the truly scariest of these scripts there are no more ideologies—no more democracies, no more socialists, no more Marxists, no principles at all. There are only corporations. Only economies. Only bottom lines. There is no difference between freedom, anarchy, and oppression. The impulse to be human is no longer of any value, and people have been grappling with this now ever since we started to see the true price one pays when you corporatize everything. Look at these last five years: this economic meltdown, when we realized the games the banks were playing with all of our lives, with all our futures, with our children's future, and how they cynically came out of it richer than ever before and not one muthafucka went to jail. That's what happens in the corporate world, bro. They make the rules. They take the human factor out of it. It's how much the CEOs can make. And they can *really* make a lot when they don't pay anyone who works for them. So that's the pickle that we're in right now. And we've got a Congress that's so fucking racist and a country that's so fucking racist that they can't even see a good idea when they trip over it, simply because a guy who happens to have black skin is presenting that idea.

And all of the places we once had that were our sanctuaries where we could go, they also have been co-opted. The music business is destroyed. We will never see a day again when a Beatles, Elvis Presley, Stevie Wonder, Bob Dylan, Aretha Franklin, or Frank Sinatra, will emerge, 'cuz there's no more recording industry. In the other arts it's the same. I love Hemingway—do you think that guy's work would've seen the light of day now? He'd be a bouncer at a bar somewhere while he scribbled stories in his off-time, stories that no one would ever buy 'cuz they could download 'em for free on some fucking Internet site. All that exists now is, "Who can we find who can sell the most tickets to the biggest swath of people?" And you usually have to aim so low to make that happen that you end up taking the whole culture down with it. So in my business it's all fucking dazzle with special effects. Everything else that might reflect the human condition is such a risk, such a gamble, and such a roll of the dice that the "smart money" is betting against it. You have to be a franchised superhero to have a movie made about you right now. What do I learn from those muthafuckas? How is my heart moved by them? How do I get some sort of a sense that life makes sense philosophically and spiritually from watching that fucking fare? We're just anesthetizing ourselves, and we're letting these corporate muthafuckas do it. And we're not fighting back because it's too big.

So what *do* you do?

Don't get me wrong—I have nothing against business, and I definitely have nothing against money. Like Barzini says in *The Godfather*: "After all, we are not communists!" And in order for business to thrive it does need to turn a profit; it is obligated to perpetuate its own existence. If it didn't, then we wouldn't even be having this discussion. And I understand that. I get that. But at some point you need to make a choice about what you're going to sell. You got to stand for something. If it's just money and power and self-glorification because you were able to make money and acquire power for yourself—if that's what you're interested in, please don't read this fucking book. Please unfollow me on Twitter. We have nothing in common, and I don't want to hear your comments; I don't want to hear your complaints. I have no fucking interest in your opinion. Does that sound harsh? Over the top? Do I not understand that I am an employee of some of the vast machines I indict here? Do I have no understanding of the price one pays when one opens his mouth as if to bite the very hand that feeds him? Because clearly history has proven that. Clearly I have opened my mouth way too much for my own good. I've burned some bridges because of the shit we're talking about right here, right now. I get it. But hey, I'm writing this book in my sixties because it really doesn't matter anymore who the fuck I piss off. So if I'm going to say something of importance to my kids, my kids' friends, and their friends, then it better be something that reflects all those heroes I've been droning on about. Wake the fuck up, muthafuckas: this is our world, and we're letting it slip down the drain.

As an actor, as a storyteller, I feel like I'm in an anointed sector of the universe because, as I mentioned, it's a true privilege to be working in the arts. So when I get around charlatans and vainglorious, narcissistic, low-life pieces of shit who manipulate the game, the system, in order to make themselves look good, get rich, feel important, and wield power to lord it over others and their intentions are nothing but corrupt, I take that personally. This is not some casual relationship I have in which I leave the important shit for others to do. This is my church; this is my crusade. This is war! I feel I'm in a war with the desensitization of all these things I've described. And that's what corporatization does. Especially when it imposes itself upon our very culture. I mean we're at the point now in which you can't tell the difference between a reality show and F. Scott Fitzgerald. *Duck Hunt* or whatever the fuck that shit is that parades as storytelling these days—that's how efficient the corporatization of our culture has become. *My* premise is that people are smarter than that, that if you give them a steady diet of good shit, they will love it, maybe even more than the shit you give them that assumes they're asleep at the switch. My faith in people's innate class and intelligence is far, far more respectful than the impulse to simply appeal to the lowest forms of discourse. That is the bar I would like my kids to assume for their dreams.

What my sons and daughters and all our kids—and us included—have to come to understand is that we now move in an entirely superficial, consumer-driven reality. It's like a fuckin' *Matrix* world. So there's nothing more than what brand of sneakers you have, which is the only thing of importance left. It happened because they've been inundated with it since they were children. This generation is one born out of corporatization that aimed to turn each and every one of them into nothing more than a consumer. That's the goal. With consumers, the more a consumer thinks, the worse that consumer is. He's not going to buy anything. He's not going to buy $300 sneakers because a dude's name is on it. He's not going to turn on *Fuck-A-Duck*. He's maybe gonna watch a classic movie that doesn't have any commercials playing on it, and we can't have that! Where's the profit in that? Just distract, distract, distract, and while distracting, throw in some product placement, 'cuz God knows, it ain't easy keeping those stockholders in their Porsches. The job now is to undo what corporations have done. We have to take back that which is precious in our society and the beautiful institutions of arts and sciences that made up our lives. That's the job. And if you're a young artist with all that powerful testosterone and estrogen coursing through your veins, you can do it. You can get into the arts and rescue our culture and reinvent it with human values and human dignity as its guide.

The hard part of trying to help my kids chart a course to success comes with the detritus of what all this obsession with progress has yielded. Gone are the days when you could appear in the next Tennessee Williams, Eugene O'Neill, Edward Albee, Arthur Miller, Harold Pinter, or Samuel Beckett play. All the dudes who might have written the next great American play are now writing for cable television, 'cuz that's where the money is. So rather than coming up through the great edifice of the New York Theater as I could do when I was staging my assault, that road is all but closed. And it's not as if, if you are a singer-songwriter like my daughter is, you can be signed by a record label and be provided all the resources they once provided to turn an unknown into a brand. The record industry isn't even a shadow of its former self, so that road is all but closed. And it's not as if you can count on that one chance in a thousand that is making, starring, or directing an original film that might find its way to the marketplace—that road is all but closed. Publishing? Journalism? These are the venerable institutions that are on their last gasps, that are doing everything they can to prevent the inevitable, that are all but a historical footnote.

So what do you tell them, these bright, beautiful, fair-haired dreamers who possess every bit as much talent, intelligence, and integrity as any generations before them? Where do they begin? What is it that they plug into? In fact, the more I obsess about answering these questions, the more I come to think we are probably in as revolutionary a moment as has existed in many aeons. For what does one do when the tide of technology has all but washed away all of the traditional edifices? Where do you turn but to yourself, your own gifts, light, passion, and determination to express yourself and, in so doing, leave something for the next generation to be inspired by? For that is immutable, nonnegotiable. It's the way this old world's been working since Jesus was a corporal. So if there ain't nuthin' but cynicism wherever you look, and if that just don't cut it for ya, then the time for reinvention is here. Have at it, kids. The future depends on it!

Oh and hey, sorry to be the one to break this to ya, but ever since we stood upright, life's been filled with tons and tons of bad news, tons and tons of things that don't break your way, and tons and tons of things that you would love to be able to control but, at the end of the day, you realize you have zero control over. So you're always only partially in control, but you're also always partially in a state of prayer. It all ends up being a compendium, a little bit of good fortune mixed in with a little bit of perspiration and determination mixed in with a shitload of persistence. And even then there's no guarantees of results, although chances are you'll begin to see little victories, and the big ones will come from things you couldn't have imagined. You are going to lose people; you are going to lose things. You are going to lose arguments, wars, possessions. You are going to lose a lot. Even if you're a winner, you are going to lose. But if you remain idealistic and cling to good values, you will know how to make the highs less high and the lows less low.

There was this famous radio show my dad used to listen to back in the fifties that featured all the top, top people in Hollywood. It was a badge of honor to appear on this show, so the host could get anybody and everybody he wanted. His last question in the interview would invariably be, "What is your advice to the young so-and-so?," depending if the interviewee was a director, a writer, or an actor. And I remember like it was yesterday when, one time, he had on Edward G. Robinson. Now, Eddie G. was as smooth a muthafucka as ever came down the pike—by the way, his real name was Goldenberg, a Russian-born Jew—so when the host got to that final question, Eddie said, "I would tell the young actor to develop tastes for the finer things in life and to study them and to begin to surround yourself with them. The best wines, the best paintings. If you're gonna buy books, buy limited series, one-of-ones, collectible things. Fine food."

The host dude was more than a little flustered by that response, and so he said, "No, no, no. I was asking what is your advice to the *young* actor who is just starting out?"

"Well yeah," Eddie said, "that's my advice."

And the host came back: "But how is the young actor supposed to be able to afford those things?"

To which Eddie G. said, "Well that's just the problem. If you don't get into wanting those things, you'll never work hard enough to get them." Huh! Fucking visualization! Who coulda guessed it would come from the cigar-smoking gangster Rico in *Little Caesar* and the tough-as-nails Rocco in *Key Largo*?!

That whole Edward G. Robinson approach to living is to put yourself in a position in which you are forced to reach beyond your grasp, forced to cover your bets, and if you fall short, you crash and burn. But if you don't, you've done quite well. That was the encapsulation of the way Eddie G. lived his life, and of all the advice that got handed down from that show, this is what resonated the most. I reached for the sky; I reached for the stars. I said to myself, "I'm gonna go Eddie G. Robinson–style, man. Someday I'm gonna live in a place that I like. I'm gonna put my kids in schools that are a stretch for me," because I'm going to make this visualization happen through hard work.

You'll find what works for you as long as you get up the balls and go for it. We need you, man, to save our culture, one person at a time. And you'll be fine if you make each little failure your friend. Look at it as a necessary phase from which all the growth emanates, otherwise you learn nothing, you will never experience "success," however it is that you define it.

CHAPTER 25

The Power and the Glory

Considering what it all felt like at the start, I have no right in hell to have ever gotten close to this place where I find myself. I have tried assiduously to make a note to myself and, thus, to you, my friends, how improbable it is in the great universal scheme of things that all of this could have come to be. Because from where I sit, there is no rational reason for this almost "Unbearable Lightness of Being," which, like the novel by Milan Kundera, challenges Nietzsche's notion that all things have already occurred and will recur *ad infinitum*, instead affirming that each person has only one life to live and that everything only happens once and never again. Clearly, this has been my life, wherein I should have been counted out of this fight long, long ago. Clearly, the scope and breadth of what I now find to be the situations of my life have exceeded even *my* lofty and ambitious dreams. Clearly, all the things that set me on my journey, regardless of what they looked like at the outset, have evolved and morphed into a foundation upon which I finally stand.

What I truly thank God for, aside from my amazing family and a most colorful band of brothers and pals, is the fact that I've lived long enough to see things, things that so many of the people I cherished along the way never got a chance to see. And although the events I've chronicled at such length here are sources of infinite satisfaction and pride, it's the inside stuff and not the events to which I refer, not the things you find on a résumé or in a bio. What gratifies me most about the time God has given me is how I have come to feel inside when the glare of day is done and it's just me and the night and the music. For it is there that I truly see footprints of a lifetime of just looking, searching, hoping there was a payoff and the diligence to do whatever necessary to earn it. Yes, I am terribly proud of so many of the events chronicled herein, tangible things that will be left behind to be considered and examined by generations down the road. And yes, I am amazingly blessed to have done the things I've done, seen the places I've seen, been around the people I've had the pleasure to meet, to work with. But as gratifying as all that is, what I was certain I would never achieve is peace—peace tied into a sublime realization that I am not in this alone, that I am a part of God's plan, placed here but for a blink of a moment but also with obligations to justify the very miracle of my being. So thank you for the gift of longevity. Because, without a doubt, I was always gonna be the last guy to finally get the joke, what was I put here to do? How do I leave here confident in the knowledge that I did something, no matter how big or small, to simply leave a fingerprint, a clue or two, that the dude paid his rent? To even have a shot at that, the slightest of shots even—that, to me, is it: the all, the everything, the Big Casino. Einstein, one of the smartest dudes ever, said, "There are two ways to live your life. One is as though nothing is a miracle. The other is as though everything is a miracle."

It's pretty clear to me how many times and ways I beat the odds in spite of the fact that I was often my own worst enemy. And even though, as I mentioned, there at first seems to be no reason why I had been given so many chances and not been ejected from the game long, long ago, I understand it now. So the obsession becomes: How do I show my gratitude? How do I do that in such a way so that it's not just lip service, not just a guilt payment, but instead it's something that truly moves the needle? What do I know that's worth sharing? What, if anything, have all these incredible blessings yielded, that can brighten another life a fraction of how these multitude of blessings brightened mine? And in the feverish search to unearth this "thing," gal dang it, if I didn't get even luckier by being given the opportunity to write a book, a book that forced me to go back to the beginning and look for threads, clues, and the actual DNA of things. And fuck-a-duck, if it wasn't staring me in the face from the get-go, looming large all throughout, no matter where the detours of my life took me!

A drunk walks out of a bar and puts a dime in a parking meter, and the thing hits sixty, and he says, "Oh my God, I lost a hundred pounds!" No, it's not stand-up comedy. My north star, my beacon, my one abiding source of comfort through the best and the worst of times was the stories, the listening to and the telling of stories. And even though my liaison with storytelling started out more as a cure, a salve for a compendium of misaligned, outsized attributes that always seemed to short-circuit any peace in my real life, stories, for me, while remaining the one constant theme, also became so much more. Because with each coming of age, with each passing milestone, with total unease and confusion finally giving way to tidbits of clarity and the ability to give myself a break, stories not only just stayed with me; my love for them intensified. And my relationship with them, though growing less codependent, became more and more sublime. Because what started out as a means to escape eventually became this highly anointed endeavor, this ultra-exclusive club in which really cool, really smart people who I admired fell all over themselves to achieve membership.

Ultimately, it dawned on me: blessed are the storytellers, because they can bridge oceans, marshal great forces, inspire and instruct, transcend all limits, transform hearts and minds. They can break down barriers and be the common thread for disparate humanities, reaching across distant borders. They can provide for that commonality I talked about earlier, and like the perfect note in a masterpiece of music, when heard the world over, they can resonate at a vibration all can hear with identical clarity. That is the "collective consciousness" and, to my mind, "the holy grail." It explains why music looms so large in our workaday lives, even though the bean-counters dismiss it as "non-essential." And painting. And dance. And, yes, for sure, movies! To traffic in a universe that is constantly in search of that universal truth, that perfect note . . . there is a nobility in that.

It was my dad who was my first storyteller, and he was a great one. And with all the dudes he dug, from the guys who made *Gunga Din* to the guy who wrote *For Whom the Bell Tolls*, he was showing me that as shitty as any of his days might have been, coming home at night to "those guys" was the great equalizer. They elevated the proceedings and gave it joy and meaning, imparting a knowledge that other guys were trying to figure out the same shit as he was, which in and of itself is a comfort. Yes, we all live, and we all die. We all get sick, and some of us get well. Some of us have money, and some of us don't. But we all are human. I aspire to wanting to make the recognition of that undisputable fact the main theme of my life. I am in search of that perfect note that is so fundamental, so primal that it holds identical value for everyone, from the poorest man in Zambia to the most anointed in Xanadu. That, to me, is a calling. Because it is helpful. Know how I know? 'Cuz I've seen how it's touched me. I've looked into the eyes of people who are simply desperate to share with me what one of my movies meant to them; I've seen how it has touched them. For there is only one place on God's little acre where we find true and real commonality—in our humanness. And the moment you truly see that you are not the first, not the only, not some freak for feeling what you're feeling, then darkness is replaced by light and loneliness is replaced by peace, gratitude, and community!

I'm here to tell you that from the year 2000 onward, by using the tools that were taught to me and the blessings that were bestowed on me, whether earned or unearned, I saw this succession of one dream after another becoming real. To the point at which I can't even articulate a thank you profound enough to begin to measure up to the magnificence that has become my life. All I can do is look for little ways—little ways to show my gratitude, my appreciation, my disbelief that, considering where I started, this is where I ended up. I can't save the world. Nor would I ever be foolish enough to try. But I do love people, and I love to be able to think that dreams and reality can be fused, because I have been a witness to it. And I'm not in some panacea state in which I am exaggerating or romanticizing. I share all this as if to say, "Here's what I've seen. Here's what it looked like when it all started. Here's what it looks like now. This part of the curve was good, and this part sucked, not only from my point of view but also from a global point of view." And at the end of the day the only real choice I have regarding what to do with all this knowledge, all this perspective, all this goodwill is what I choose to do about it. Because I need to find a way to show my appreciation. It's time to take the advice I gave to my kids: stop waiting for the studios, the networks, or even for the government to do it.

The great dramatists have forever and always been ahead of the curve at illuminating the values that were worth aspiring to and, in turn, those that spelled chaos and destruction, be it in our literature, our theater, or our movie houses, and they managed to teach these immutable lessons while entertaining—no small feat. But today, when all the "smart money" is betting on special-effects action movies and movies that can be made into friggin' rides at amusement parks, the business of doing the kind of storytelling that truly enriches the human condition is becoming more and more marginalized. And the more thin and one-dimensional the premises for these flicks seem to get, the more money they seem to throw at them. I mean, when you spend $200 million to make a movie, you better fucking make a billion dollars in profit. And in order to do that, you better make the stupidest piece of shit you can fucking make because you're really going to want to attract every fucking body you can, in this universe and the next. Anybody can do that. That's just P. T. Barnum, man. That's just like, "How much shit can we throw up against the wall to get these rubes to unload fourteen bucks a ticket? Twenty-one if you throw in 3D or IMAX!" So where there was once nuance and sophistication, big ideas seeping with style, you now only have spectacle, which doesn't leave a whole lotta room for the David Leans, the Alfred Hitchcocks, the John

Fords, the Frank Capras, and the Akira Kurosawas. The new corporate movie moguls are sipping champagne and dancing on their graves.

So please forgive me if I seem to take some of this shit personally. 'Cuz to my way of thinking—and trust me when I tell ya I am prepared to be the *only* muthafucka thinking like this—I gotta feel as though I'm working on something every day that kind of keeps all the right conversations alive. Whatever happens after I die, hey, it's none of my fucking business. All I know is I'm going to do everything I can while I'm here to say, "This shit is not okay. The complete marginalization of the little guy is not okay. The guy on whose back this country was built and run—it's not okay to fuck with that guy. He needs to be respected. He needs to be celebrated and loved and nurtured." From that little two-bedroom flat I was born into, I know how hard it is to keep a fucking family sustained. I know a rigged system when I see one. I know what kind of cynicism is bred from pure greed, from the accumulation of wealth at all costs, no matter how wealthy you are to begin with. From corporations trying to break their own records while they break the backs of workers, of veterans, of the elderly, who've only invested their whole adult fucking lives just trying to simply be good Americans. And if some Romney-minded muthafucka wantsta tell me free enterprise trumps compassion, generosity, the simple dictum that the luckiest need to be the first among the spreading of the luck, then bring it, muthafucka! I'm right fucking here!

I am far and away not the first among us to pronounce how fortunate we are to witness the emergence of this new Pope. He is the embodiment of those sentiments. And although I don't physically kneel in that particular church, I kneel with all my heart to his core teachings. And, further, I remain one of the dwindling masses who thank God to live in a world where Barack Obama can be the heart and soul of this country I love so much. Because he is a man who has spent all of his political capital just adjudicating for the common man, and in the face of every single thing they could throw at him, he remains calm, classy, and incredibly humorous—one of the greatest political wits since JFK—all this in the face of *the* worst, most blatant racism along with the highest degree of disrespect for the title Commander-in-Chief I have seen in my lifetime, a title our founders granted to him. Men and women have left their blood in a shitload of dark and lonely places so you can disagree with me about this, but let's be clear: no one should confuse that right with the dignity and the sanctity of an office that came as a result of two fair and democratic elections. I am a fan. He has managed to maintain his poise, his grace, and, most importantly, his vision in the face of profound ugliness. It cannot be lost on us that he is the Jackie Robinson of executive politics. And like Jackie, he never complained, never engaged with the haters, never took his eye off the ball. What he did do is finally begin a worldwide discussion about a whole lotta shit that nobody wants to talk about, chief among them being the redistribution of resources. I'm not going to say wealth, because I don't mind wealth as either a concept or a fact; I just mind what one chooses to do with it. Because with great power comes great responsibility. Don't tell me you're a pious person—just show me. Don't hide behind some empty nonexistent spiritualism because, like *Elmer Gantry* says, "Ya can't go to church on Sunday and cheat at business all through the week!" Spiritual? Gimme a fuckin' break. You better know if you're truly spiritual or not, 'cuz I got news for ya: God does! And there comes a moment in every muthafucka's life when the ability to buy a first-class seat to the other side ain't no longer negotiable!

So after all is said and done and when all the dust finally settles, what I truly believe would be the best use of my last fifteen, twenty years on this Earth, or whatever time God chooses to give me, is to reclaim and rededicate the simple beautiful things in this life that no amount of money can buy. And I am convinced that this can only come about by appealing to people's better angels, their deeper longings to be part of something bigger than even themselves, where they have a seat at the table, a voice that money can't drown out, a knowledge that they are giving their children the best lives they can. And this means that in order to put some skin in the game, I better be willing to make an investment I can afford. I may not pull it off, but I'm good with that.

I'm calling this little venture of mine Wing and a Prayer Pictures. And in what will come as no surprise, we're gonna make movies. In fact, I'm betting we're gonna make the best damn movie company since MG-fucking-M. 'Cuz I'm betting on the artist. I'm betting on the storyteller. I'm betting on the folks out there—just plain, ordinary folks who want something a little smarter, a little classier. Something that truly engages their better angels. And by the time this book is published, I'm betting we'll be well under way. 'Cuz I just can't give my kids and my kids' friends a bunch of shit that says, "Ain't nuthin' 'less you got some skin in the game!" I gotta walk the walk! I gotta pave a parking lot and put up a paradise. 'Cuz if not me, then who?! And if not now . . . well, you know what I'm sayin'. Fuck waiting for the world to change you; you start by trying to change it. And if you are pure of heart and your intentions are good, you can't lose. Even if nothing happens, you can't lose. Because whether you are successful or not, what better way is there to spend your one and only life than working every day purely from passion, love, respect, and awe?

Oh, and by the way, just so I get off on the right foot, here's a little tip for all you talent out there: make sure your people show you everything that is offered. There's a rule at my management company that my whole team is cool with: if a script comes in with an offer for me, no matter what they think of it, whether they think it's good for me or not, they send it so I can make *my own* decision about whether I do the project. As talent, if ya wanna keep watching the movie business get more and more mediocre, then keep leaving it to your agents, your managers, and your fucking lawyers to make your decisions for you! But if you do that, I better not ever hear you complain how shitty the movie business is, 'cuz you ain't part of the solution; you're part of the problem. 'Cuz you can bet dollars to donuts you ain't seeing the good stuff, 'cuz they don't wantcha to, 'cuz there ain't no *money* in it for 'em. So yeah, if my theory holds any water and it's true that our beautiful culture is truly *de*volving, believe me when I tell ya, there's plenty of blame to go around.

Listen, man, righteous indignation aside, ain't nothing gonna ever happen by just identifying the problem—the walk is in need of being walked. I'd love to suggest that every artist who's coming out of school, every journalist, every actor, every musician, and every dancer stand up and say, "No, this ain't art, this contributes nothing to our culture." It's possible. The only thing that's getting in the way of it are market forces. That's all it is. Ever. 'Cuz I submit to you that there's just as many Bob Dylans, Stevie Wonders, and Joni Mitchells getting born every day as there ever was. The only thing that separates an artist like that and us knowing about an artist like that are market forces. So we got to change the hearts and minds of people. We gotta wake people up. We can't keep going down this road where we allow ourselves to be completely desensitized and buy into the fact that fucking Coca-Cola is good for us and a Romney-type is a great leader, all because of billions of marketing dollars that tell us he is. While, if he had pulled it off, a couple of hundred people would have gotten *much, much* richer during his eight years in office while the rest of us would go fuck ourselves.

No one person is going to be able to change the world. No one gesture is going to be able to change the world. But if enough of you decide, "I'm not gonna buy into any of the paradigms, any of the edifices that only worship false idols," well, then, maybe we can turn this ship around and start sailing to higher ground. I'm hoping this book at least starts a conversation in places where it might not have started before. And if it doesn't, who gives a fuck? I'm gonna die anyway. Shit, we all are. All I'm sayin' is: here's what I see. You agree with me, you don't agree with me—whatever, no problem. But hey, nothing ventured, nothing gained. And look, if ya don't like my version of the good, the bad, and the ugly, then go find your own. Just don't settle. Your life is worth more than that. And as far as I can tell, you only get one.

Yet we can do all these things and still be happy. That's really the point, isn't it? For me, happiness is this vision of me walking down the street on my way someplace. Doesn't even matter where. I got my wife on my left and my two kids on my right, and we're laughing our asses off. That's the image that trumps everything. That's my contingency plan, and knowing I got that, then it doesn't matter whether I'm an actor or a plumber, whether I'm wealthy or just getting by. All that matters is . . . I'm happy.

Don't let them steal that from you.

That's winning. That's Easy Street, Baby!

acknowledgments

If you've made it this far, you already know the many people who I thanked, and I did so with sincerity. As for this book, much thanks to Katherine Latshaw of Folio Management for her belief in this project and especially for hooking me up with Ben Schafer at Da Capo. Thank you, Ben, for sharing the vision I had for this book. Also, much gratitude to all the folks at Da Capo and Perseus who worked hard behind the scenes, especially John Radziewicz, Lissa Warren, Kevin Hanover, Sean Maher, Christine Marra, George Banbury, and Justin Lovell.

A special thanks to Michael Largo, without whom there *is* no book—we started off with a job to do and ended up hecka pals!

And thank you, Ian Gibson, for taking good care of GDT so he could take such good care of RP.

But to my intrepid team, starting with the inimitable Erik Kritzer and the inspirational Brian Wilkins. And the young guns, Kyle Einsohn, Patrick Havern, and David Katsman. And a special thanks to Ryan Bundra, who ran point for me on the evolution of this book. And Ben Levine and Jay Cohen and Brett Norensberg. And Michael Selby, Craig Baumgarten, and Josh and Randy Crook, all of whom dwell in places that make dreaming big just another part of the day.

And to my kids, Blake and Brandon Perlman, around whom keeping it real is the only option and in whose company all is good!